The College History Series

University of Baltimore

Thomas L. Hollowak

The College History Series

UNIVERSITY OF BALTIMORE

THOMAS L. HOLLOWAK

ARCADIA
PUBLISHING

ISBN 978-0-7385-0594-7

Published by Arcadia Publishing
Charleston, South Carolina

Printed in the United States of America

Library of Congress Catalog Card Number: 00-104928

For all general information contact Arcadia Publishing at:
Telephone 843-853-2070
Fax 843-853-0044
E-Mail sales@arcadiapublishing.com
For customer service and orders:
Toll-Free 1-888-313-2665

Visit us on the Internet at www.arcadiapublishing.com

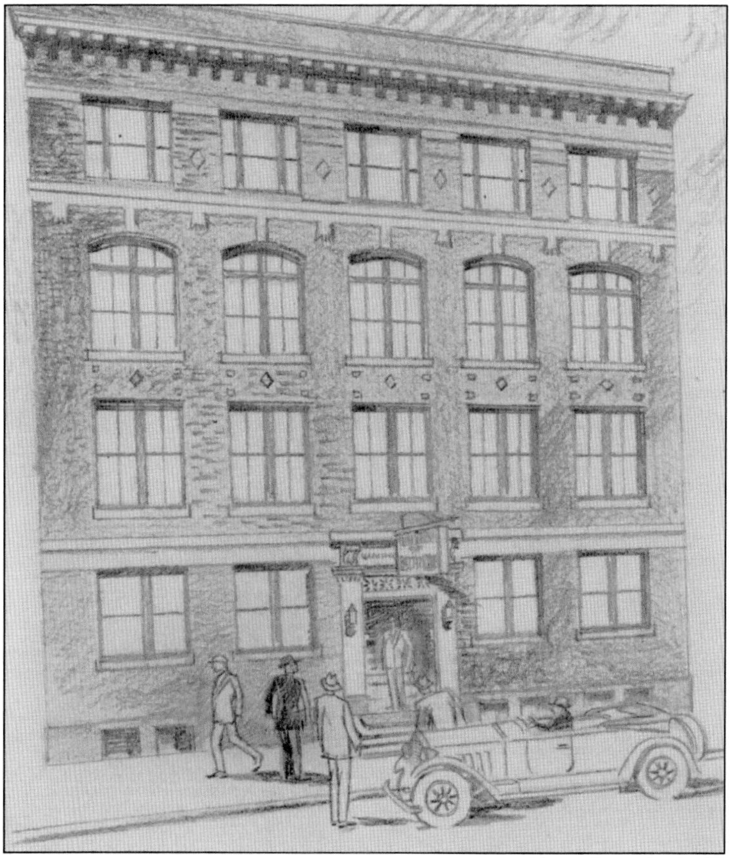

HOWARD STREET HALL. This is a 1932 drawing of the former Baltimore College of Dentistry, which was purchased in 1929 by the trustees to provide more classrooms for the increased student population.

Contents

Preface		6
Introduction		7
1.	Founders and Leaders	11
2.	Administrators, Faculty, and Staff	17
3.	Students	37
4.	Activities, Clubs, and Organizations	51
5.	Athletics	73
6.	Alumni	85
7.	Friends and Visitors	99
8.	The Campus	107
Acknowledgments		127

PREFACE

Since 1925, the University of Baltimore has set itself apart by providing both affordable and accessible opportunities for men and women to prepare for success in law, business, accounting, and the professional applications of the liberal arts. UB's hallmark has always been a fine faculty supplemented with working professionals as adjunct instructors who have focused on the application of knowledge from the classroom to the real world.

UB's future will include providing more professional degree opportunities for individuals who require advanced graduate education beyond the master's, such as the new Doctorates of Communication Design and Public Administration. The new millennium will challenge UB to bring its degree programs to men and women far from its core campus on North Charles and Mt. Royal. While using the Internet and interactive television to keep UB accessible, our faculty and staff must still maintain the high degree of personal attention and interaction of the classroom experience.

It is the past that makes the present and future possible. When I first came to the University of Baltimore in the fall of 1968, I heard many wonderful stories about UB people—people like longtime President Theodore Halbert Wilson; Dean Cliff James of the School of Business; Kathleen Joyce, the registrar; Hugh Higgins, vice-president and treasurer; and Dr. Nell from the psychology department. I quickly learned that we were privileged to have had and enjoyed many dedicated and beloved employees.

I was also privileged to serve as provost under the wise leadership of Dr. Thomas Pullen. When I succeeded him, he made the transition of leadership a most gracious and easy time for me. I also had the privilege of getting to know Dr. Wilber Dehuff, acting president before Dr. Pullen, and Dr. Theodore Halbert Wilson, president of UB for 21 years prior to Dr. Dehuff.

All were wonderful people and great friends to legions of UB students. They left behind memories we cannot lose.

In an effort to make one more mindful of UB's past and our institutional heritage, UB archivist Thomas Hollowak has searched out records of the past 75 years and compiled the pictorial history that follows. We hope it will stir fond memories for many, causing alumni, university retirees, and present employees to search their files, attics, and memories for more glimpses of the past. Perhaps, this book will encourage them to honor us with the privilege of storing them in our university archives so that future generations will be able to share in their experiences at UB.

—H. Mebane Turner

INTRODUCTION

The history of the University of Baltimore has been one of constant change. The founders, whose names are Maynard A. Clemens, P. Lewis Kaye, William H. Wilhelm, R. Loran Langsdale, Victor R. Jones, Howell A. King, Alton R. Hodgkins, Stewart Lewis, and Clarence W. Miles, incorporated it on August 8, 1925. They were a group of professional businessmen interested in providing greater educational opportunities for employed men and women in Baltimore. The university was originally planned as an evening professional school, but a day division of the business college was started in 1926. When the university opened on October 1, 1925, the student body was composed of 62 students in the School of Law (including 3 women) and 114 in the School of Business Administration. Three years later, in 1928, the university's first students graduated.

Academically, the university has expanded from these evening professional schools offering courses in business and law to a fully accredited university. Mergers with Eastern College in 1970, Mount Vernon School of Law in 1970, and the Baltimore College of Commerce in 1973, together with the establishment in 1972–73 of the Graduate School and the College of Continuing Education, allowed the university to become a middle-size, comprehensive urban university. In 1975, as the result of an action of the 1973 Maryland General Assembly, the University of Baltimore was brought into the state higher educational system as "an upper division academic institution, that is third and fourth collegiate year and post graduate studies." It was also instructed to maintain "professional schools and graduate programs" and placed under the administrative direction of the Board of Trustees of State Colleges. In 1988, it became part of the University of Maryland System (now known as the University System of Maryland).

As an upper division, graduate and professional school, it is comprised of the Yale Gordon College of Liberal Arts, the Merrick School of Business, and the School of Law. The university's institutes and centers include the Institute for Language, Technology and Publications Design; the Center for International and Comparative Law; the Center for Negotiations and Conflict Management; the Hoffberger Center for Professional Ethics; the Information Systems Research Center; the Jacob France (Business) Center; and the Schaefer Center for Public Policy.

The academic expansion begun in 1926 when the Day Division was established was followed by the organization of a junior college in 1937. The increasing demand of high school graduates to obtain a liberal arts college education at relatively low cost led the university, in the fall of 1961, to expand its two-year junior college into a four-year college of liberal arts. When, in 1961, it became a four-year institution, the school offered day and evening classes. It offered its first graduate programs in 1974. Since 1975, it has been an upper-division college and graduate school. The college was named in 1982 for Yale Gordon, a University of Baltimore alumnus and businessman who understood the central importance of the humanities in higher education and in the life of a community. Thus, with his wife, he established the Peggy and Yale Gordon Trust, which supports organizations, including Gordon College, dedicated to advancing the humanities. Along with this endowment from the Gordon Trust, support for the college comes from a Challenge Grant from the National Endowment for the Humanities and by endowment grants from the Hearst Foundation, the Helen P. Denit Foundation, the Klein family, and others. Support for developing the General Education Core Curriculum was provided by a planning grant from the National Endowment for the Humanities and by the Fund for the Improvement of Post Secondary Education.

In 1945, the College of Business Administration was reorganized as the School of Business, Industry, and Management. In 1965, the two-year Accounting and Business Administration programs were expanded into four-year baccalaureate programs. In 1967, the undergraduate division of the university became a candidate for regional accreditation. The University of Baltimore Business School received three major gifts from the Merrick Foundation from 1982 to 1996. In addition to the naming gift in the early 1980s, grants were provided to endow the Jacob France Center and a business and economic research facility, and to support the Advantage MBA scholarship program. The Merrick School of Business is accredited by the International Association of Management Education (formerly the American Assembly of Collegiate Schools of Business) at both undergraduate and graduate levels. The school's accreditation was reaffirmed in 1995.

The School of Law added its day division in 1969 and began seeking the approval of the American Bar Association. Currently, with a student body of approximately 1,000, the University of Baltimore is the largest law school in Maryland. Admission is highly selective with nearly 6 applicants for each of the 225 places in the day and 80 places in the evening classes.

The University of Baltimore School of Law has more than 12,000 graduates. A significant number of alumni are prominent in the legal, governmental, and business communities in the Baltimore-Washington area, as well as around the country. In addition to those alumni who work in private law firms, UB graduates sit on the bench at every level of the Maryland Judiciary and work as state's attorneys and U.S. attorneys. School of Law graduates also work at numerous federal organizations, such as the Departments of Energy, Health and Human Services, Justice, the FBI, and many more. They also work in organizations such as the Maryland Disability Law Center and the office of the public defender.

Since 1969, President H. Mebane Turner has been at the University of Baltimore's helm and has guided its growth and change. During the past 30 years our mid-town campus has expanded and contributed to the revitalization of the Mount Royal neighborhood. We are an integral part of what makes this city work. The University of Baltimore is a part of the fabric that is Baltimore, a reflection of the vitality, the heritage, and the hope for the future. The university's history is unique in its service and contributions to Baltimore, and it is for this reason that it is Baltimore's university.

Physically, the university has grown from a four-story row house to a complex of buildings and athletic facilities many times the school's original size with plans for future expansion. The first classes of the university's School of Law and College of Business Administration were held in a four-story row house at 625 St. Paul Street on the southeast corner facing Mount Vernon Place. The success of the school in attracting students resulted in an on-going need for the physical expansion of the school. As early as 1926, a temporary annex had to be procured at St. Paul and Centre Streets. By the time the first classes graduated in 1928, it was apparent that a larger building was needed. In 1929, the trustees purchased 840 North Howard Street, formerly the home of the Baltimore College of Dentistry, and when classes resumed in the fall, they were held in the building renamed Howard Hall. The Howard building served the needs of the university until after the Second World War, when a dramatic increase in enrollment again made expansion necessary. In 1947, the former Baltimore Athletic Club at 1420 North Charles Street was purchased to provide additional recreational facilities, a cafeteria, classrooms, a student lounge, and offices.

It was not long before the demands on Charles Hall for additional classroom space made it desirable to provide campus facilities for varsity athletics and other undergraduate activities. In the spring of 1952, the university purchased the 45-acre tract of land bounded by Belvedere Avenue, Green Spring Avenue, and Rogers Avenue. The site, which had been formerly occupied by St. Paul's School, provided room, not only for immediate but also for the probable future expansion needs of the institution. By 1959, more classrooms were needed. The property on the corner of Charles and Oliver Streets, immediately adjacent to the Charles Street building, was acquired and a new four-story building was erected and occupied in the fall of 1961. The new building is connected by corridors with the Charles Street building. Langsdale Library was begun in 1964 and completed in 1966. The library was named for R. Loran Langsdale, who was president of the board of trustees for over 25 years and among the last surviving members of the school's founders. The former garage, located on the corner of Charles Street and Mount Royal Avenue, was purchased for a planned Academic Center in 1970. Renovation of the 1906 building began shortly thereafter, and the center was dedicated on December 9, 1971. In 1982, the Law Center was completed, and the plaza at the corner of Maryland and Mount Royal Avenues was completed two years later. The plaza ties together the Law Center, Academic Center, Langsdale Library, and Charles Hall to create a unique urban campus. In the 1990s, the Merrick School of Business was relocated to a new building at the corner of Charles Street and Mount Royal Avenue, while the School of Communication and Design was located across the street in the Charles Royal building. In the spring of 2000, the Schaefer Center was relocated to the St. Paul Street building that formerly housed the university's Educational Foundation and Alumni Services. The latter was moved to a newly renovated property at 1130 North Charles Street.

The expansion of academic and campus facilities is not limited to traditional classes and buildings, but also an array of online programs and increasing virtual university. "Web your way to an MBA," electronic reserves, and distance education are examples of technological advancements in education that helps the University of Baltimore usher in the new century. Despite its 75 years, the university still holds a unique position in the life of the city and state by providing a solid, affordable education for students from the local city to those who come from any number of countries throughout the world.

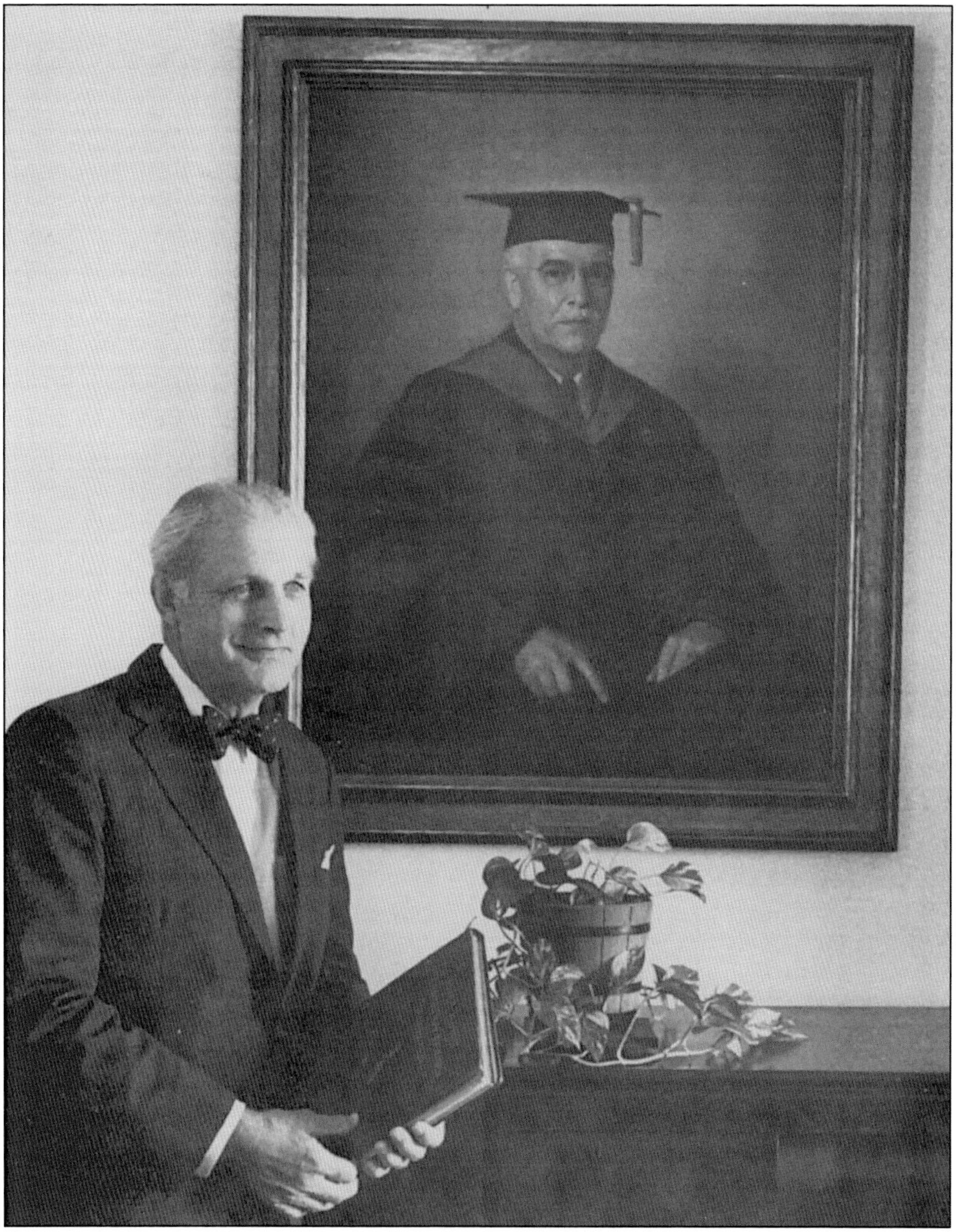

Two Leaders. University of Baltimore President H. Mebane Tuner stands before a portrait of President Emeritus Theodore Halbert Wilson.

One

Founders and Leaders

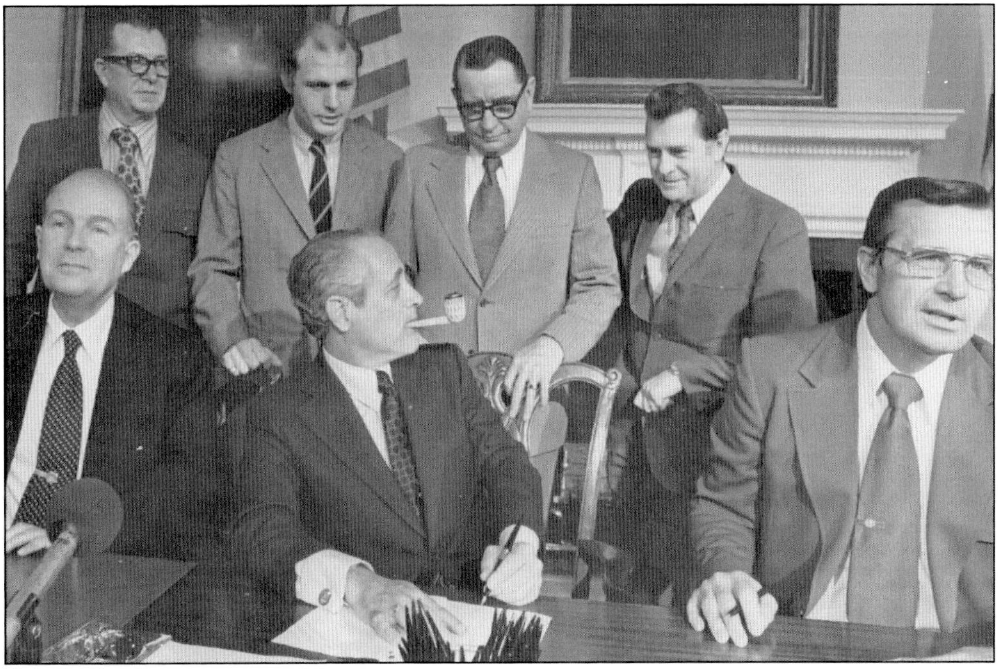

UB Becomes a Public Institution. On May 24, 1973, Gov. Marvin Mandel signed into law Bill 586, which provided for the university to enter the state system, effective January 1, 1975. Taking part in the ceremony are the following, from left to right: (seated) Sen. Williams S. James, Governor Mandel, and Lt. Gov. Thomas Hunter Lowe; (standing) Dr. Wesley N. Dorn (executive director, MCHE), President H. Mebane Turner, Senator Roy N. Staten, and Dr. Joseph F. Keimig (assistant executive director, MCHE).

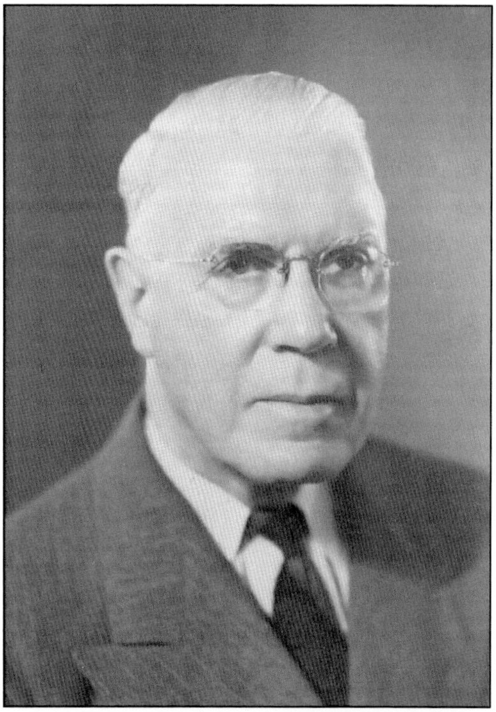

Maynard A. Clemens. In June of 1925, Dr. Clemens met at the University Club with Eugene Edgett, Clarence W. Miles, and Howell A. King, who was associated with the School of Business Administration at the University of Maryland. The details of the proposed university were thoroughly discussed and a tentative plan was formulated. Maynard Clemens's idea became a reality in August 1925, when a charter was granted under the general laws of Maryland to establish the University of Baltimore.

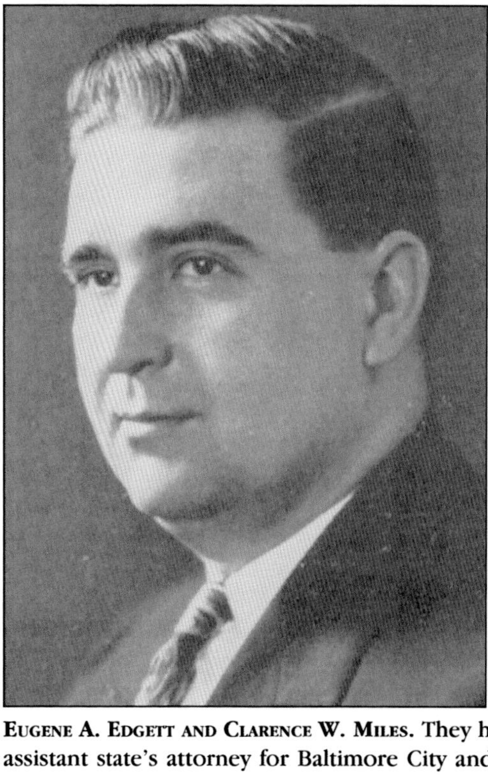

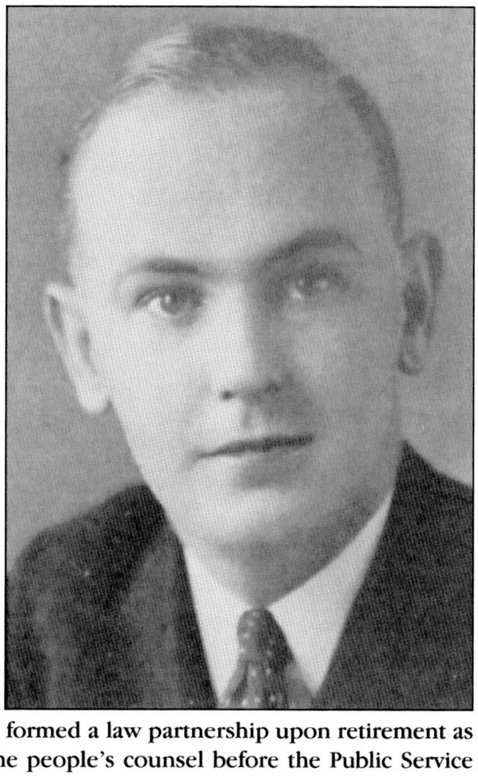

Eugene A. Edgett and Clarence W. Miles. They had formed a law partnership upon retirement as assistant state's attorney for Baltimore City and the people's counsel before the Public Service Commission, respectively. Mr. Edgett served as the assistant dean of the School of Law, and Mr. Miles was chairman of the Executive Committee.

Wilbur F. Smith. Dr. Smith became the university's first president in 1926 and held the position until his retirement in the fall of 1933, when he became president emeritus. Dr. Clemens approached Smith in 1925 and asked him to become the first president of the University of Baltimore. However, since Smith had one year before his retirement as president of Baltimore City College, it was agreed that Maynard A. Clemens would serve as chancellor from 1925 to 1926.

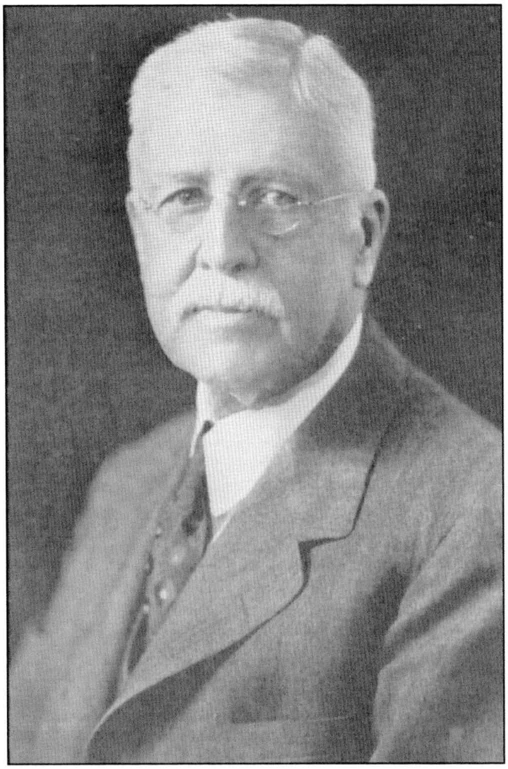

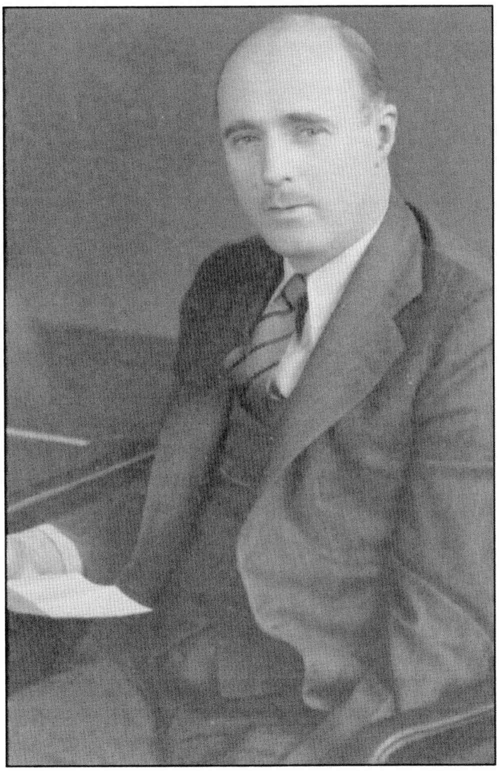

Howell A. King. One of the founders of the university, he served as executive dean before becoming the second president upon the retirement of Wilbur F. Smith in 1933. King served as president until 1935.

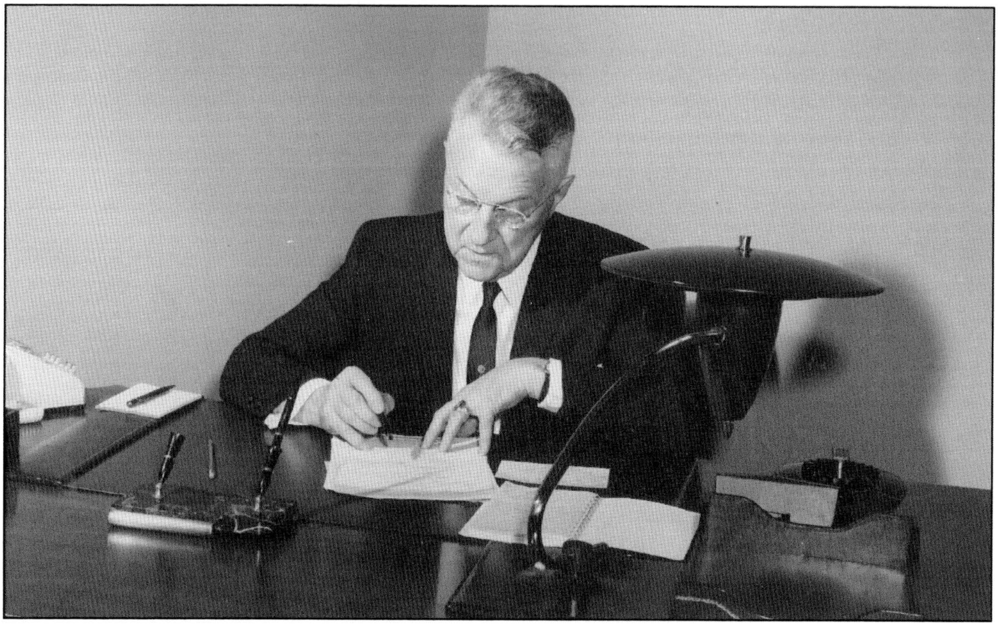

Wilmer A. DeHuff. After Theodore H. Wilson retired in 1961, the board of trustees appointed Dr. DeHuff as the acting president in 1962, in which capacity he served until 1964.

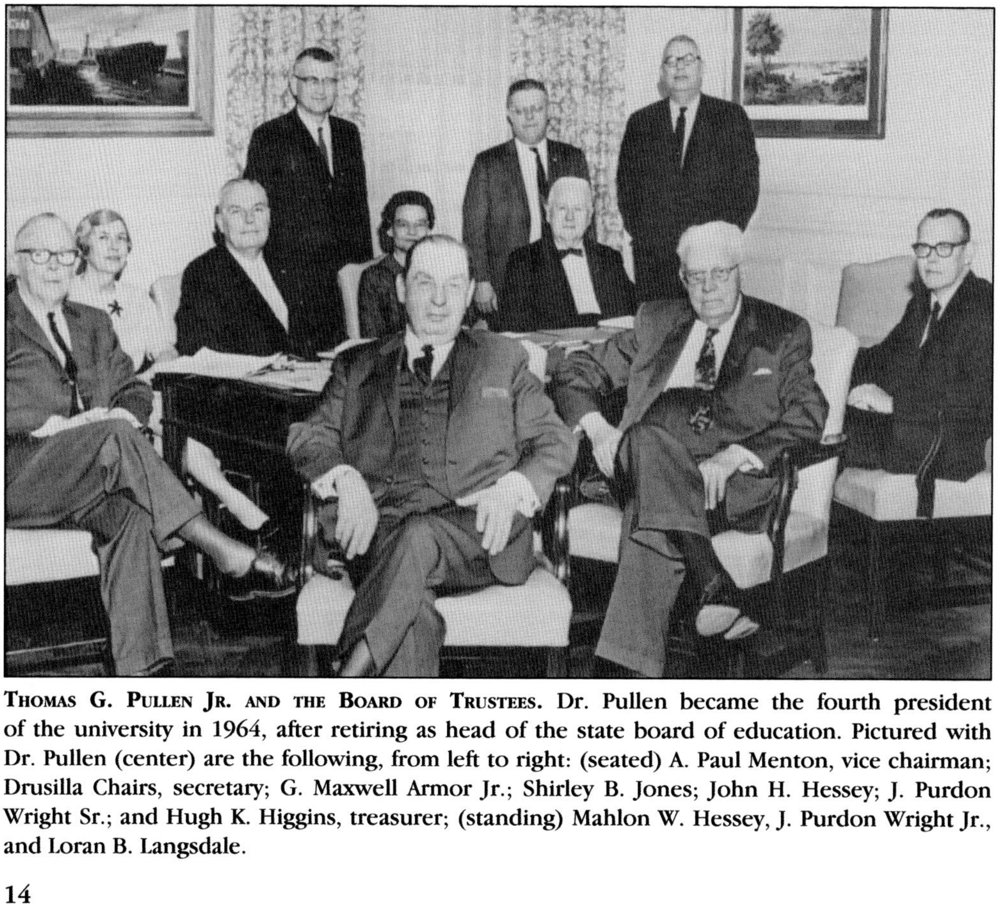

Thomas G. Pullen Jr. and the Board of Trustees. Dr. Pullen became the fourth president of the university in 1964, after retiring as head of the state board of education. Pictured with Dr. Pullen (center) are the following, from left to right: (seated) A. Paul Menton, vice chairman; Drusilla Chairs, secretary; G. Maxwell Armor Jr.; Shirley B. Jones; John H. Hessey; J. Purdon Wright Sr.; and Hugh K. Higgins, treasurer; (standing) Mahlon W. Hessey, J. Purdon Wright Jr., and Loran B. Langsdale.

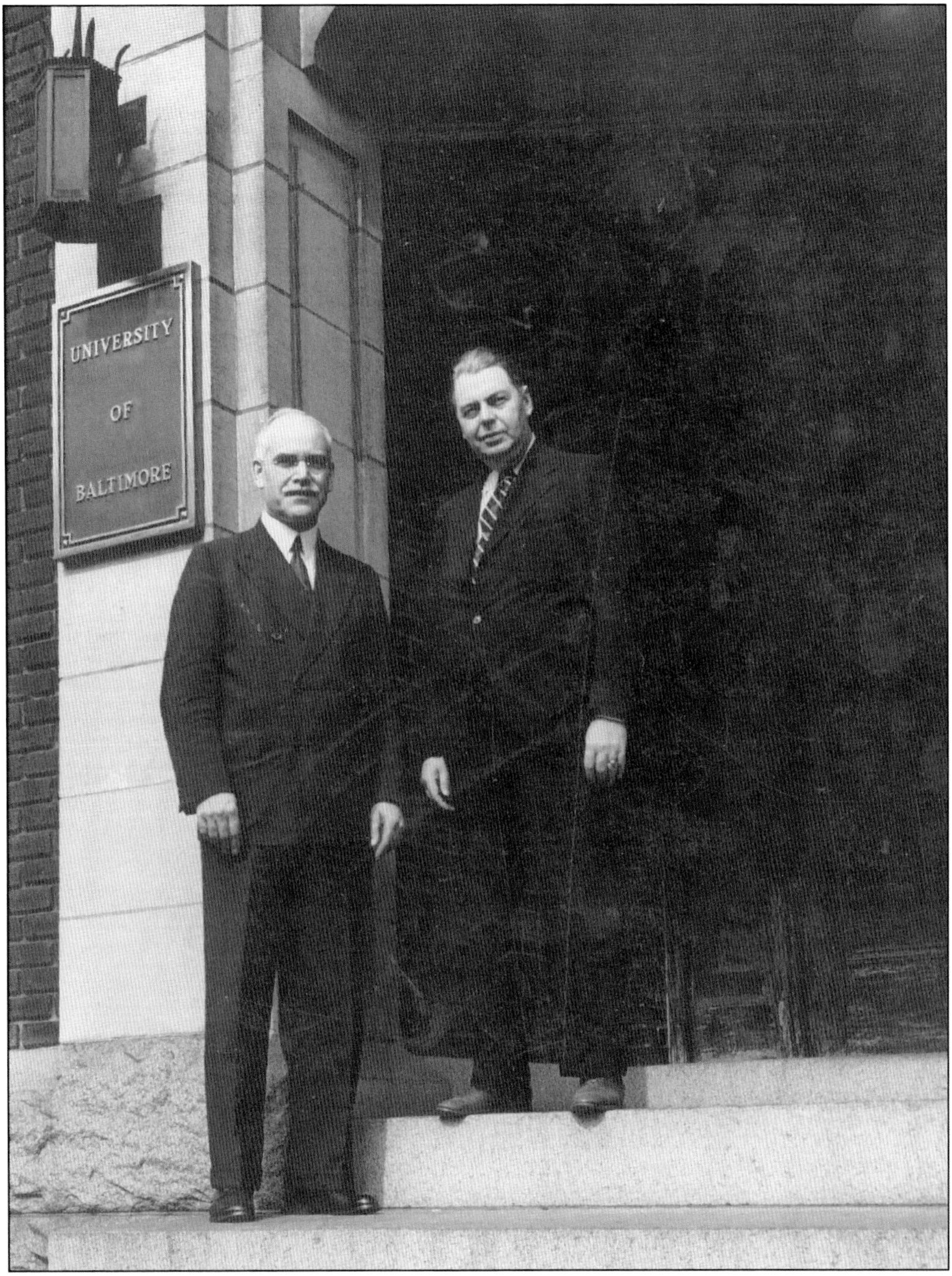

Founder and President. Photographed here are President Theodore H. Wilson (left) and Loran R. Langsdale on the steps of the newly acquired Charles Street building. Dr. Wilson came to the university in 1937 as an educational consultant and was named president in 1940. He served until his retirement in 1961. On the occasion of Dr. Wilson's 100th birthday, February 11, 1985, President H. Mebane Turner announced the establishment of the Theodore Halbert Wilson Scholarship Program. Dr. Wilson's crowning achievement was the establishment of the College of Liberal Arts. He died the following year on May 13.

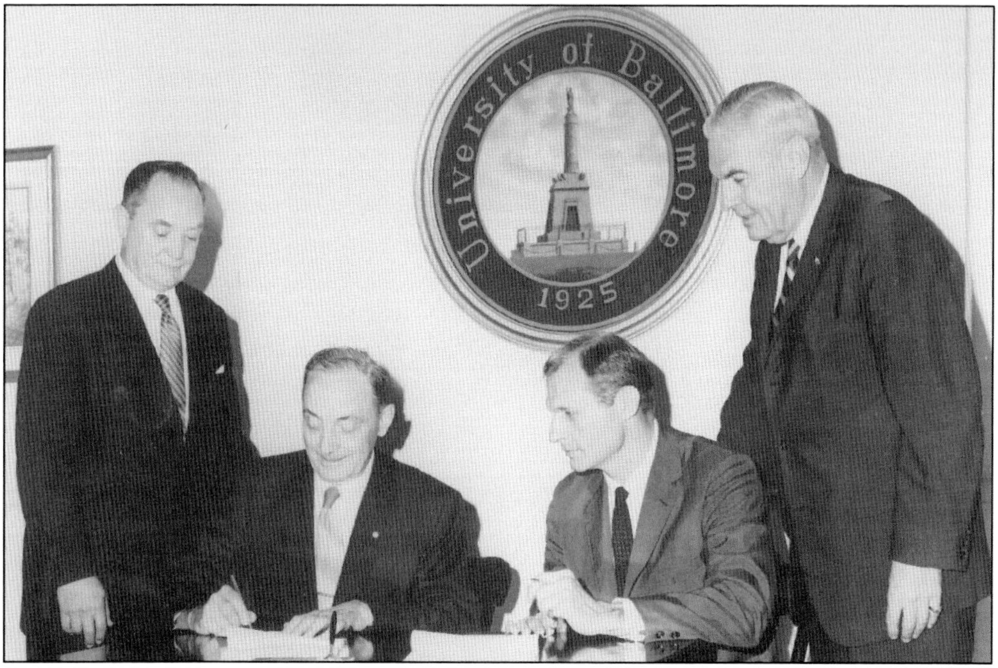

Eastern College and University of Baltimore Merged. On September 1, 1970, these people participated in a ceremony marking the merger of Eastern College, founded in 1928, which included the Mt. Vernon School of Law, founded in 1935, with UB. They are, from left to right, G. Maxwell Armor Jr. (UB chairman of the board of trustees), A. Risley Ensor (president of Eastern College), H. Mebane Turner, and Paul C. Zahn (chairman of the board of trustees of Eastern College).

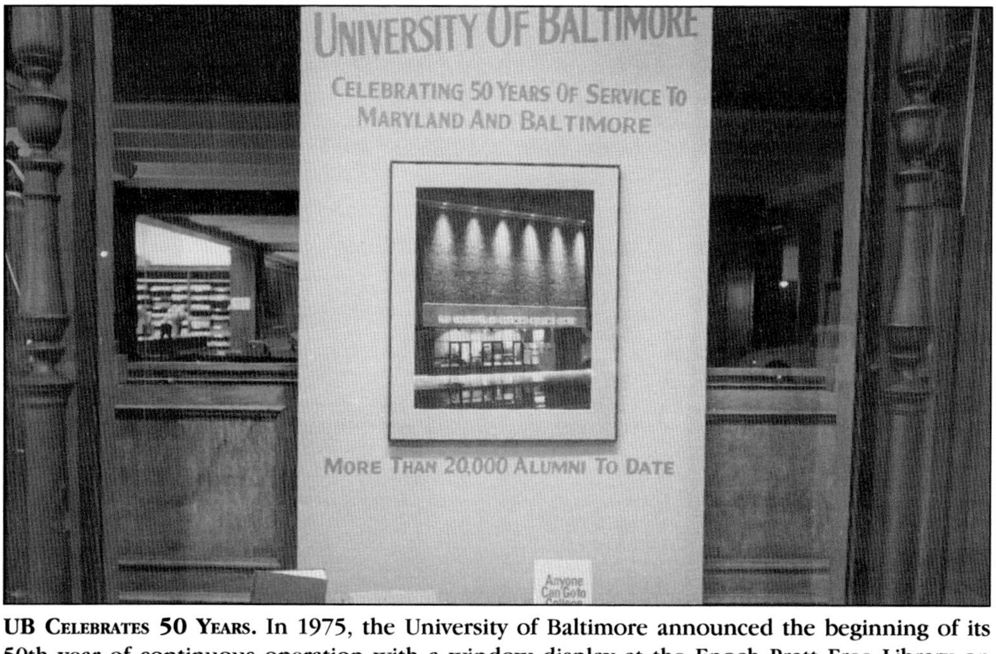

UB Celebrates 50 Years. In 1975, the University of Baltimore announced the beginning of its 50th year of continuous operation with a window display at the Enoch Pratt Free Library on Cathedral Street.

Two

Administrators, Faculty, and Staff

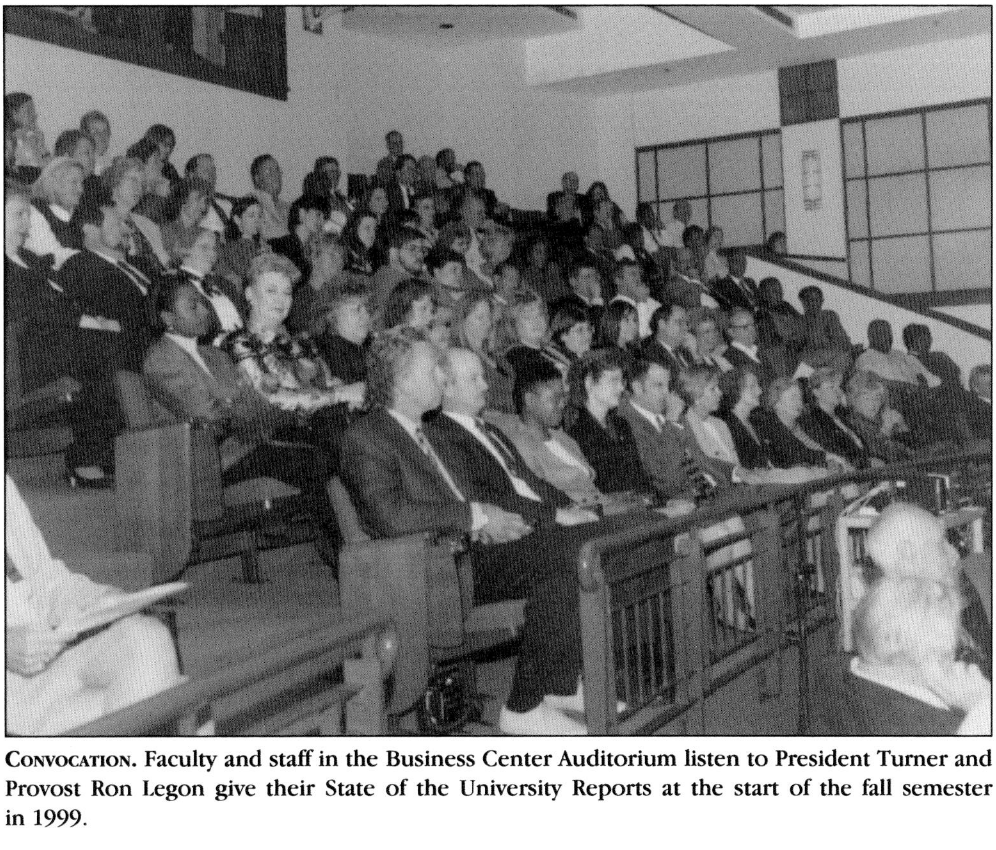

CONVOCATION. Faculty and staff in the Business Center Auditorium listen to President Turner and Provost Ron Legon give their State of the University Reports at the start of the fall semester in 1999.

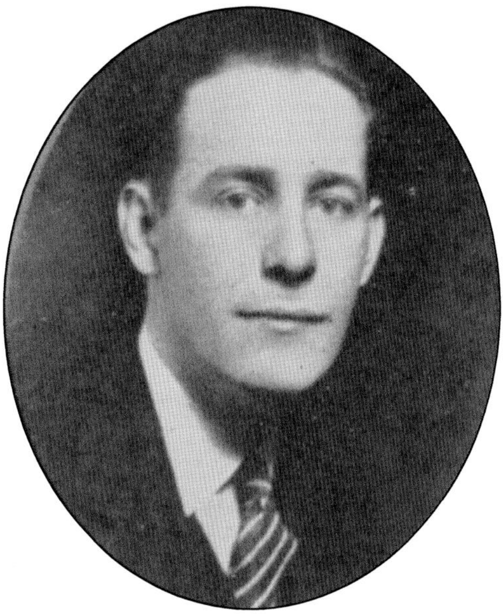 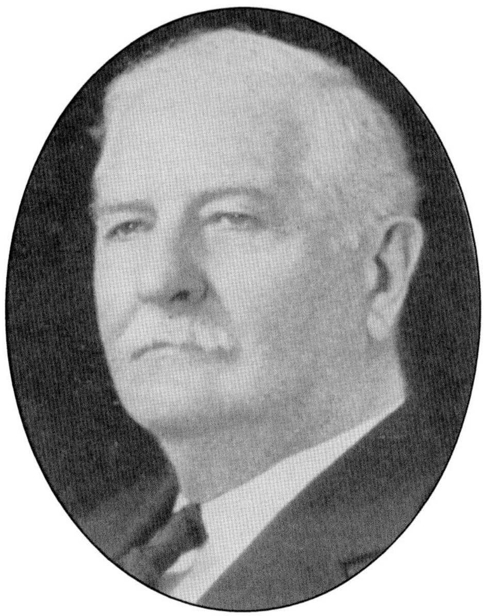

Distinguished Faculty. Among the early School of Law faculty was Herbert R. O'Conor (left), then state's attorney for Baltimore City, who taught criminal law. He later would become Maryland's governor. The Honorable James H. Preston (right), a former mayor of Baltimore, taught the class on municipal corporations.

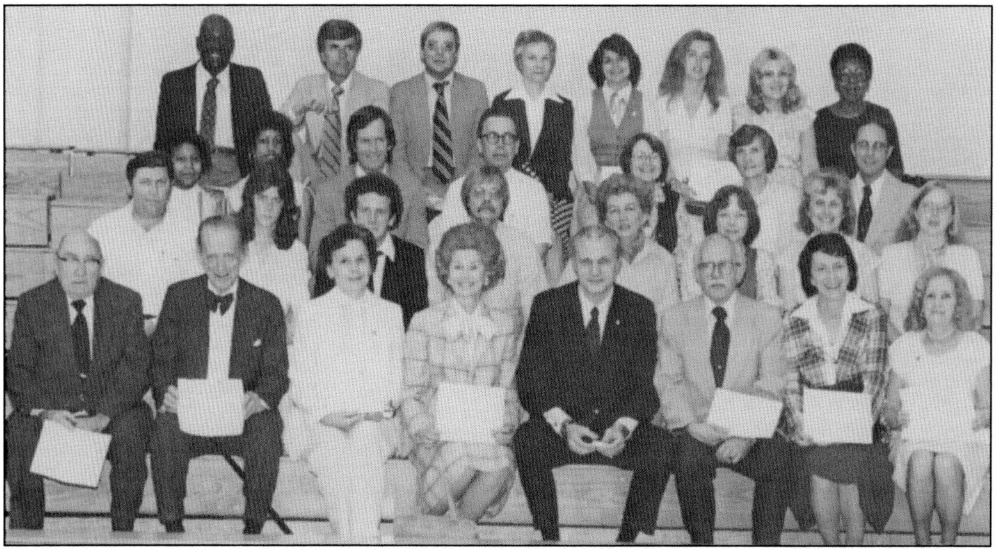

Three Hundred and Fifty-five Years of Service. In April 1979, 46 faculty, staff, and administrators were awarded certificates of service for years of employment ranging from five to ten years. Shown in the photograph are the following, from left to right: (front row) John Nicholson, George Slade, Irma Black, Dorothy Hobbs, H. Mebane Turner, Edward Fritz, Audrey Regner, and Mary Berger; (second row) Walter Strevig, Linda Shelton, J. David Ash, Ronald Bond, Betty C. Petzold, Joan Burns, Mary Pakulski, and Shirley Murphy; (third row) Linda Tate, Diane Kemp, Charles Reese, Francis Cooch, Carol Pierce, Doris Powell, and Bob Fudge; (back row) Dallas Purnell, Barry Bowen, Andrew Goletz, Mary L. Gardner, Kathie Diehl, Donna L. Pennepacker, Diane McDaniel, and Mae Ward.

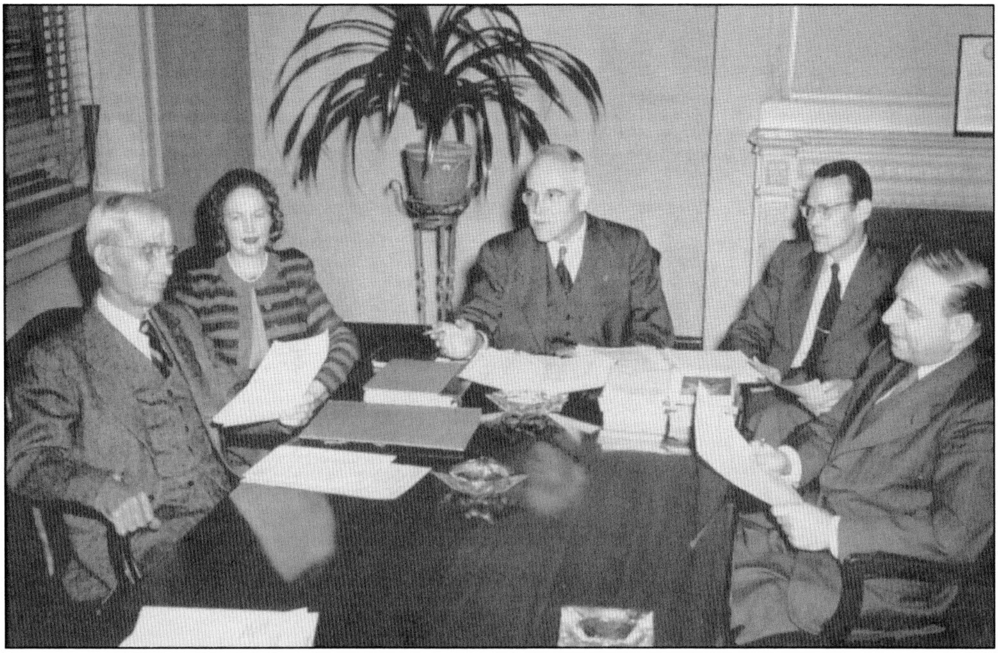

THE ADMINISTRATIVE COUNCIL. A 1951 photograph of the university's administrative council shows, from left to right, Dr. P. Lewis Kaye, dean of the junior college; Katherine Joyce, registrar; Dr. Wilson, president; Hugh K. Higgins, treasurer; and Clifford C. James, dean of the School of Business, Industry, and Management.

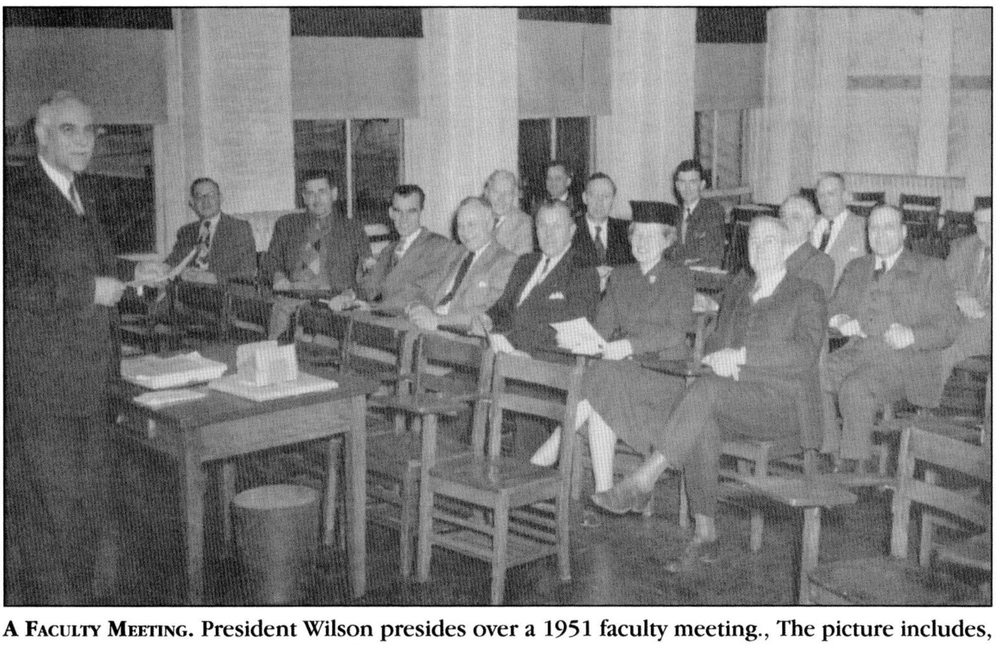

A FACULTY MEETING. President Wilson presides over a 1951 faculty meeting., The picture includes, from left to right, Dr. Wilson, Professors Russel B. Rice, B. Floyd Flickinger, Harry W. Amtower, Ernest S.Huberman, George H. Gottshall, Harvey S. Reed, John R. Spellissy, Lester Lindley, Florence C. Wilmer, John H. Webb, George A.Neeld, Raymond B. Nell, William C. Troutman, Clifford C. James, and Julius Nelson.

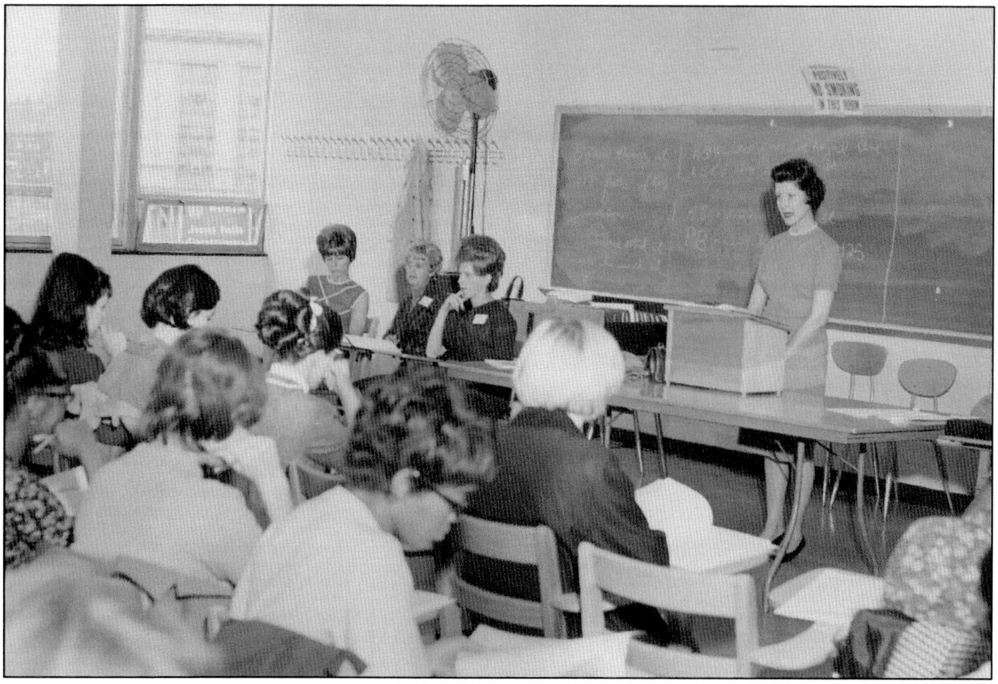

PROFESSOR GRACE LAWTON. This 1970 photograph shows Dr. Lawton teaching history and political science.

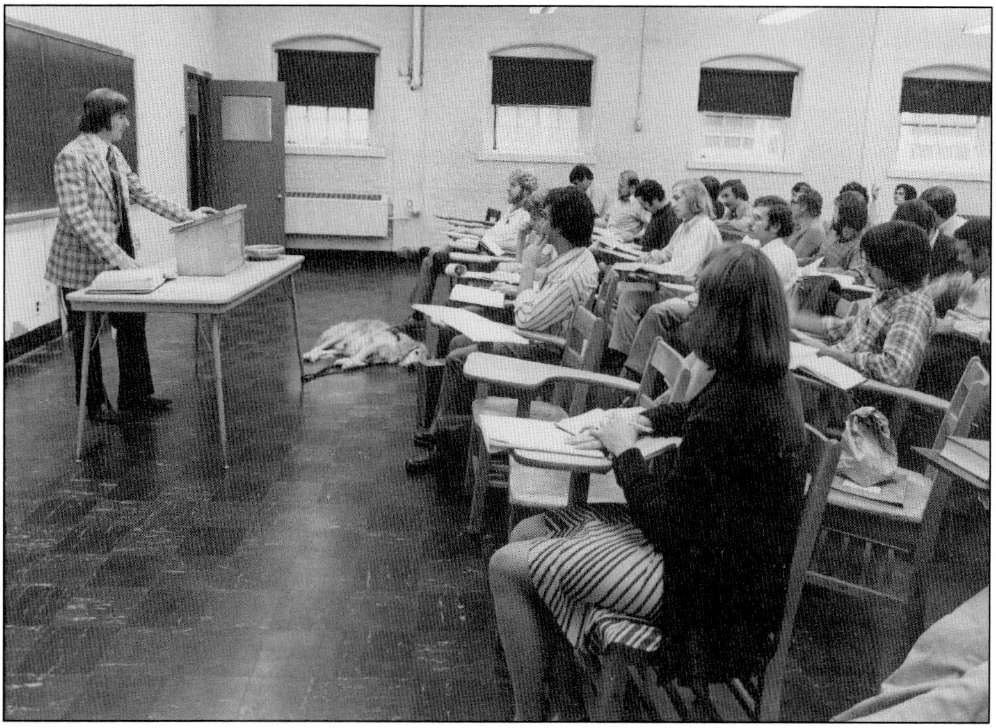

PROFESSOR JOE SMITH. Dr. Smith instructs one of his law classes as Elf, his seeing-eye dog, lies on the floor waiting for the class to end.

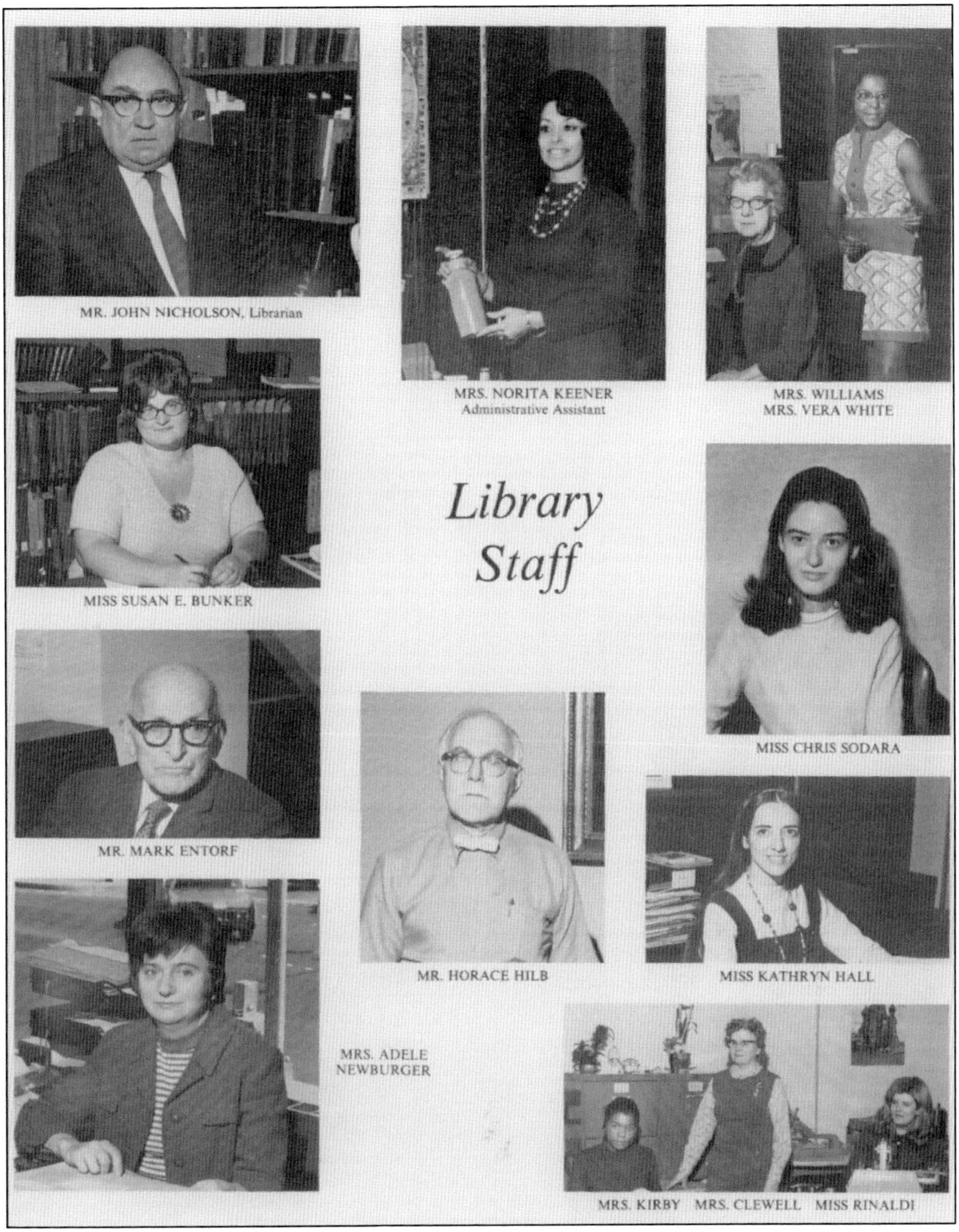

LIBRARY STAFF. A page from the 1972 yearbook, *The Reporter*, shows the staff of Langsdale Library.

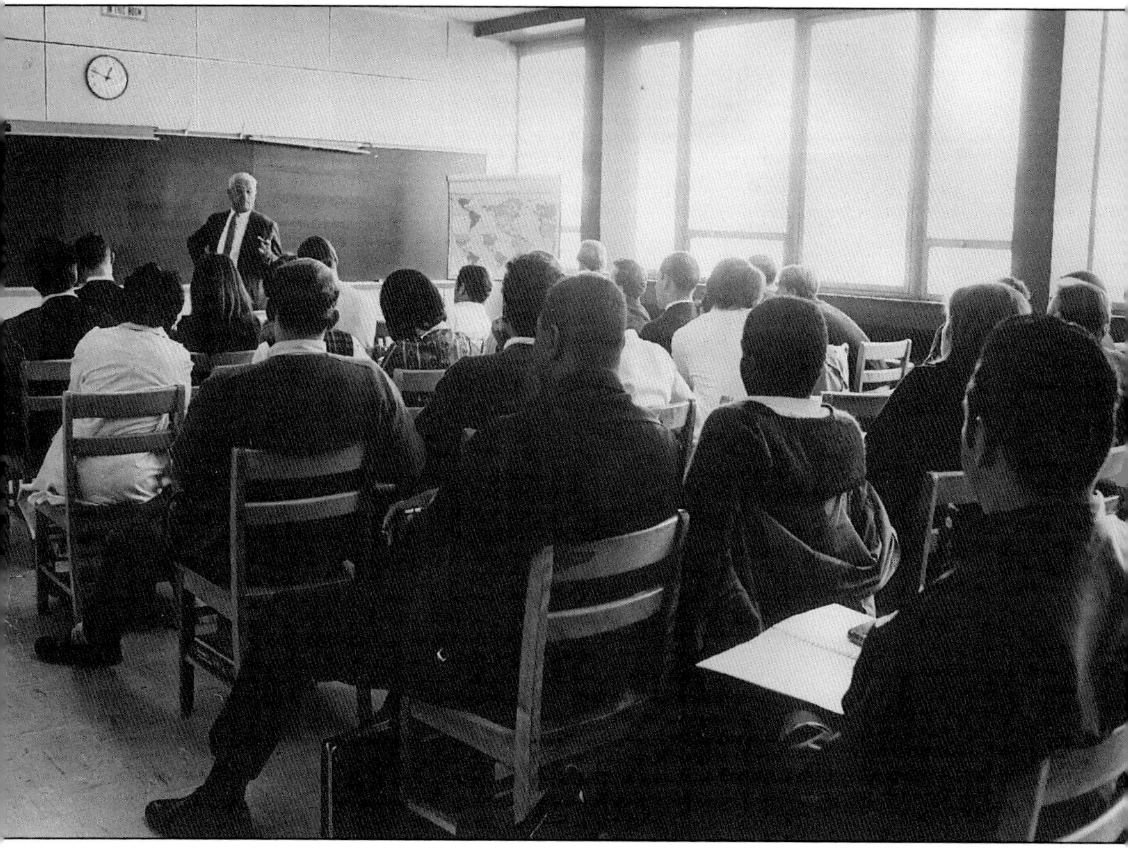

Professor Nelson Blake. Dr. Blake lectures his history class in this 1970 yearbook photograph.

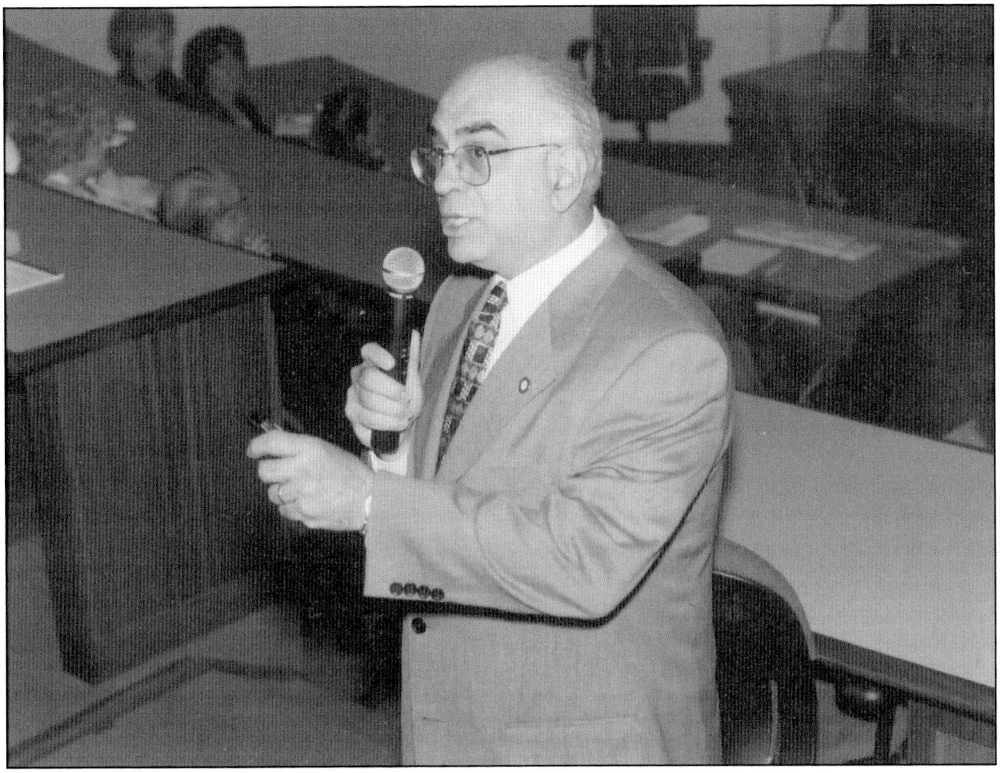

Ronald Legon. Dr. Legon was appointed provost in August 1992. Before his appointment, he was at the University of Illinois at Chicago.

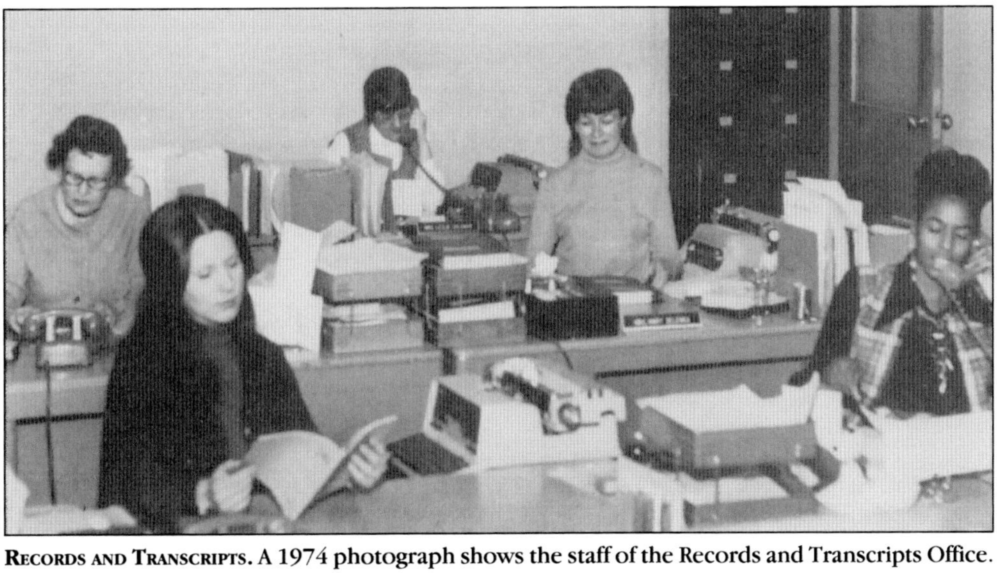

Records and Transcripts. A 1974 photograph shows the staff of the Records and Transcripts Office. From left to right are Nancy Rumsey, Leslie Coleman, Mary Zelenka, and Patricia Harris.

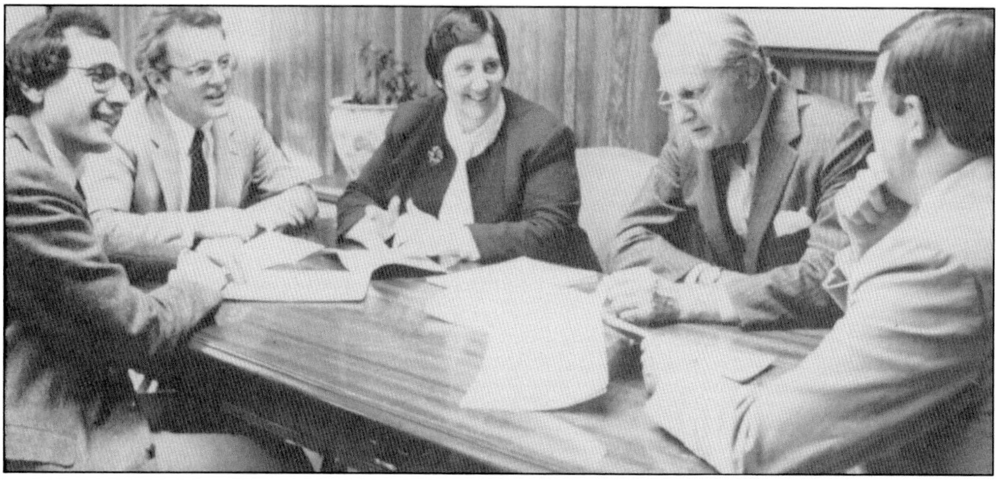

Catherine Gira. Dr. Gira taught English at the university before being named provost in 1982. In 1990, she left UB to become president of Frostburg State University. This photograph shows her with grants administrators after the College of Liberal Arts was awarded a $139,000 grant from the Fund for the Improvement of Post Secondary Education.

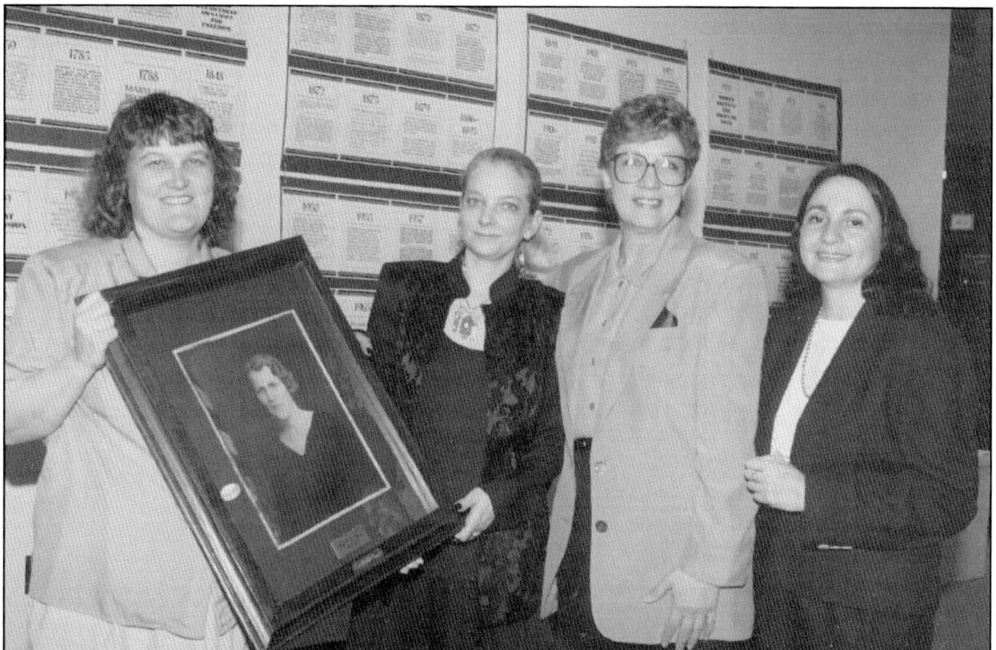

Women's History Month. The law faculty and staff celebrate Women's History Month in 1994. Pictured here are, from left to right, Pat Beahles, Leslie Oswin, Mary Boyd (law graduate), and Valerie Diamond with a photographic portrait of Mary Risteau, a School of Law graduate and the first woman to serve in the Maryland Legislature.

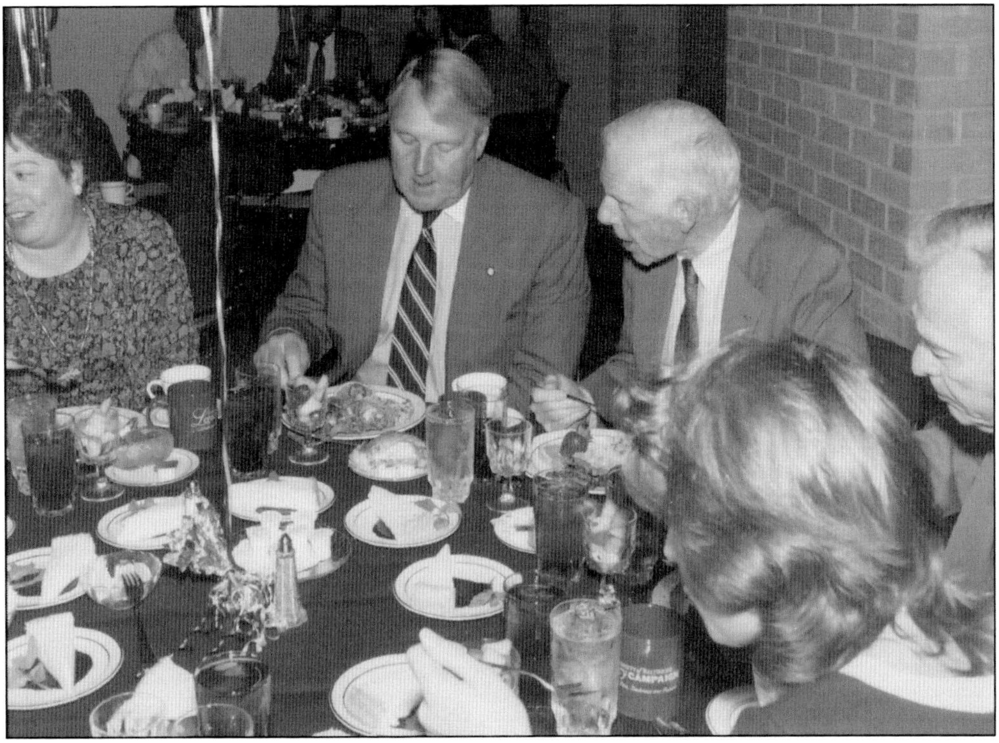

A Legacy Campaign Luncheon. After the fall 1999 convocation, a luncheon for faculty and staff was held in the atrium of the Thumel Business Center to kick-off the university's Legacy Campaign. Pictured here, from left to right, are Karen Drake, Carl Stenberg, Louis Gawthrop, Lawrence Downey, and Barbara Aughenbaugh.

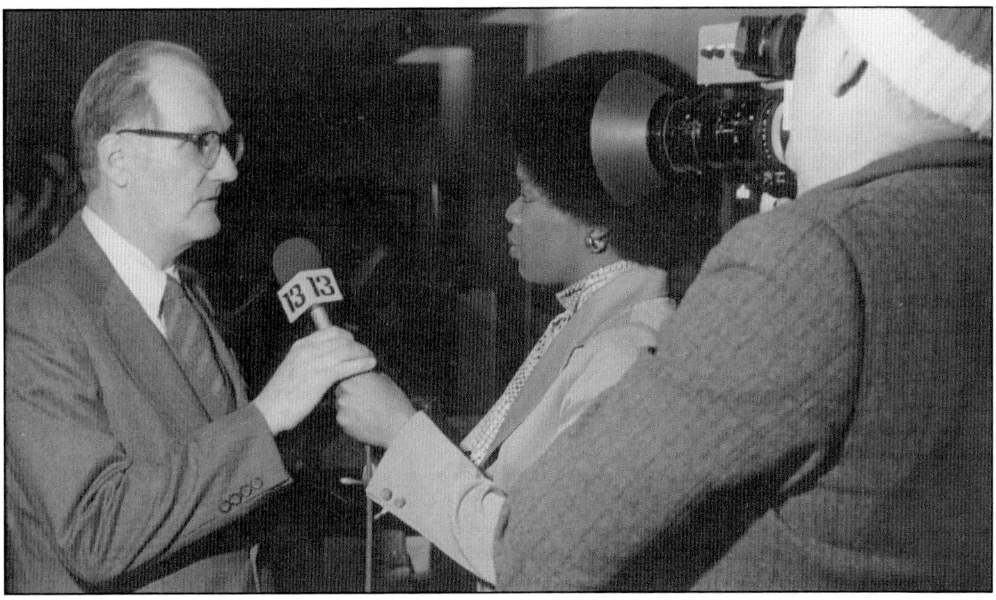

The Baltimore History Conference. In March of 1978, Oprah Winfrey (then a reporter for WJZ-TV) interviewed Professor Randall Beirne at the history conference that he helped to organize and participated in at the university.

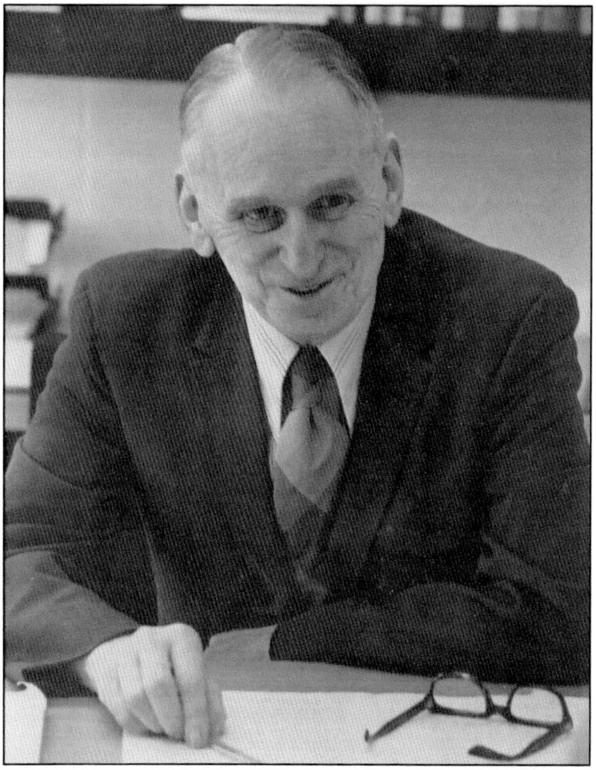

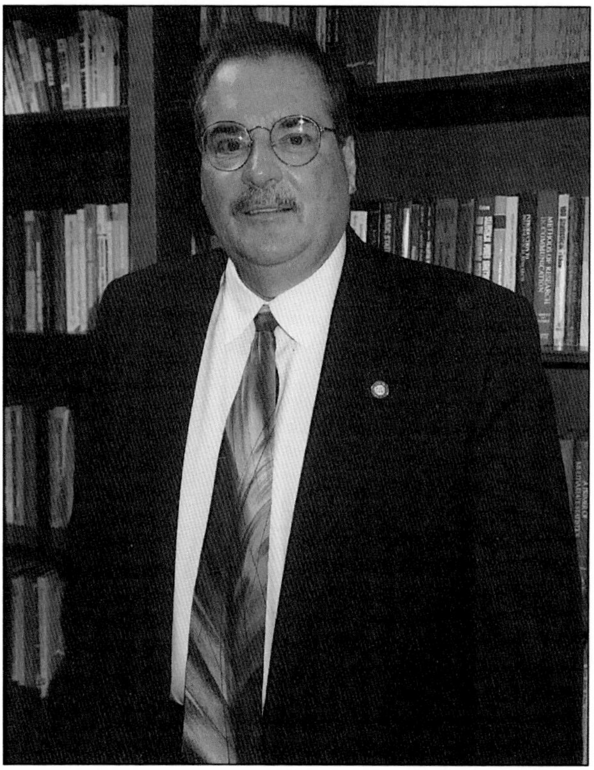

Business School Deans. Harry Watson (above) served as dean of the School of Business from 1970 until his retirement in 1973. John D. Hatfield (below) became dean of the Merrick School of Business on June 1, 1996.

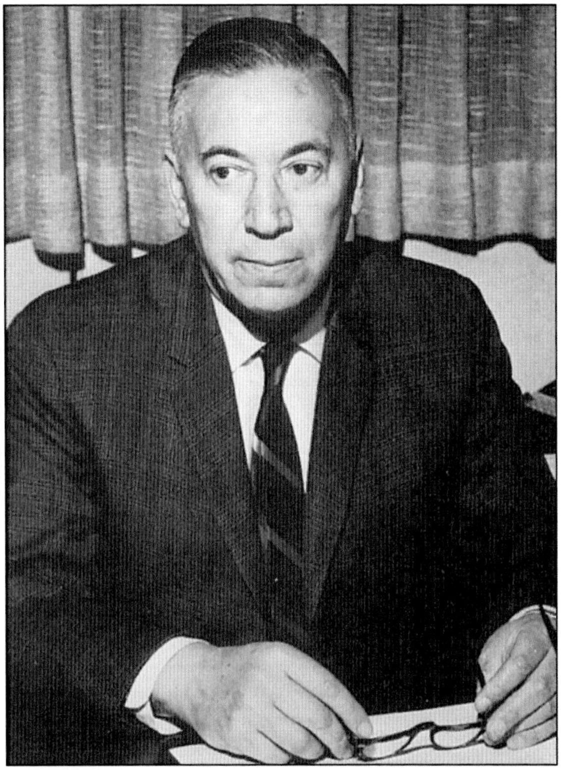

LAW SCHOOL DEANS. Dr. Joseph Curtis (above) served as dean of the School of Law from 1969 until 1978. The first dean of the School of Law was Judge Charles W. Heuisler (below), the former associate judge of the Supreme Bench of Baltimore City. He served from 1925 until his death in 1929, when Sen. William M. Maloy became dean. John H. Hessey succeeded Maloy.

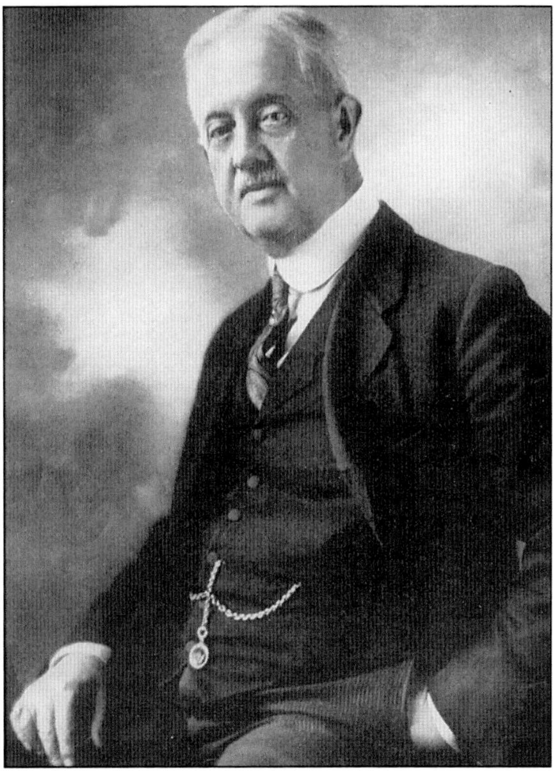

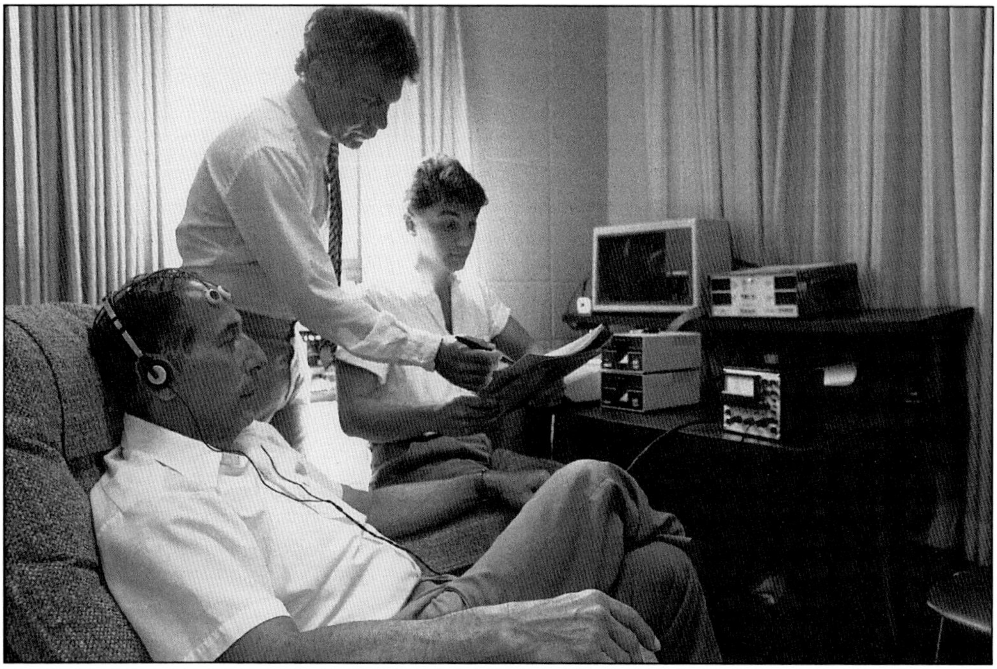

Division of Applied Psychology and Quantitative Methods. In the above photograph, Thomas Mitchell (center), program director, conducts a psychological test. with fellow Psychology professor George Lassen (left) and an unidentified student (right). William Wagman (below) reviews one of this psychology student's data on the computer screen. This program provides students with broad exposure to the theoretical, methodological, quantitative, and applied aspects of psychology necessary for careers in psychology and related fields. The faculty members have research and professional skills in counseling, psychopathology, industrial/organizational psychology, data analysis, psychological assessment, and neuropsychology.

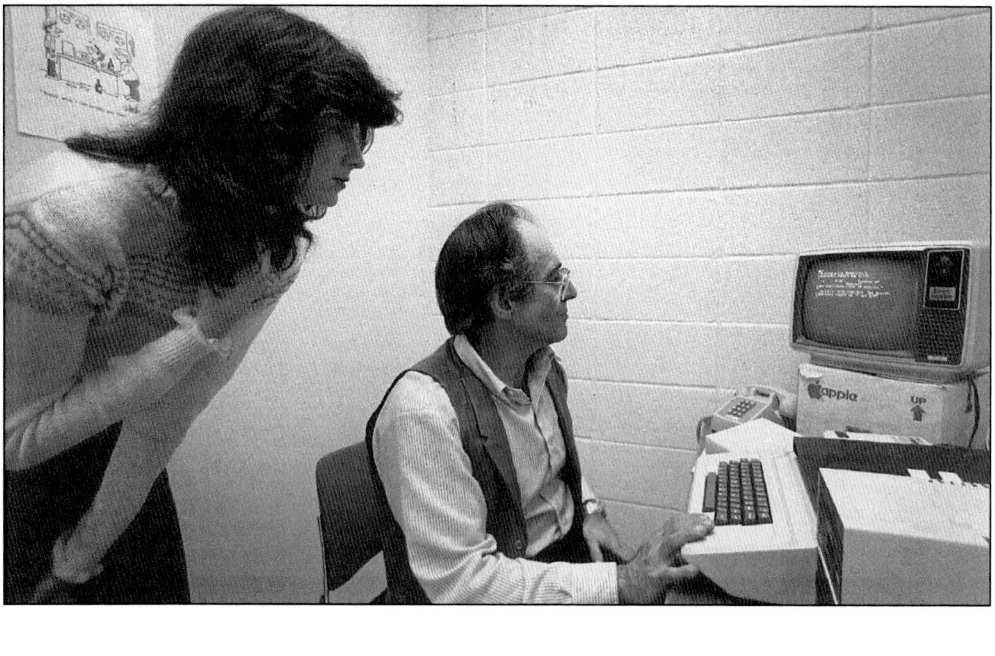

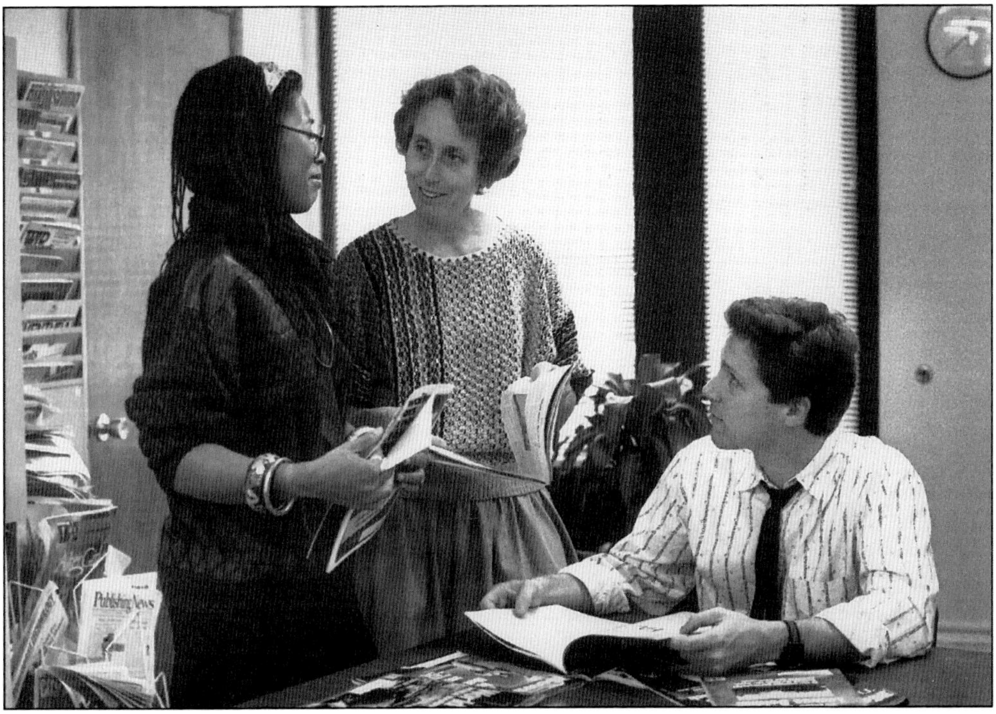

The School of Communication Design. Virginia Carruthers (center), the director of the masters program in Publications Design, advises two graduate students, Natsha Ortiz (left) and Cass Taylor (right).

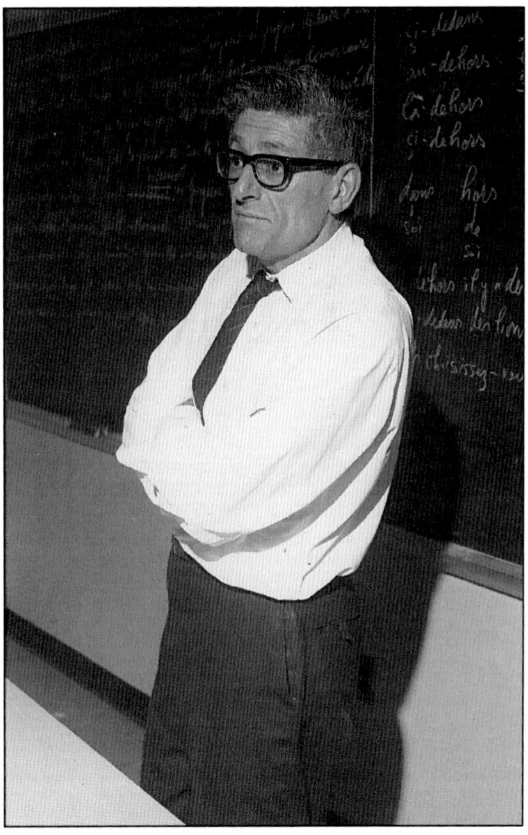

Lawrence Short. In this 1970 photograph, Dr. Short is seen listening to a student response in his language class.

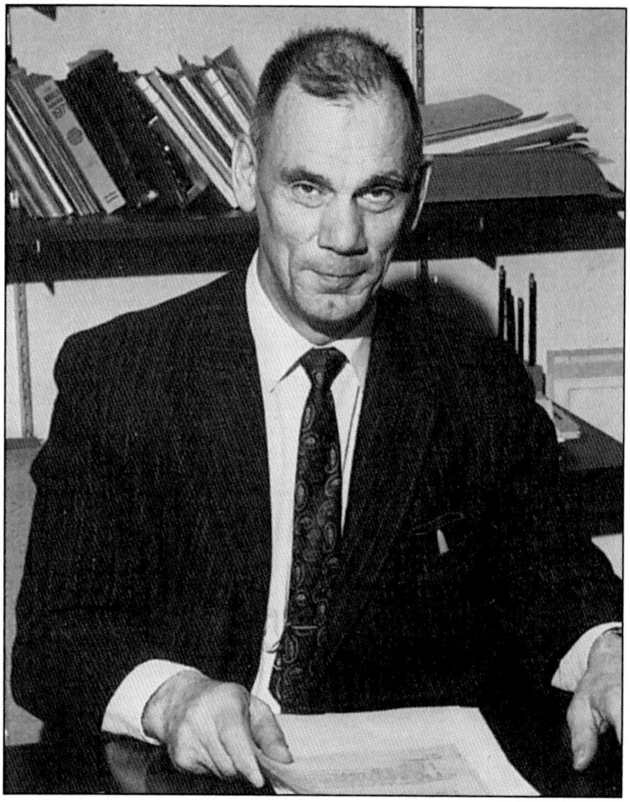

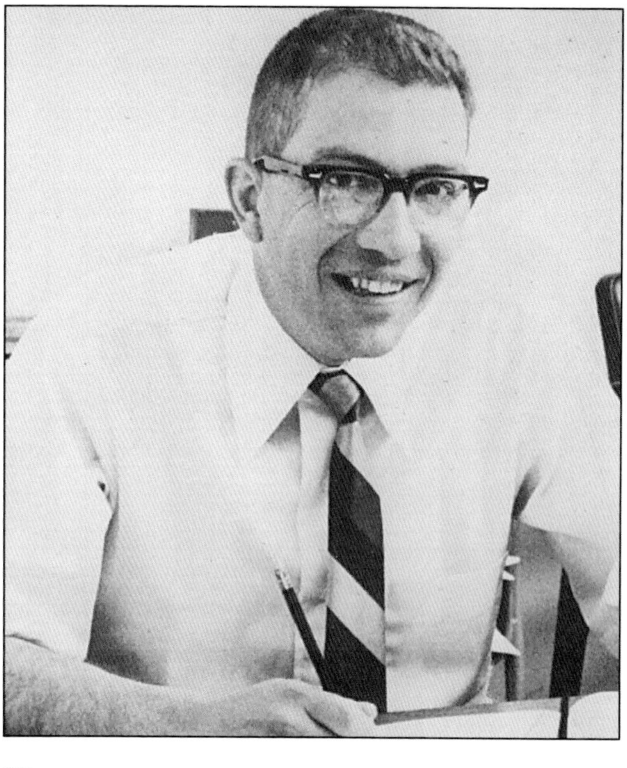

LIBERAL ARTS DEANS. Lawrence D. Bridgham (above) served as dean of the College of Liberal Arts. Fred W. Hopkins Jr. (below) served as dean of Admissions and later taught history in the Legal, Ethical, and Historical Studies Department.

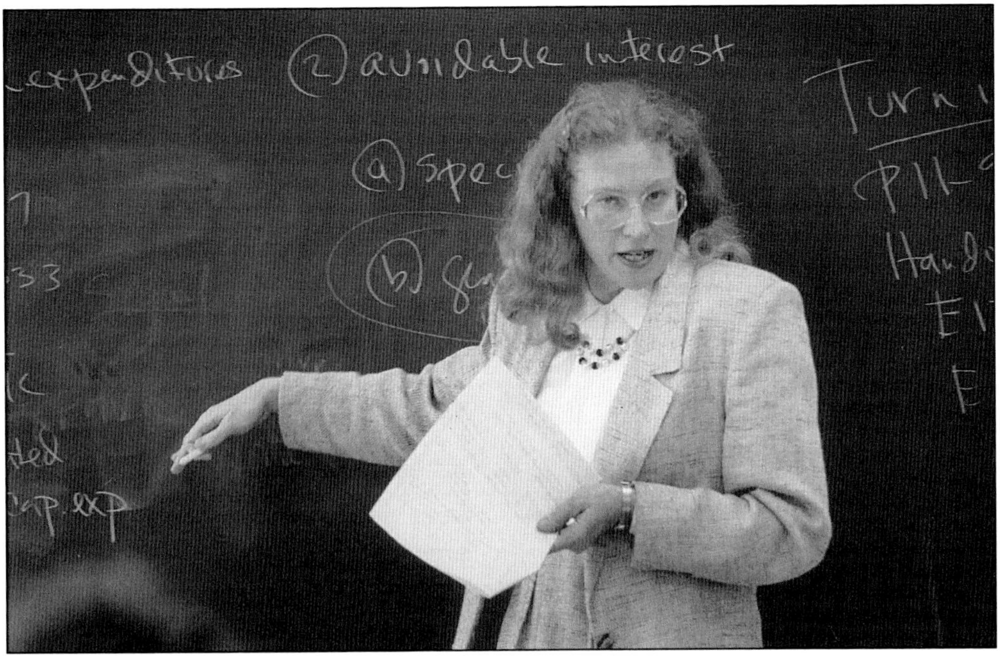

Accounting Specialist. Susan Lynn teaches accounting to students who are planning careers in the accounting profession. Flexibility is built into the program so that students are prepared for employment in the public, private, or governmental sectors. Additionally, courses leading to a position in the accountancy field prepare students for the rigors of the CPA and CMA exams.

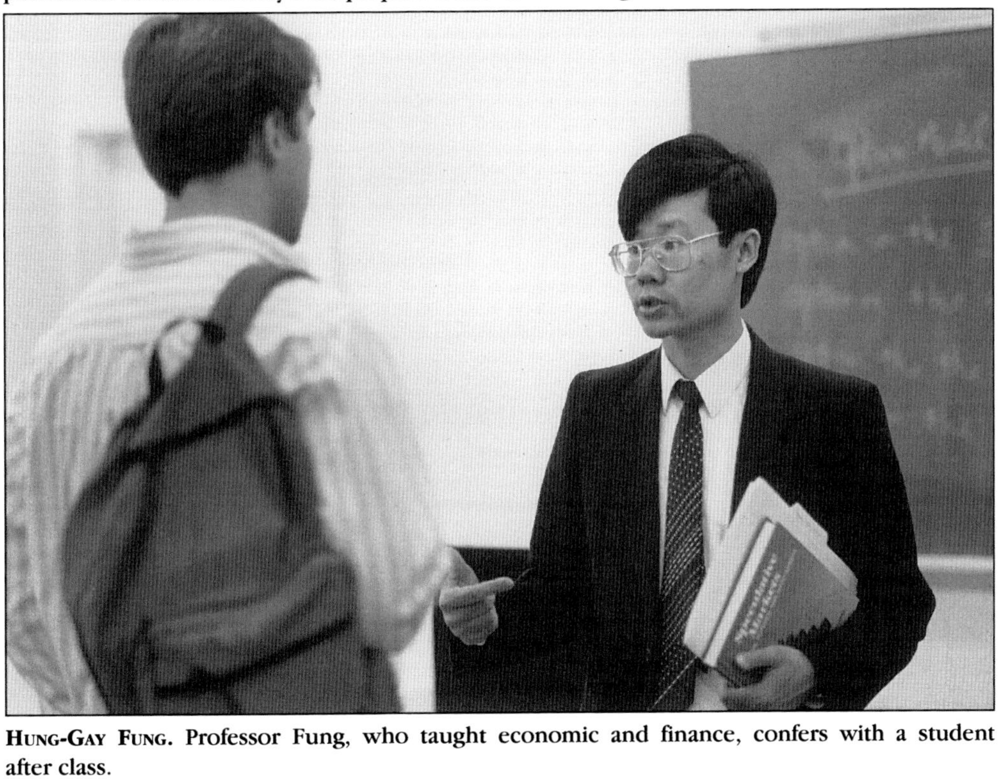

Hung-Gay Fung. Professor Fung, who taught economic and finance, confers with a student after class.

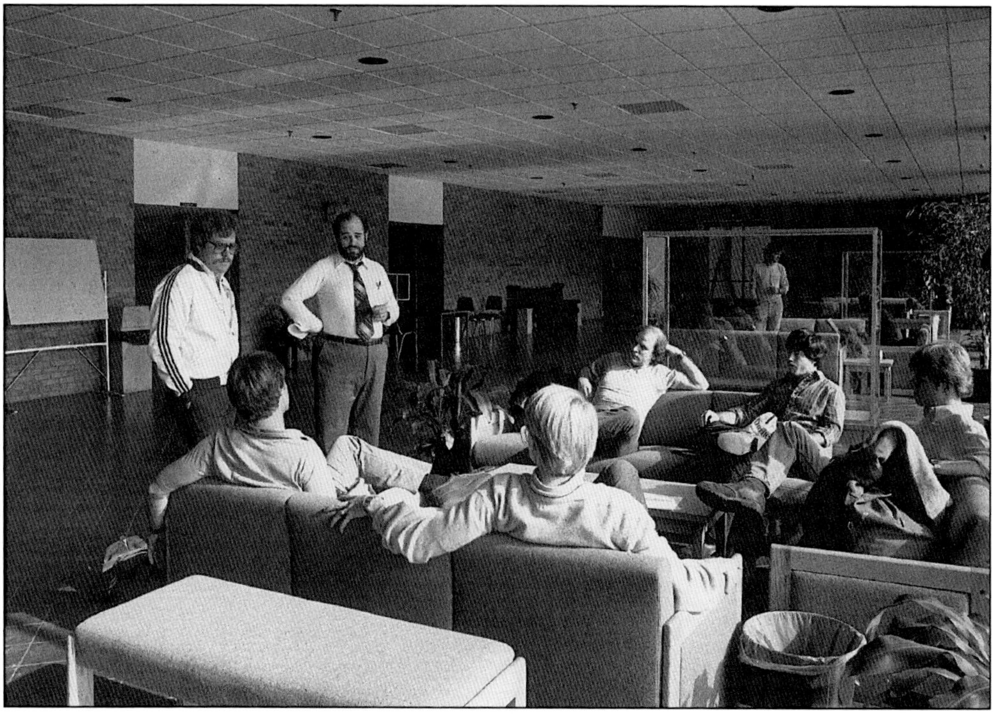

Two Law Professors. In the photograph above, William I. Weston, director of the internship program, speaks with a group of law students in the lobby of the Law Center. Perry Wallace, who taught securities law, emphasizes a point during his class lecture in the photograph below.

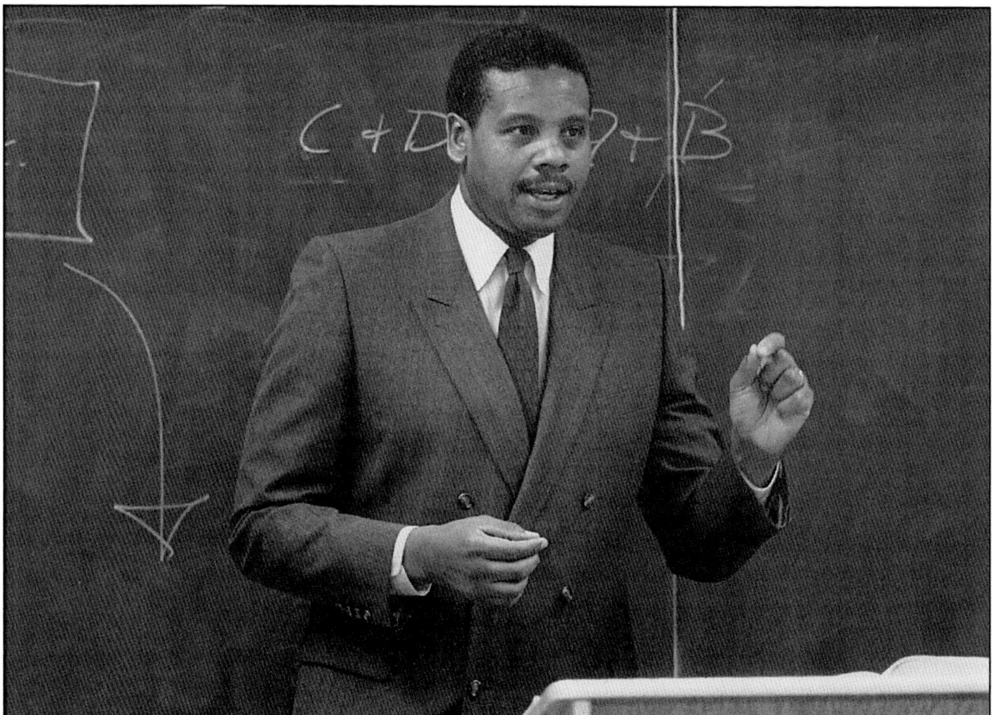

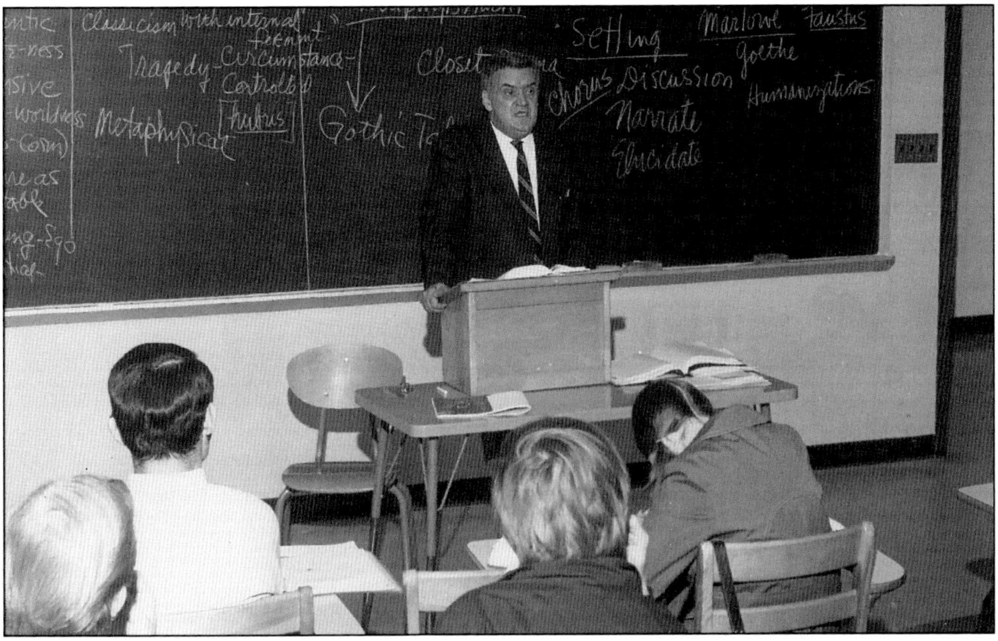

GEORGE MUTCH. Professor George Mutch instructs his English class in this 1970 photograph.

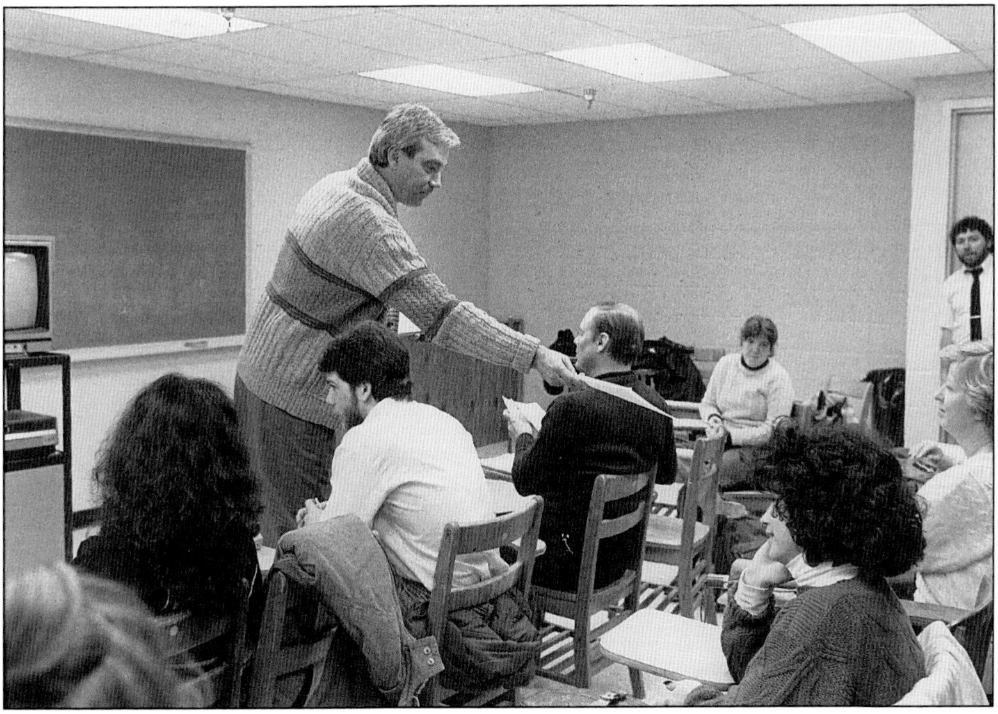

FRED GUY. The director of the Hoffberger Center for Professional Ethics since 1994, Dr. Fred Guy returns students' exams. He is an associate professor in the Legal, Ethical, and Historical Studies Department.

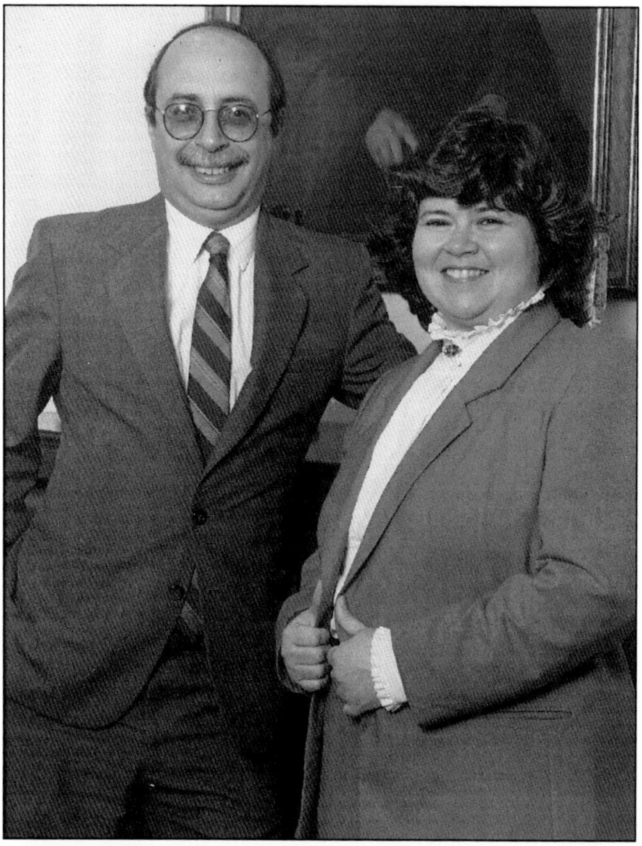

Albert and Regina Bento. Albert Bento is an associate professor of information and quantitative sciences, and his wife, Regina, is an assistant professor of management in the Merrick School of Business.

The Y2K Laboratory. The laboratory was used to assist private sector businesses and government agencies prepare for the Y2K problem with their computing and information systems. Seen in this photograph, from left to right, are Konstantin Smirnnov, research associate; Gortan Resinovic, visiting professor from the University of Ljubljana, Slovenia; Song Zhang, research assistant; Milton Jenkins, director; and Oveta Popjoy, visiting faculty.

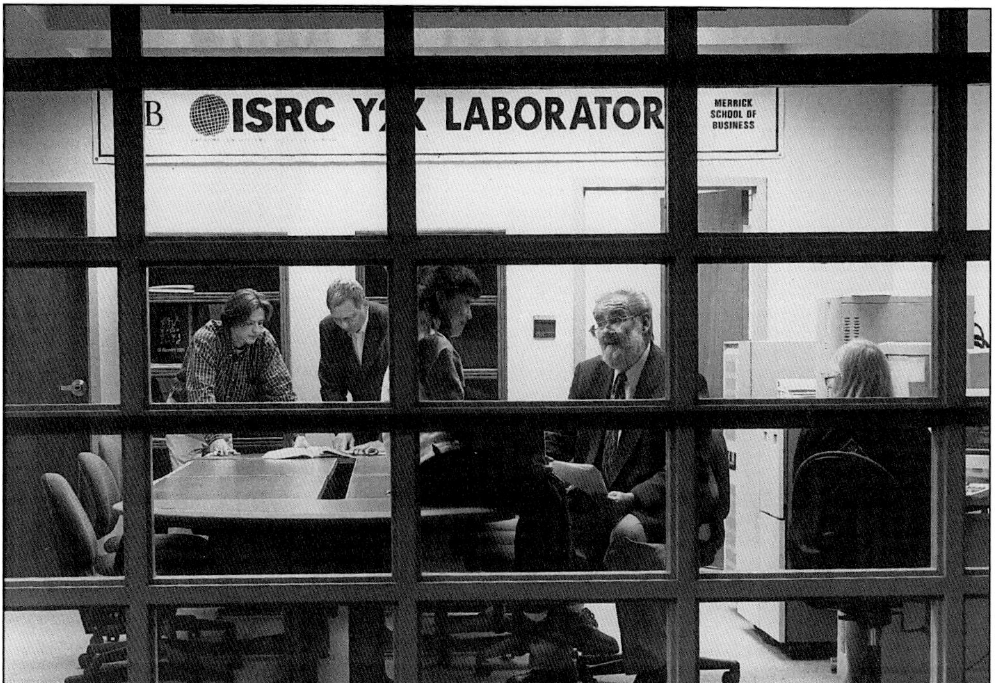

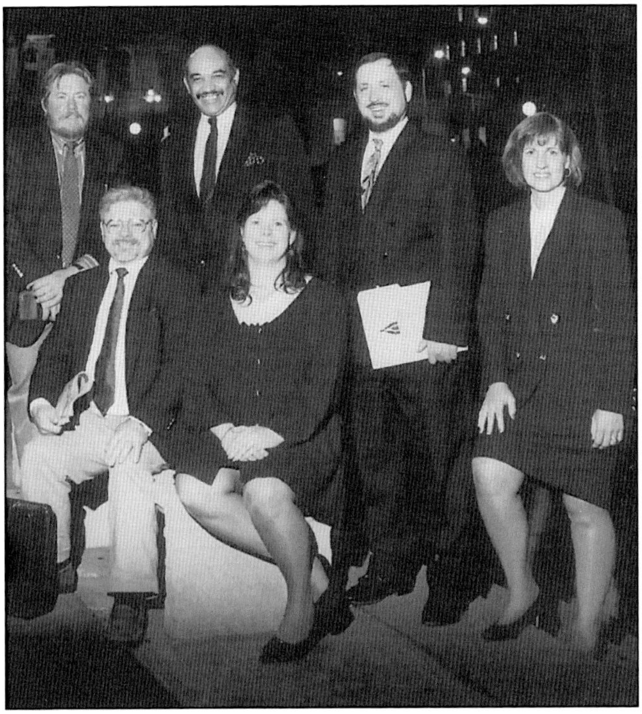

The Schaefer Center. Established in April 1985, the center was named for William Donald Schaefer, UB alumnus and mayor of Baltimore City, as a way to promulgate the university's public service mission. Its focus is researching, training, and educational programs on public policy issues of importance to the city, state, and region. Laslo Boyd served as the first director until 1987, when he joined Governor Schaefer's administration. Provost Catherine Gira then appointed Larry Thomas as the second director. In this 1995 photograph, staff members are, from left to right, Don Haynes, Dennis McGrath, Lenneal Henderson, Ann Cotton, Larry Thomas, and Diane Aull.

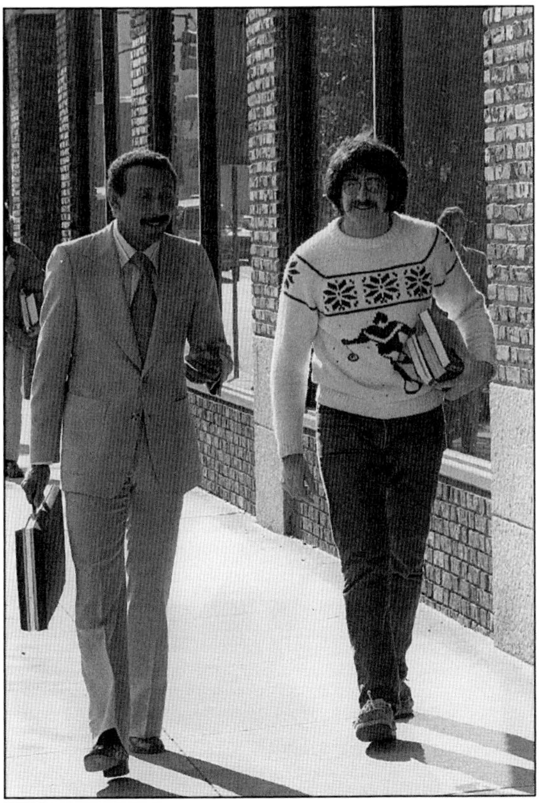

Reginald Thomas. Dr. Reginald Thomas advises an unidentified student in this 1970s photograph.

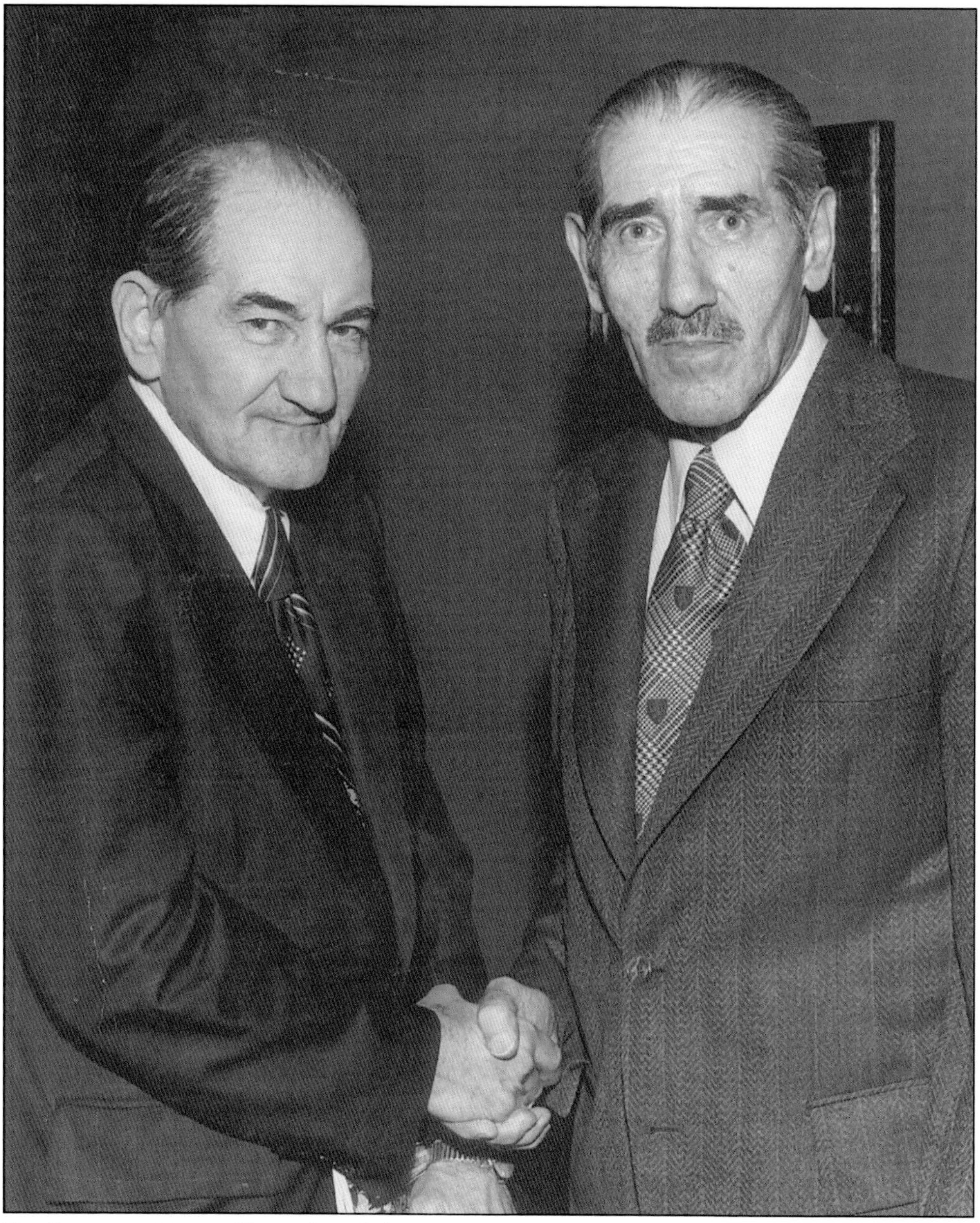

The Ginsburgs. Pictured here, from left to right, are brothers Isidore and Hyman Ginsburg, who were among the early law faculty. Hyman is famous for his "I demand absolute quiet, but if you must talk remember I can out shout all of you."

Three

STUDENTS

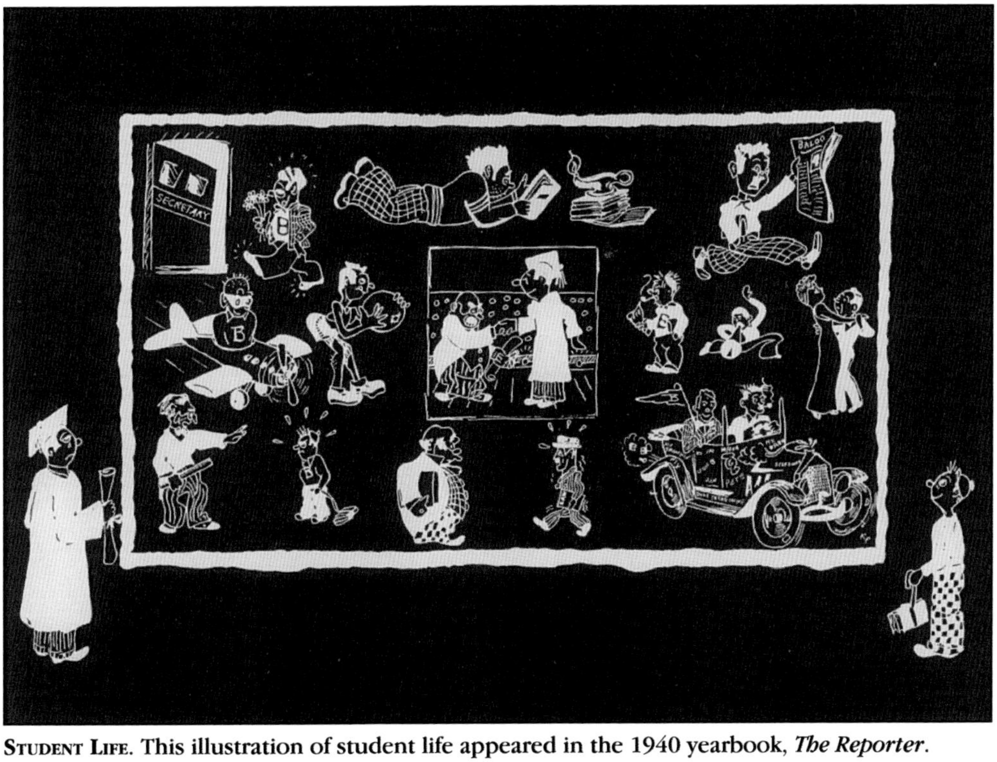

STUDENT LIFE. This illustration of student life appeared in the 1940 yearbook, *The Reporter*.

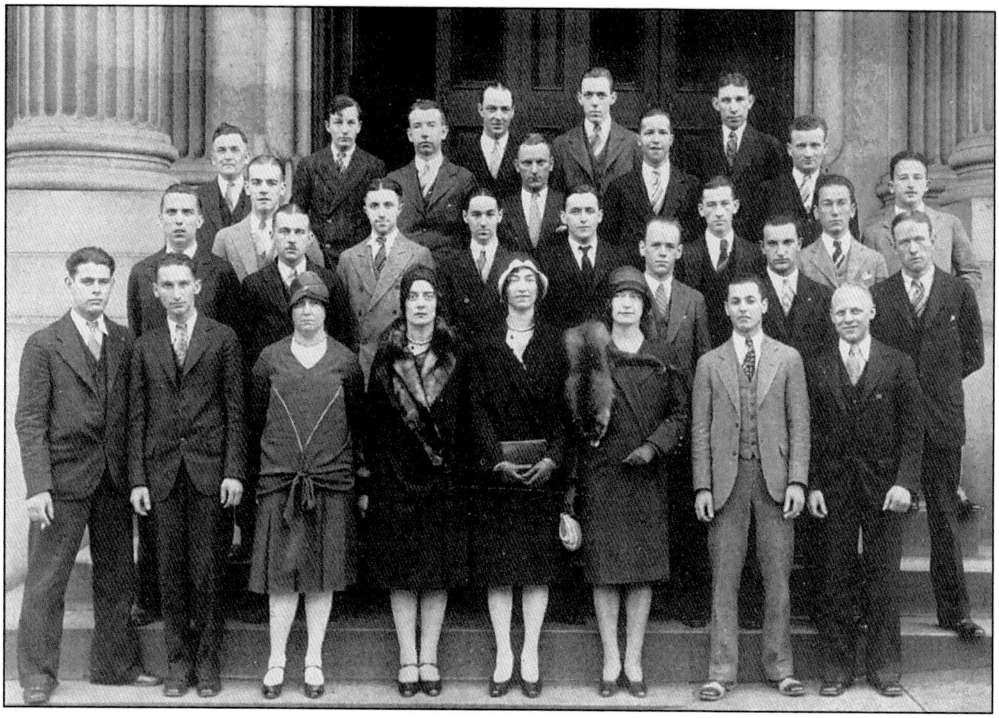

The School of Business. Students of the evening school freshman Class of 1929 pose on the steps of the Peabody Institute Library on Mount Vernon Square.

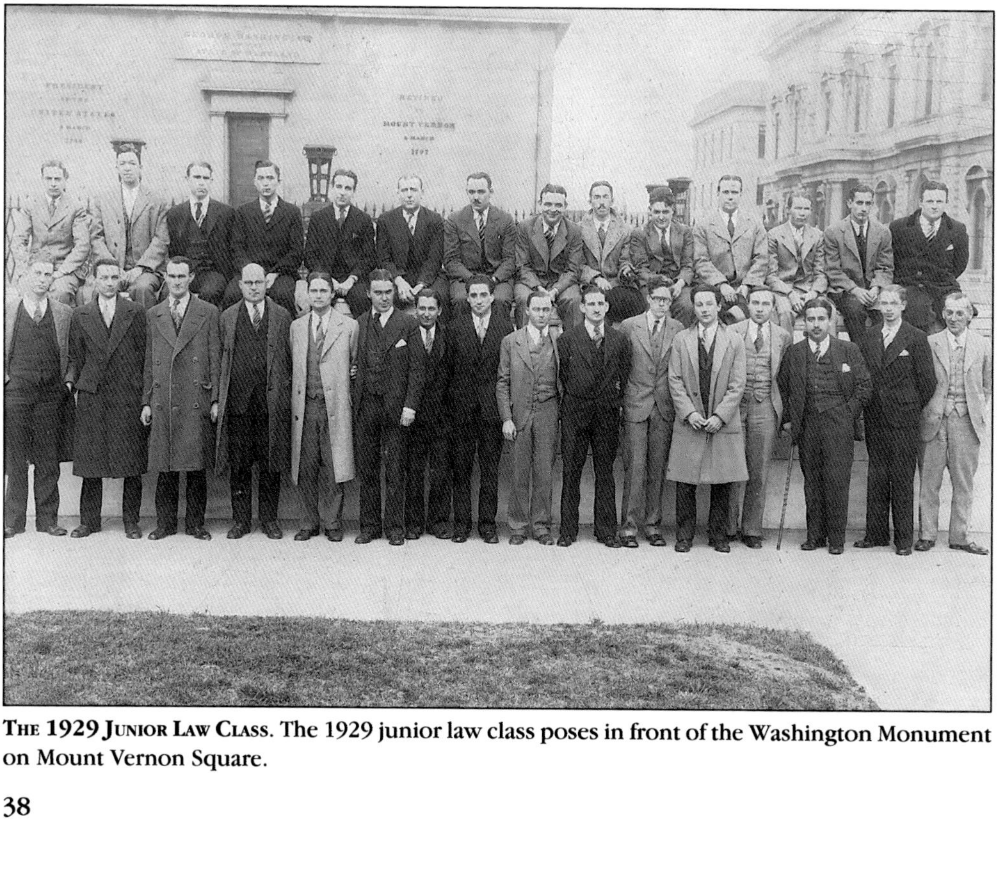

The 1929 Junior Law Class. The 1929 junior law class poses in front of the Washington Monument on Mount Vernon Square.

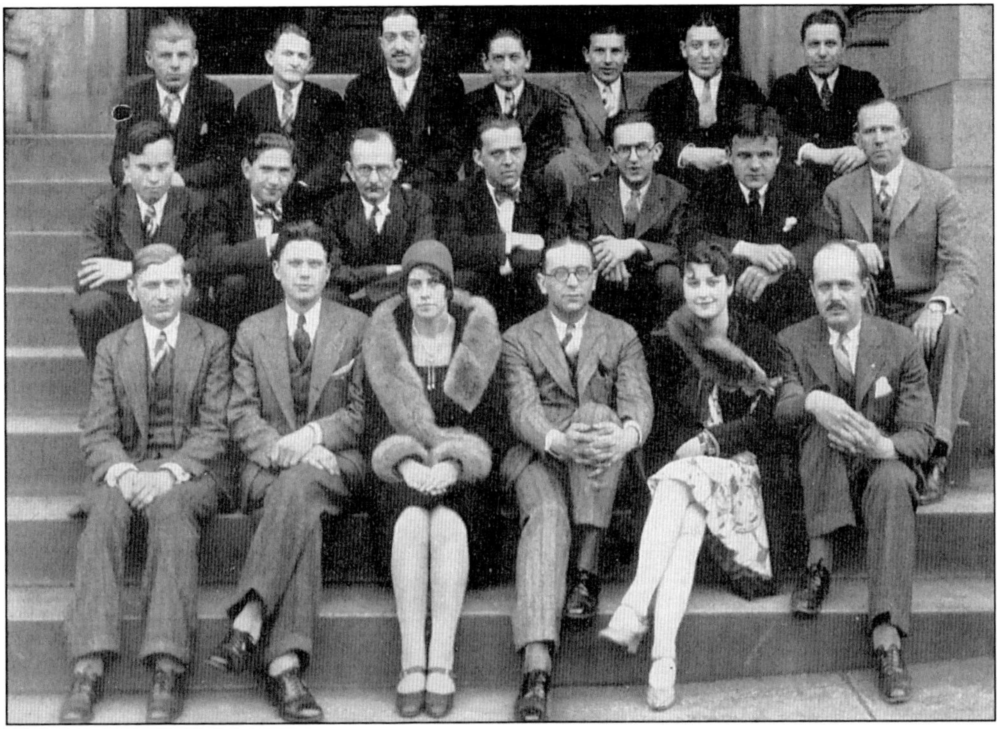

Freshman Class. In this 1929 photograph students pose on the steps of the Peabody Institute. Both the School of Business and the School of Law were open to women.

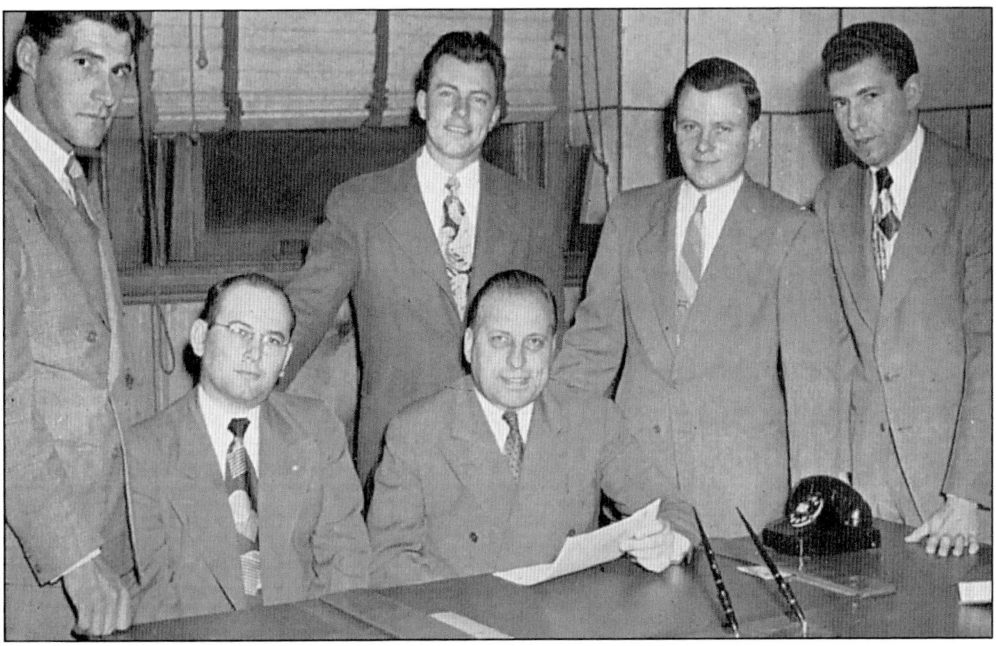

Graduates of BIM. Pictured in this 1947 photograph are the following, from left to right: (front) Otto P. Greiner, Joseph Schnaper, and Director Clifford James; (back) Edward A. Johnston, Daniel I. Long, and Abraham Meyers, who were the first graduates of the Business, Industry, and Management School (BIM) to receive a bachelor of science degree.

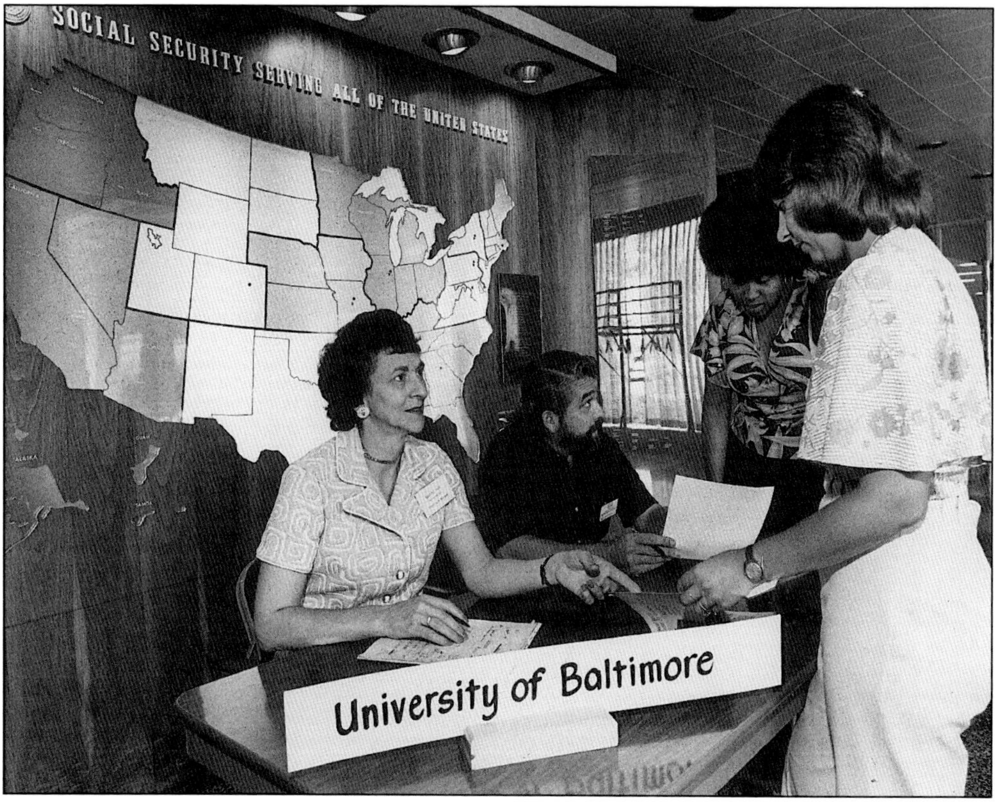

Satellite Programs. In the 1970s, the university began to hold classes at "satellite" or off-campus sights. In the above photograph, Audrey M.H. Regner (left) and George M. McDevitt, dean of students, are shown registering employees at the Social Security Complex in Woodlawn, Baltimore County. In the bottom photograph, students are seen attending a class at Fort George Meade in Anne Arundel County.

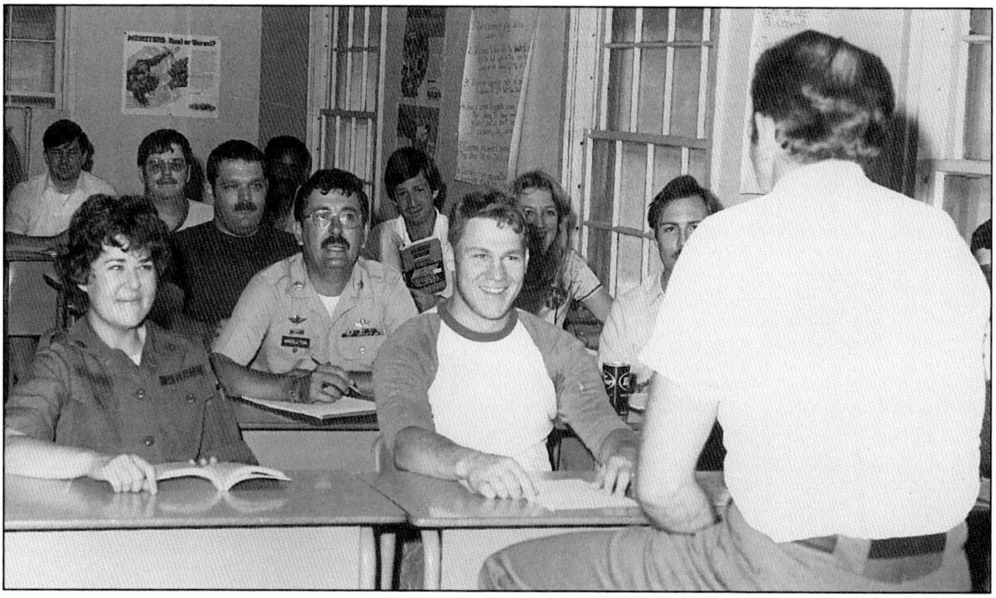

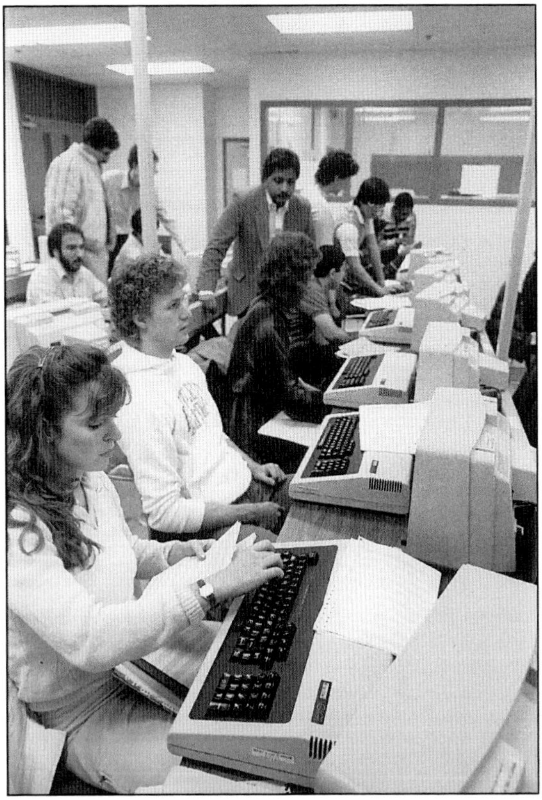

COMPUTER INFORMATION SYSTEMS. This specialization provides the student with the skills necessary to analyze, design, and implement information system in any organization. Students develop an understanding of the management of computer technology as well as the design and selection of appropriate hardware and software.

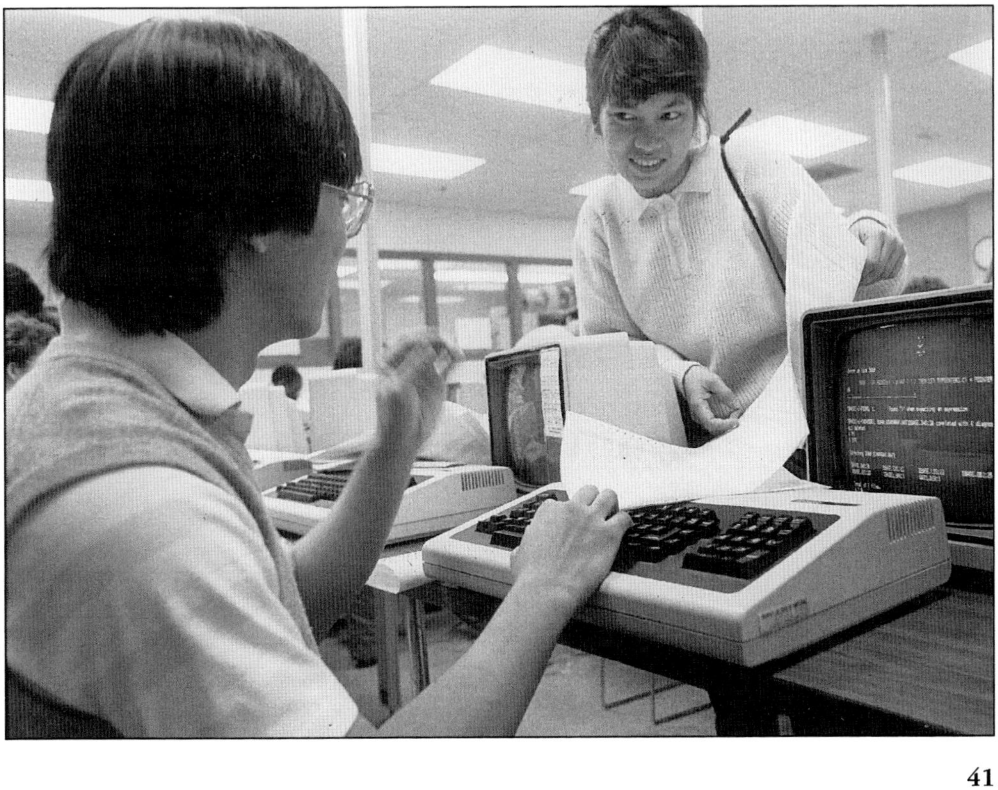

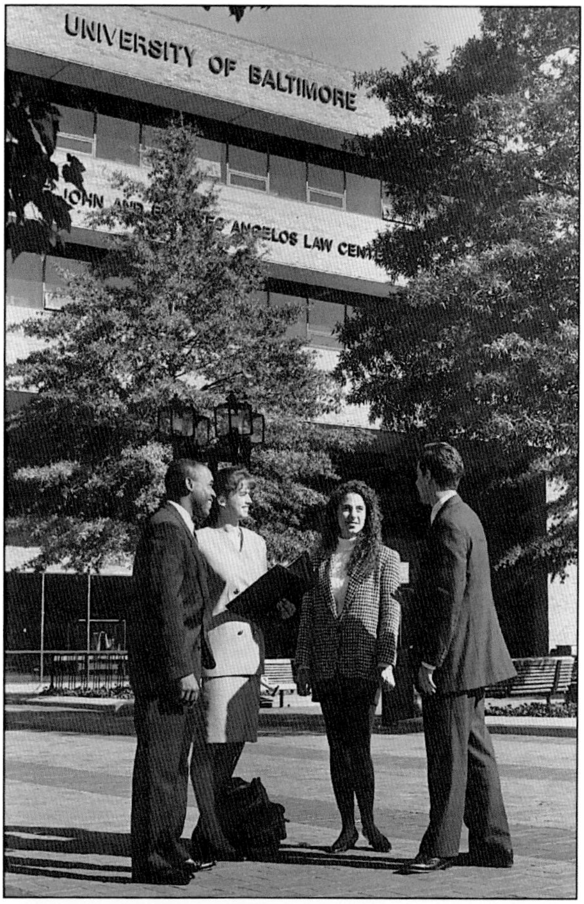

The School of Law. The law program exposes students to broad legal, economic, and social perspectives, so they become both effective and reflective attorneys who can meet the 21st century head on.

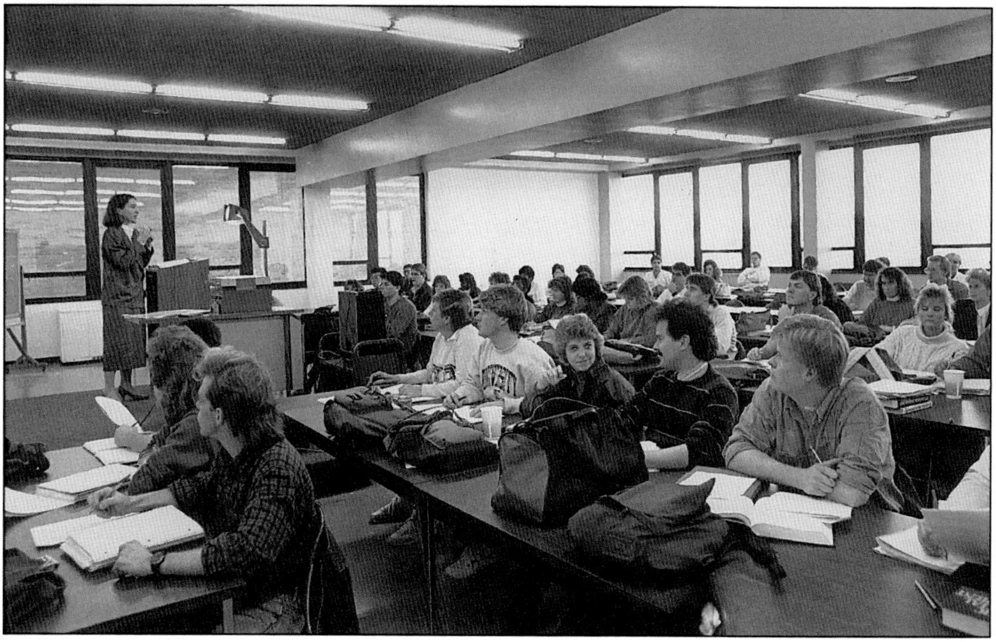

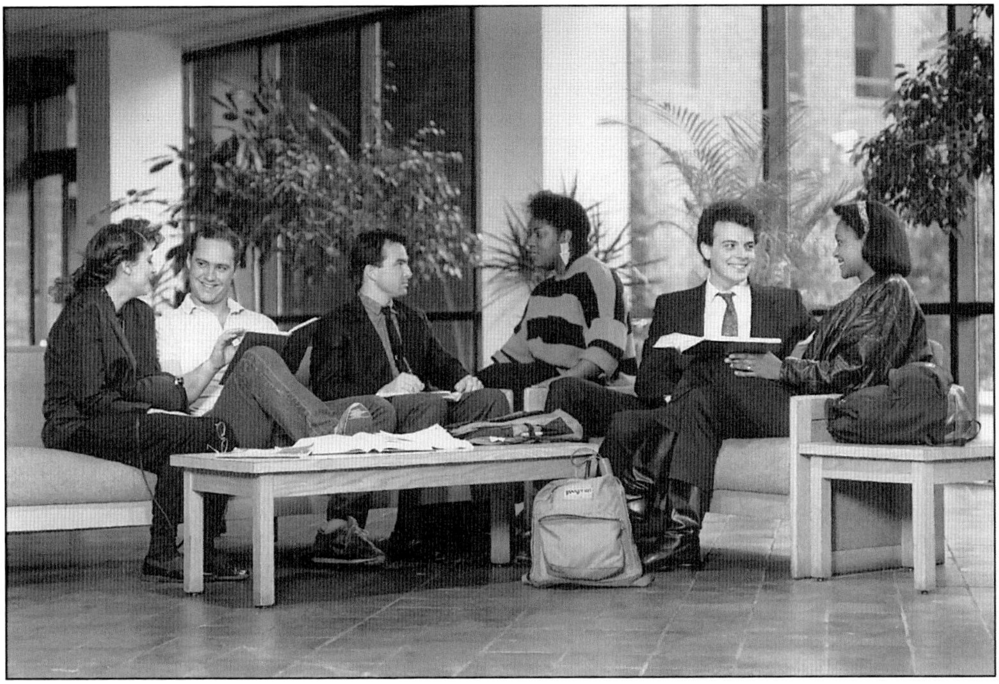

Law Students. The lobby of the Law Center (above) and the browsing area of the law library (below) offer a place where law students can get together to meet or study.

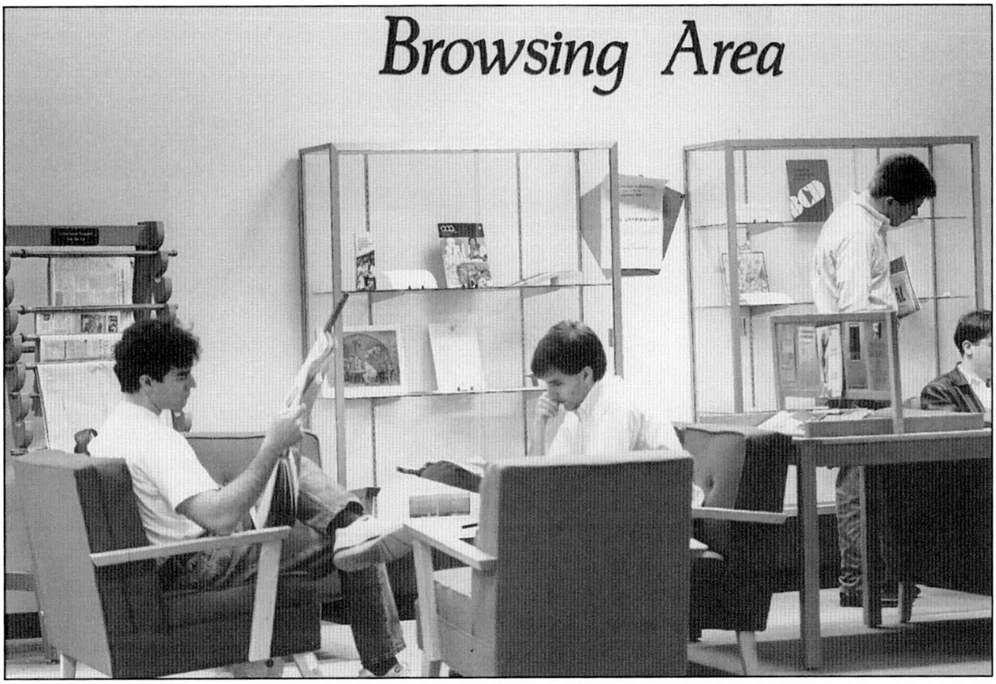

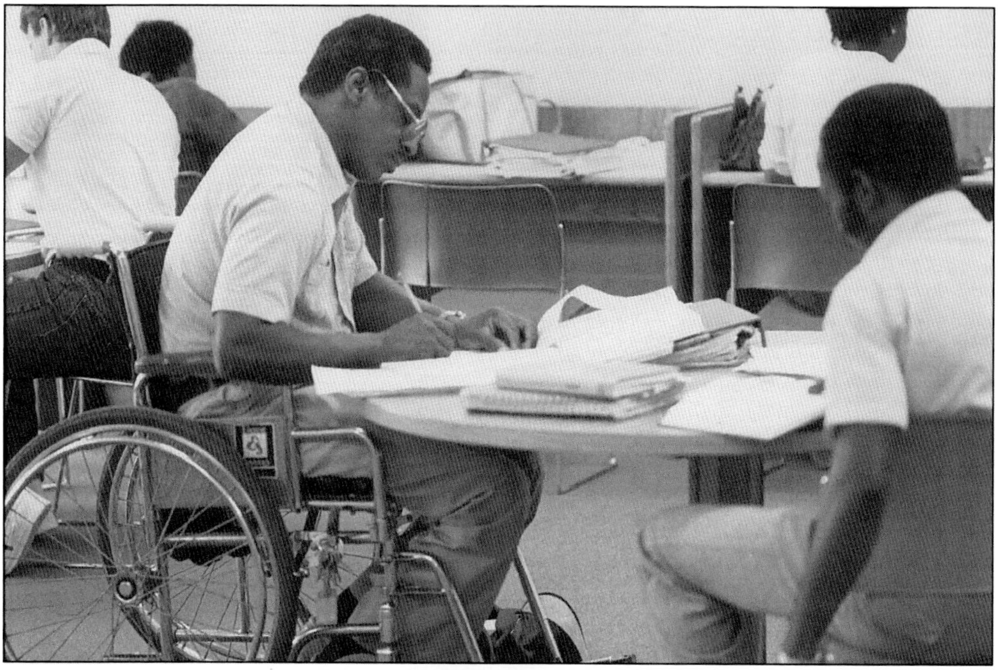

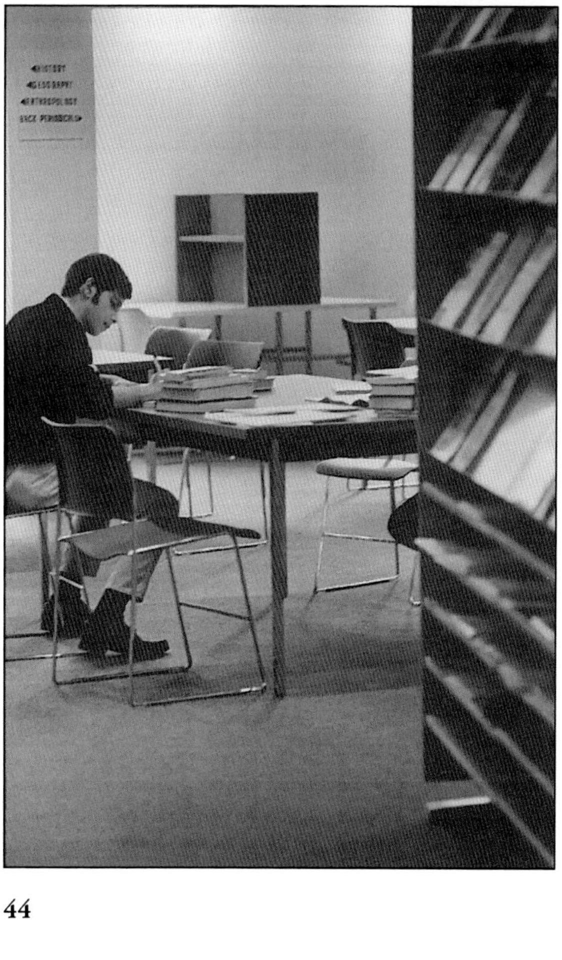

A Place to Study. The student lounge (above) and the Langsdale Library (left) offer these students a quiet place to work on class assignments.

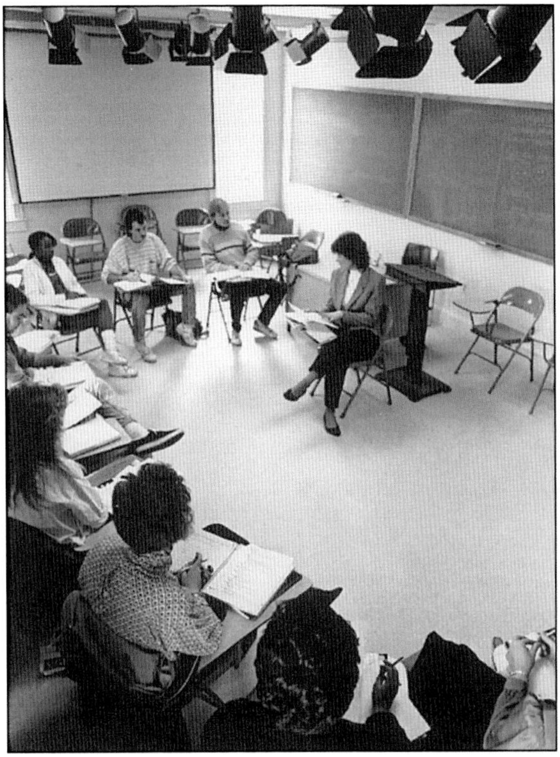

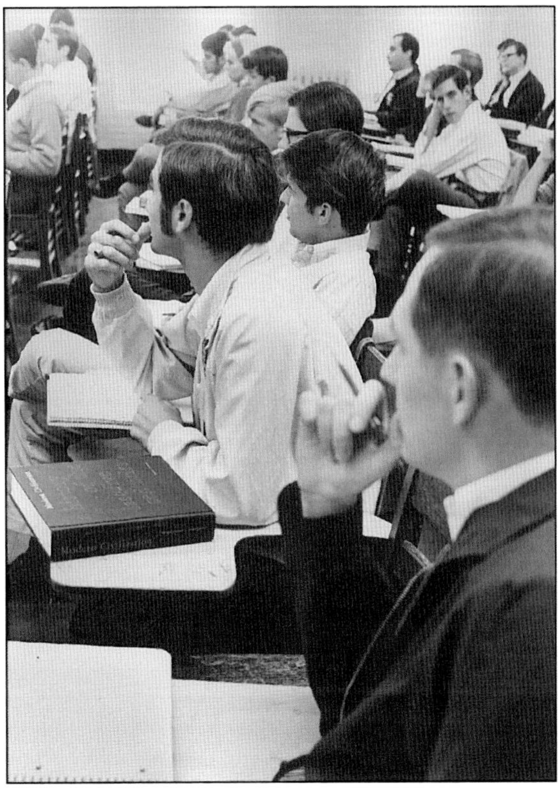

Liberal Arts. The Yale Gordon College of Liberal Arts awards bachelor's and master's degrees that combine traditional liberal arts and professional studies. This combination, emphasizing inter- and cross-disciplinary work, makes the college unique among the institutions within the University of Maryland System and allows students to pursue academic programs that prepare them for the work of the world, as well as the life of the mind.

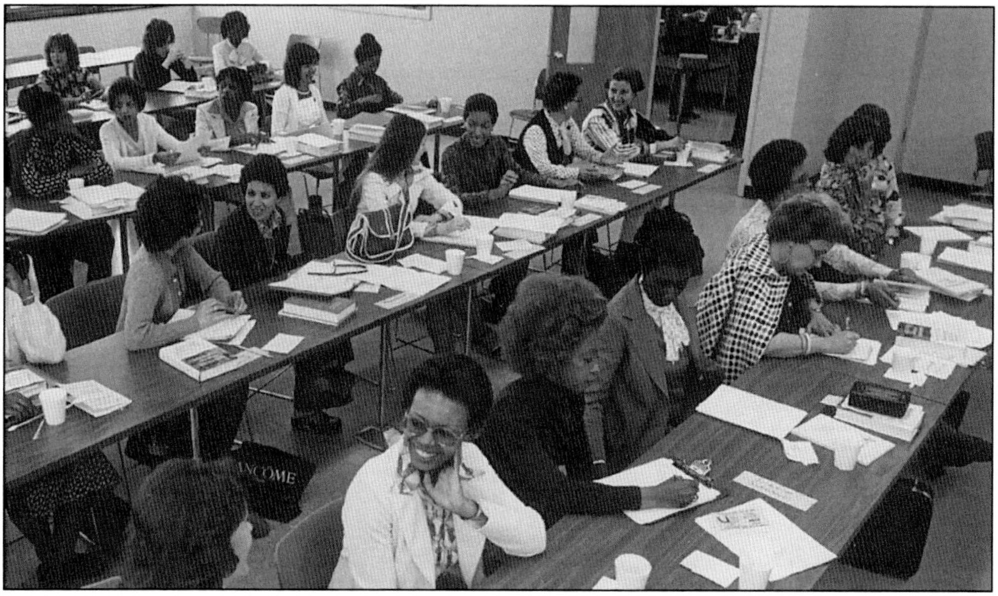

Women's Program in Management. This program was designed for women in management positions seeking significant advancement and for those interested in entry-level management positions. The program accepted its first students in June 1978. By December 1985, 142 women had completed the certificate program and 50 percent had gone on to earn an MBA degree.

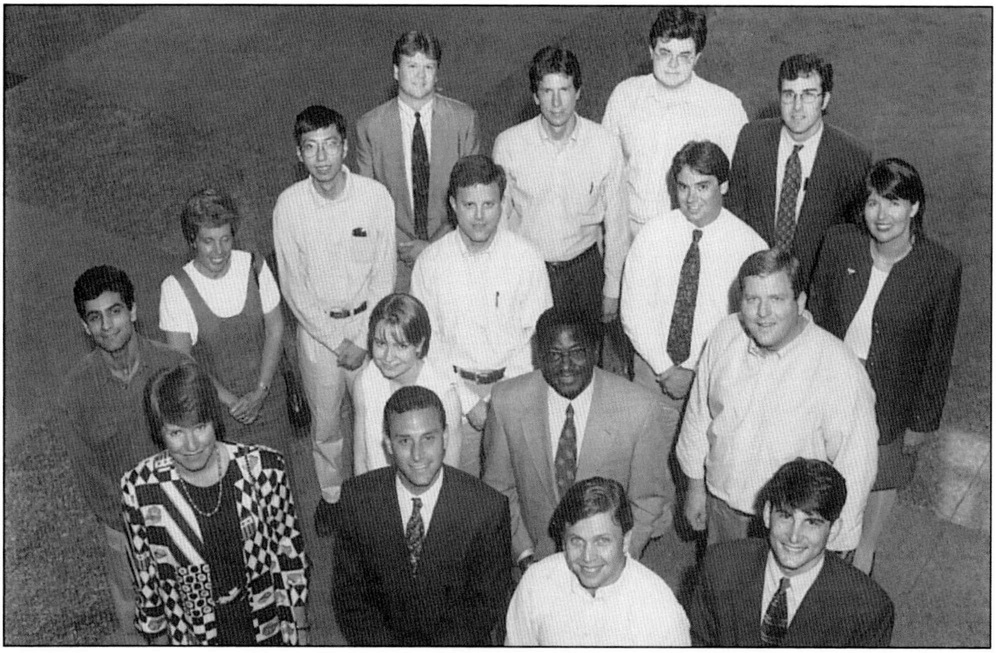

AMBA. An accelerated MBA is available through the Advantage MBA (AMBA) program in the Merrick School of Business. The first class consisted of the following, from left to right: (front row) Robin Snyder, Jason Kunzman, Jim Paterson, and Joe Sutton; (second row) Sunin Raina, Nora Kraemer, Kalida Bayo, and Jim McMahon; (third row) Margaret Colleluor, Mingming Zhao, Don Haskell, Jason Jacobs, and Susan Pfister; (fourth row) Randy Cornelius, John Godshalk, George Howell, and Michael McEvoy.

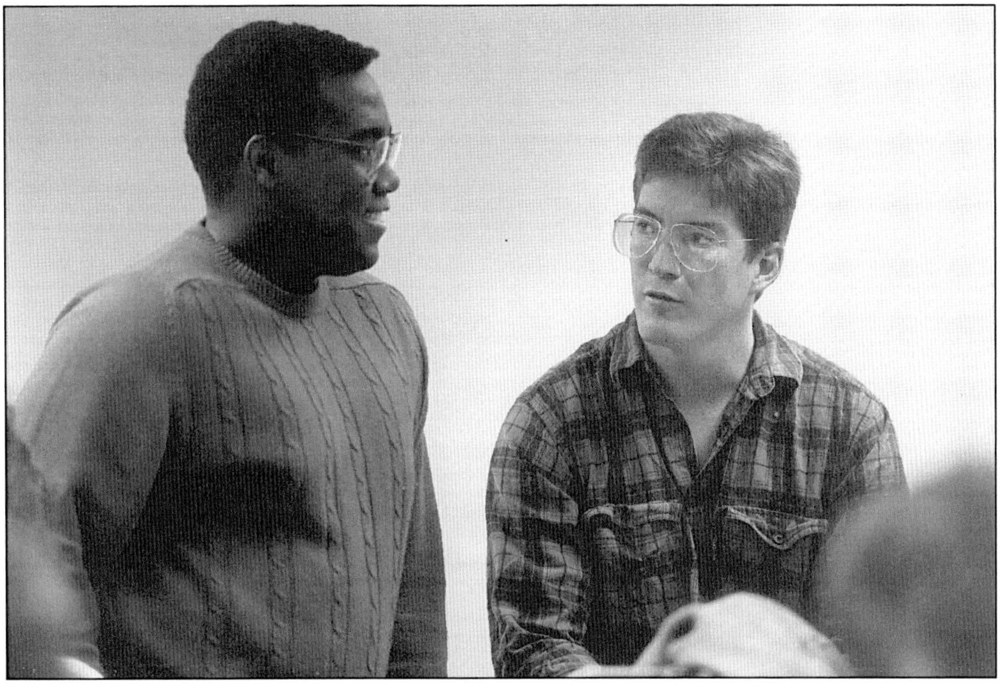

STUDENTS. The University of Baltimore currently has a student body of just over 5,000 and is one of 13 institutions comprising the University System of Maryland. UB offers upper-division, graduate, and professional academic programs.

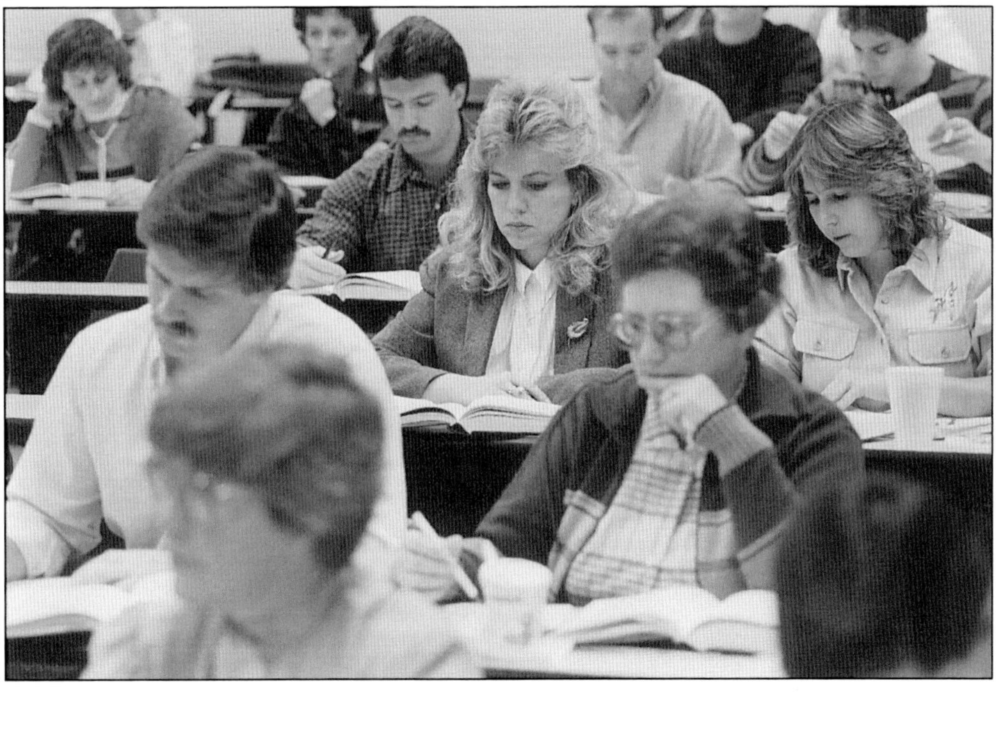

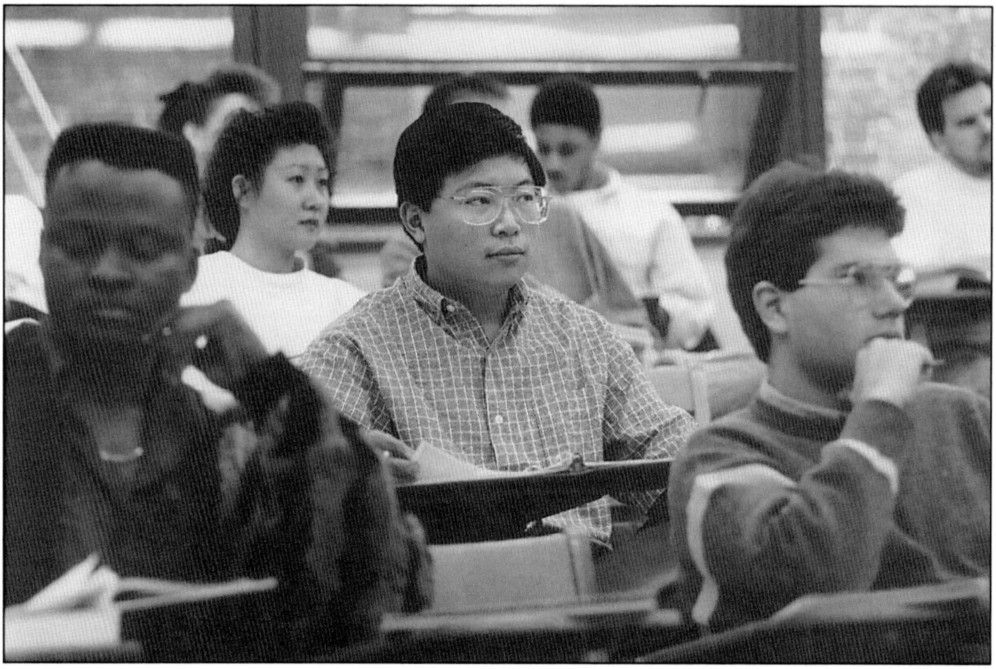

INTERNATIONAL STUDENTS. The university is host to over 200 foreign-born students and faculty members representing nearly 60 nationalities. The university's population reflects the changing demographics of the national and regional work force. Below, students representing just a few of the nationalities are, from left to right, Suhah Kocabal (Turkey), Ogla Korobkova (Russia), and Jesper Nielsen (Danish.)

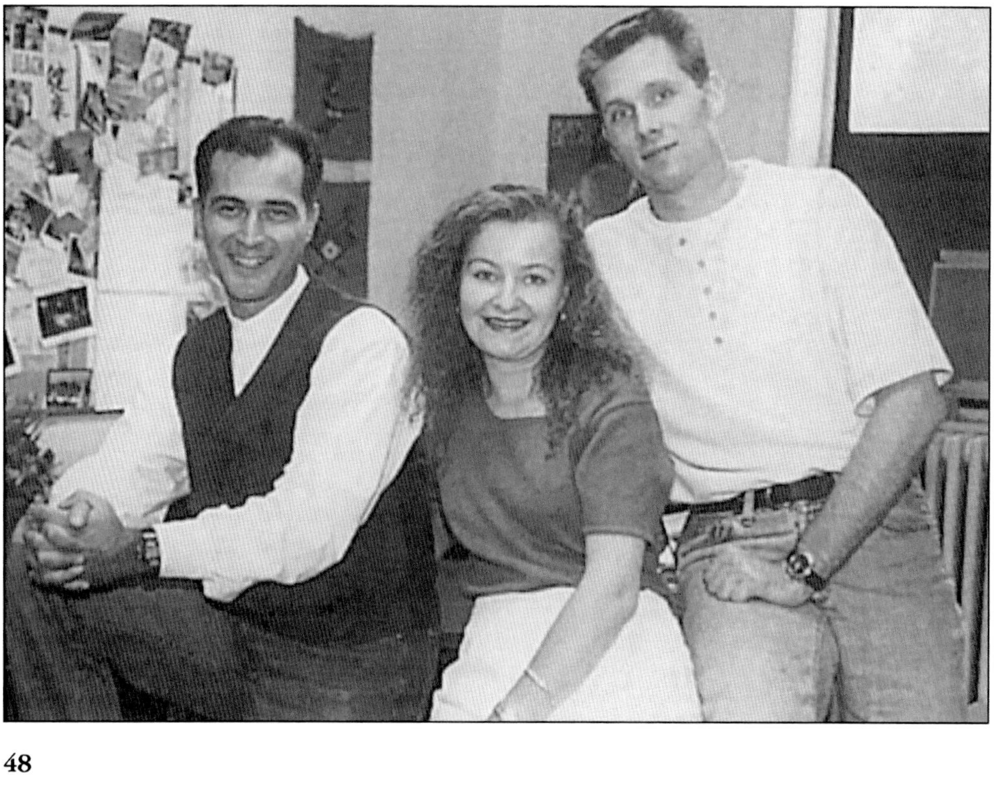

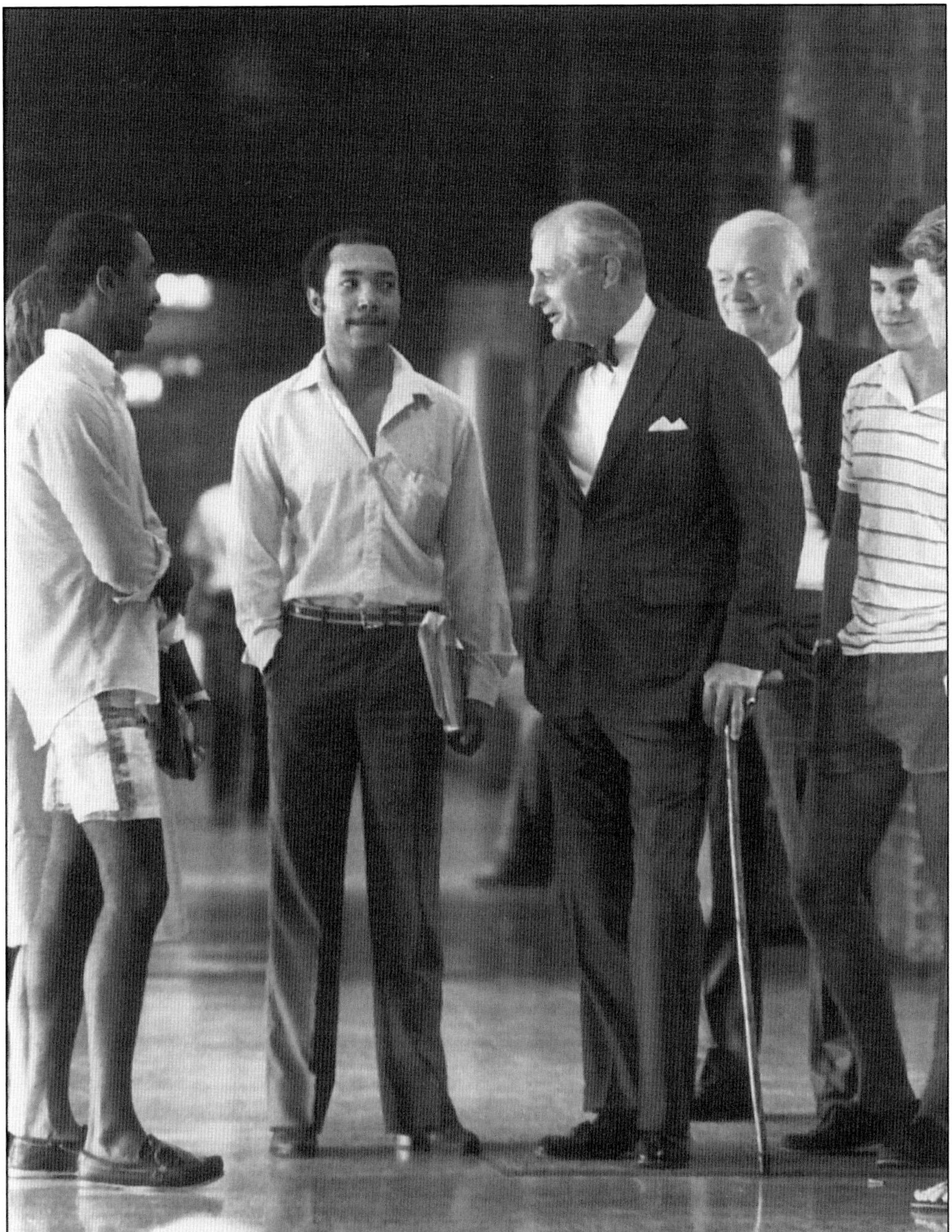

TIME TO CHAT. President Turner (third from the left) stops on the way from a meeting to speak with a group of students.

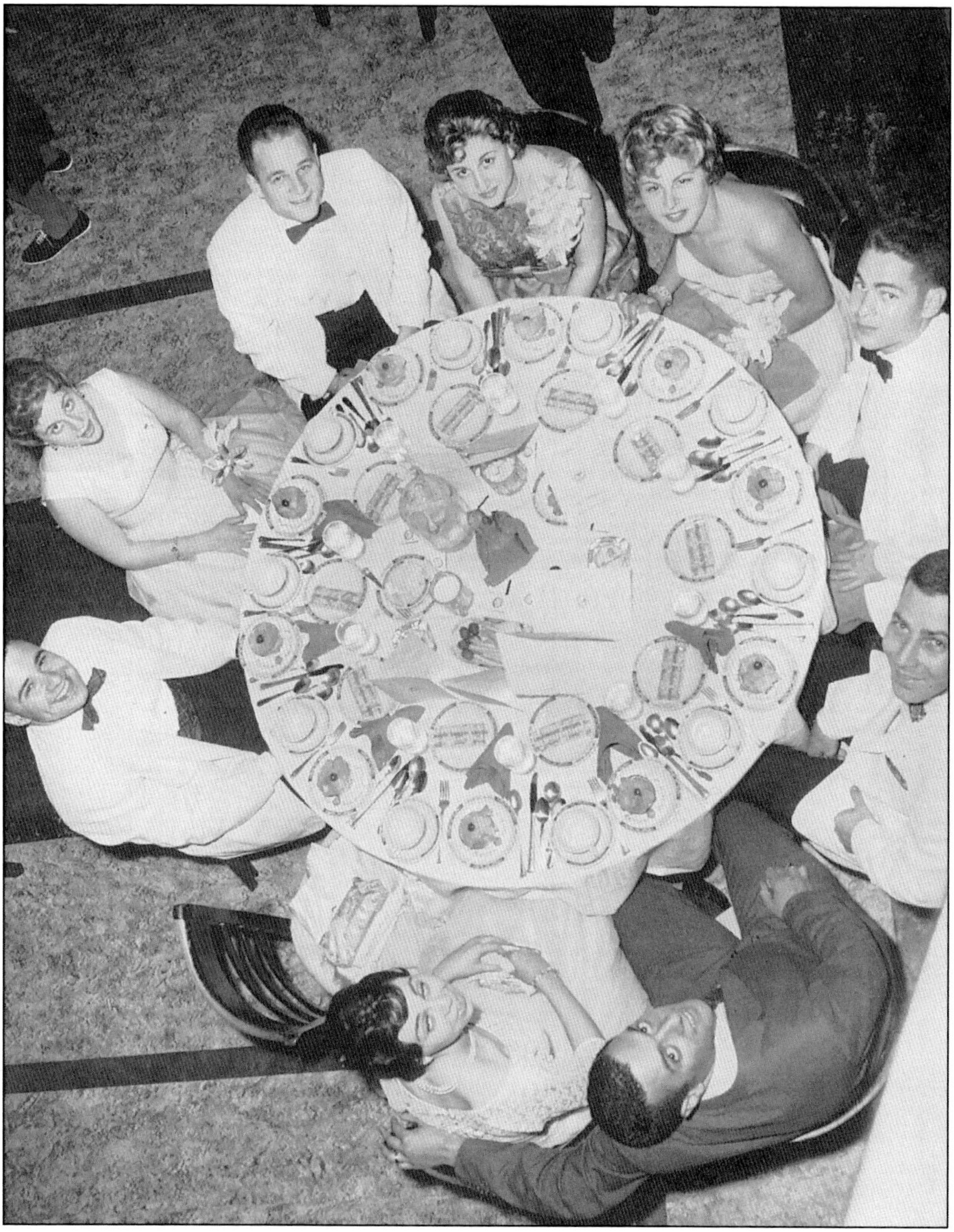

Senior Dance and Banquet. The Class of 1960 gathers for the annual senior dance and banquet.

Four

Activities, Clubs, and Organizations

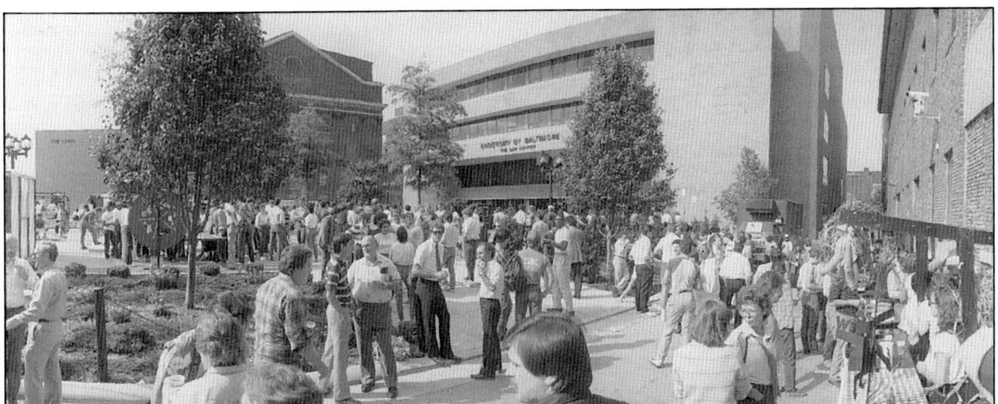

Block Party. Since its beginning, the University of Baltimore has provided more than a place to earn a degree in higher education. Shortly after its founding, a wide-range of fraternities, social organizations, and activities were begun to enhance university life. The tradition of the block party began in 1974.

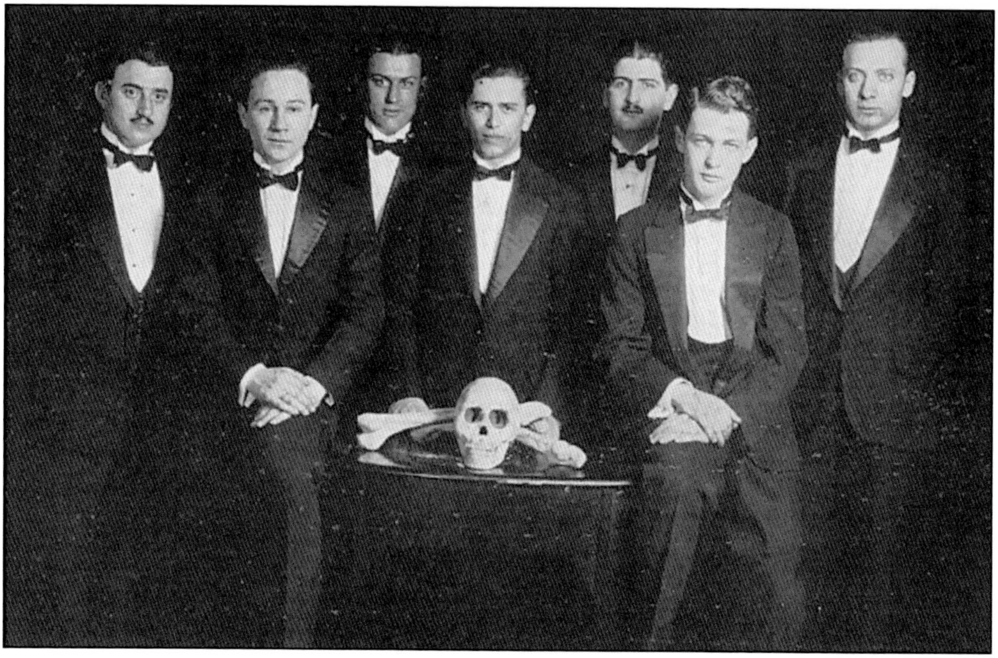

Alpha Delta Omega. A national social fraternity, the Supreme Chapter was chartered shortly after the University's founding. These members in 1928 are, from left to right, Leo Storch, Aaron H. Fagan, J. Yale Gordon, Philip Shapiro, Irving Shapiro, Emanuel J. Kirsh, and Leon S. Goldberg.

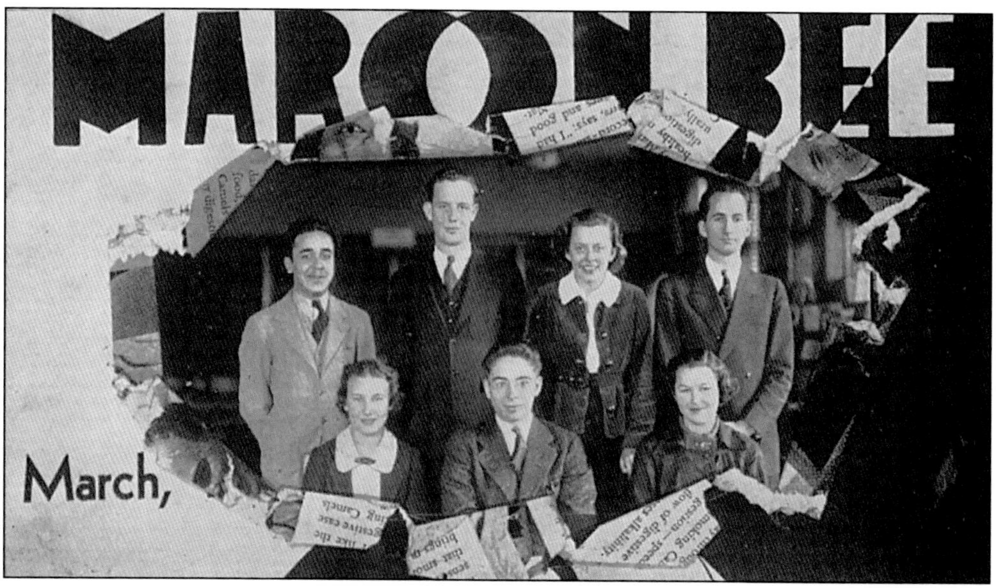

***Maroon Bee.** Maroon Bee* was published monthly by the students in this 1937 photograph.

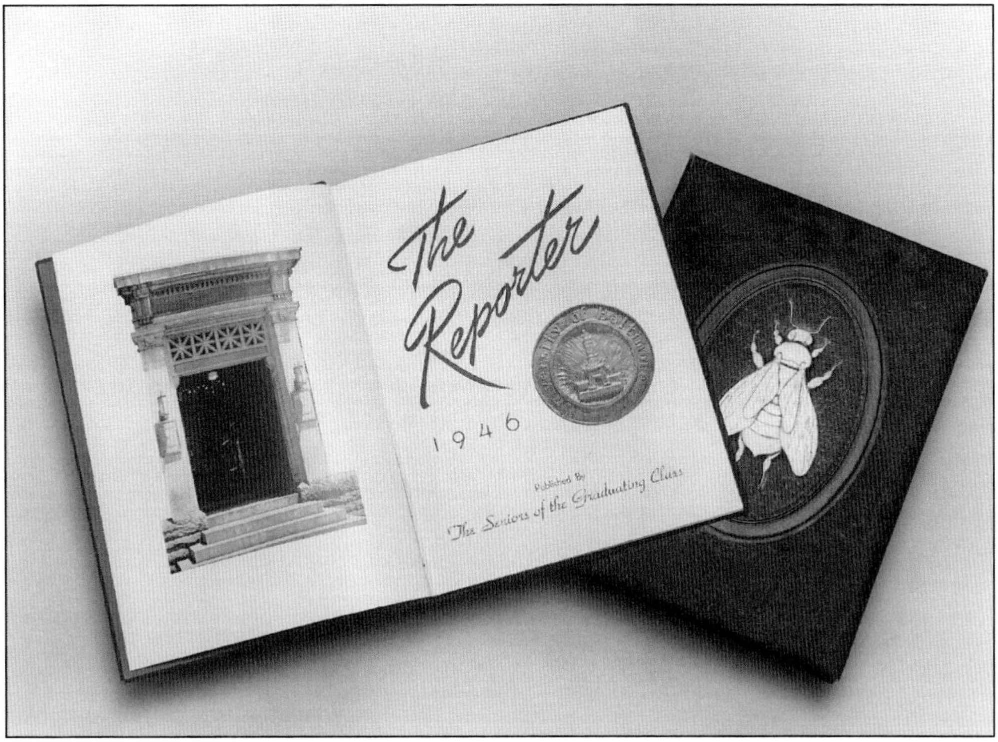

***The Reporter*.** Published by the seniors of the graduating class, *The Reporter* was published yearly from 1928 until 1975.

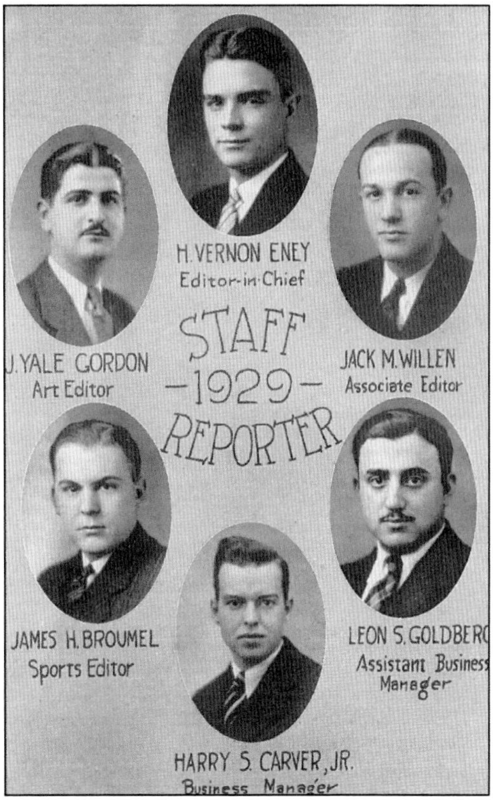

***The Reporter* Staff, 1929.** Among the staff were two illustrious members: H. Vernon Eney, who would become president of the Constitutional Convention of Maryland, and J. Yale Gordon, for whom the School of Liberal Arts and Gordon Plaza was named in 1982.

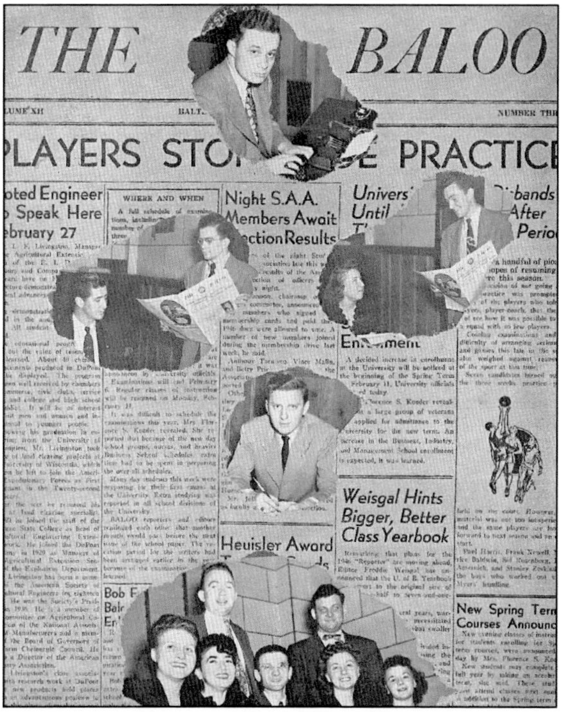

The Baloo. The student newspaper was published weekly by and for the students of the university. The 1946 staff are as follows, from left to right: (top) Bill Zorzi, organizer and managing editor; (upper middle) James A. Sprigle, day editor; Vince Mailin, night editor; Lenore Krug, exchange editor, and John Steadman, sports editor; (lower middle) John E. Meyers, business manager; (bottom image, front row) Mary D. Wittstadt, business staff assistant; Betty Bless, reporter; Anthony J. Tarntino, advertising manager; Lillie G. Hahn, reporter; and Dorothy M. Hass, business staff; (bottom image, back row) Bill Hannon, reporter; and Leon Amernick, reporter.

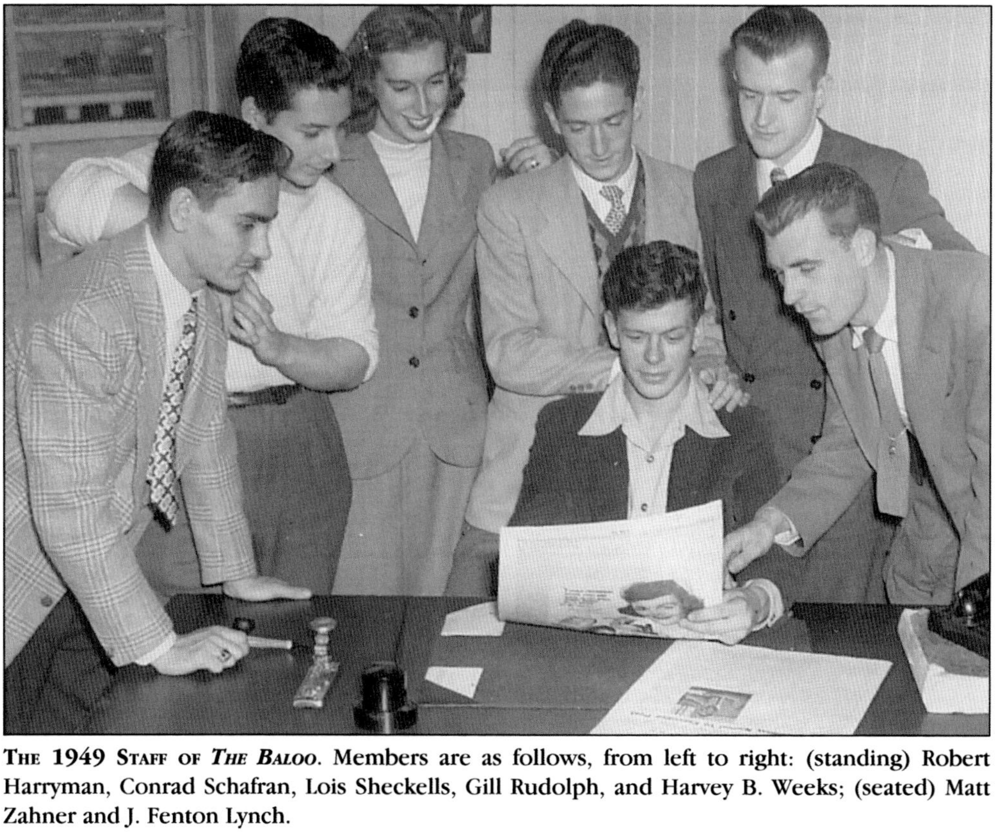

The 1949 Staff of *The Baloo*. Members are as follows, from left to right: (standing) Robert Harryman, Conrad Schafran, Lois Sheckells, Gill Rudolph, and Harvey B. Weeks; (seated) Matt Zahner and J. Fenton Lynch.

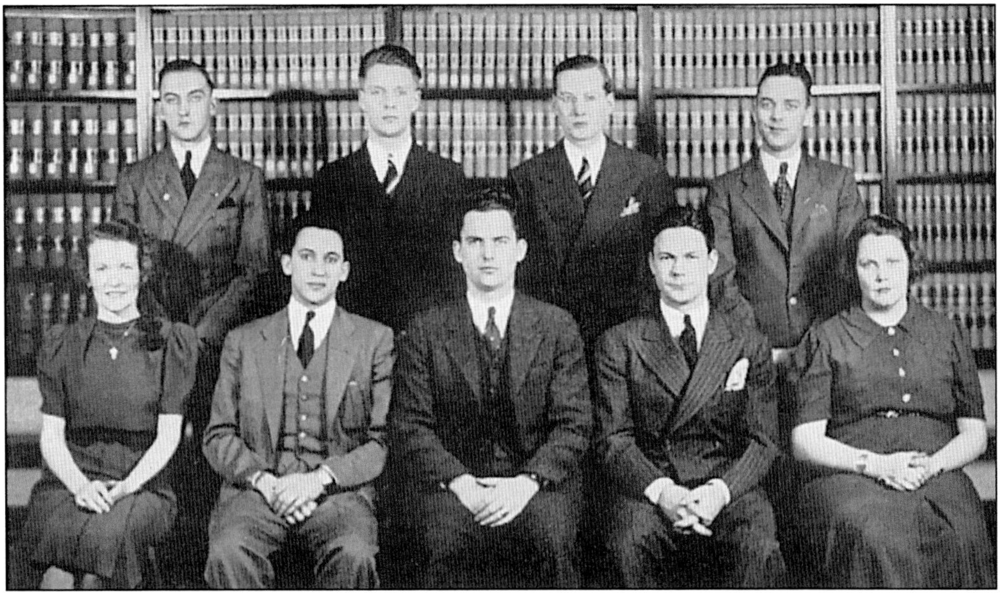

Members of Beta Alpa, 1939. Beta Alpa was an honorary fraternity open to members of the senior class in business administration who maintained an average of 88 or higher during their three years.

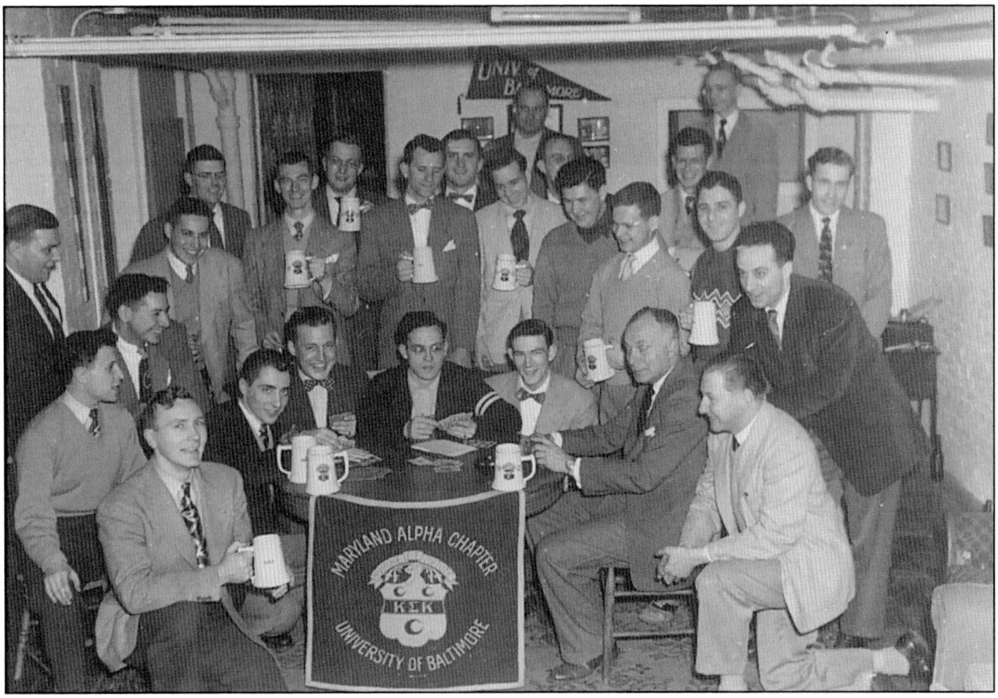

Kappa Sigma Kappa. Founded as the university's only international social fraternity, Kappa Sigma Kappa's chief objective is to provide good wholesome social entertainment for the students, as well as support for all extracurricular activities sponsored by the school. The Maryland Alpha Chapter was established in 1947.

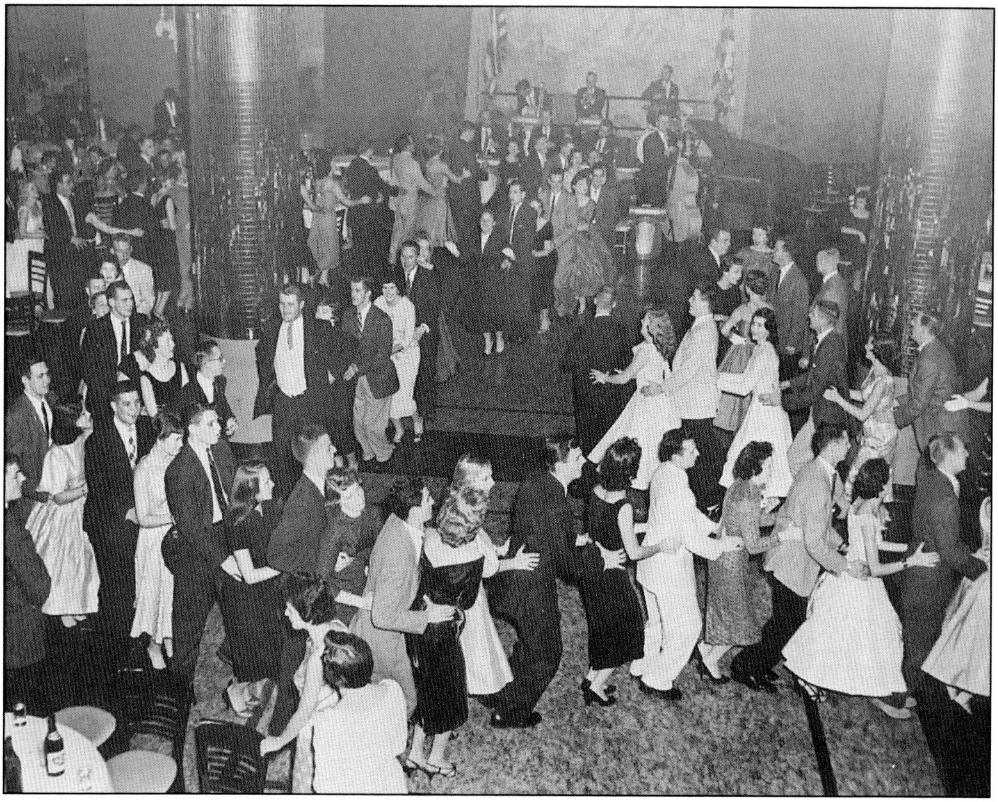

Seniors Dancing into the Night. The Class of 1958 forms a conga line at the annual senior dance and banquet (above) but by the fall of 1962 (below), members of the senior class at their dance were twisting again like they did last summer.

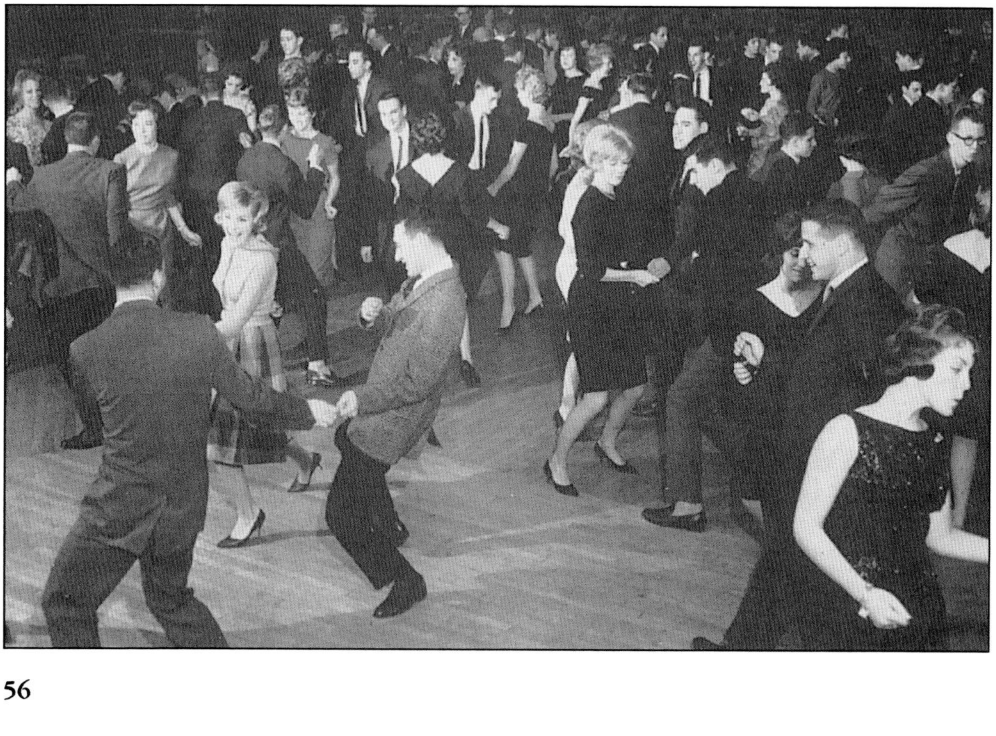

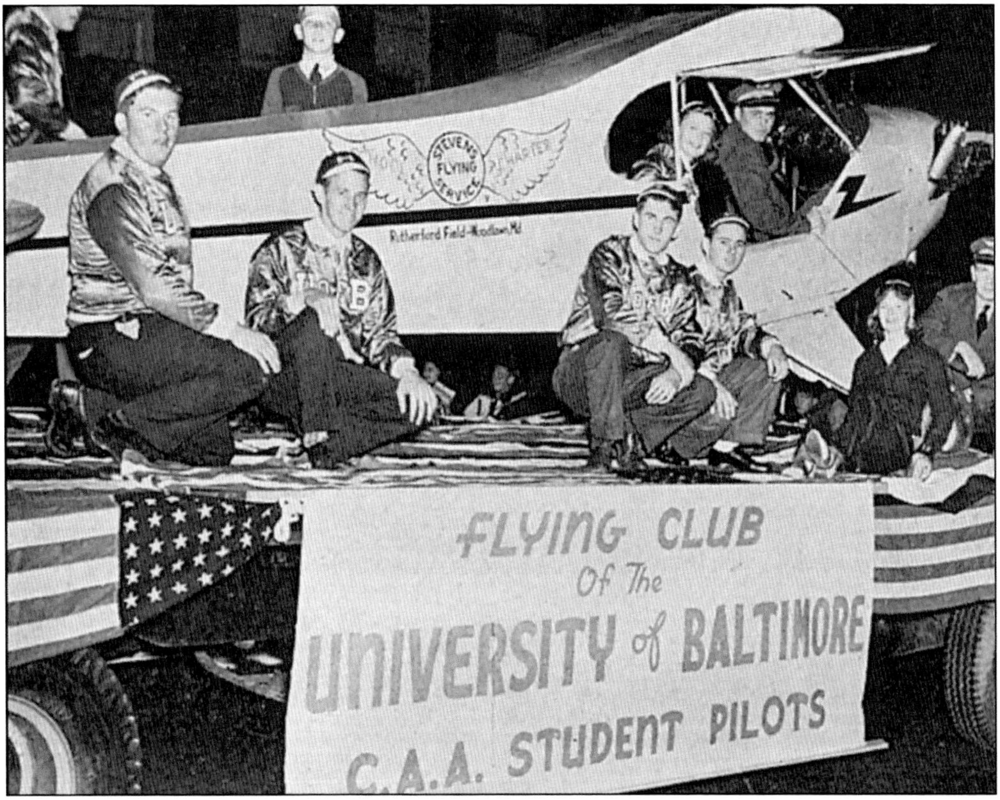

The Flying Club. In this 1941 photograph, CAA students proudly present their float in a local parade. This pilot training program was conducted at the airport in Hanover, PA, where students were housed at a nearby inn leased by the university. Over 100 pilots were trained for the Army Air Corps.

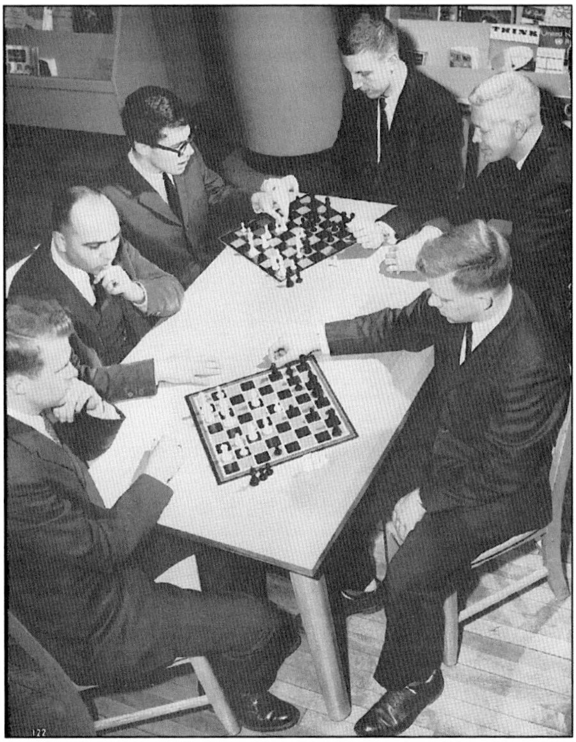

The Chess Club. Pictured here are the 1961 chess club members.

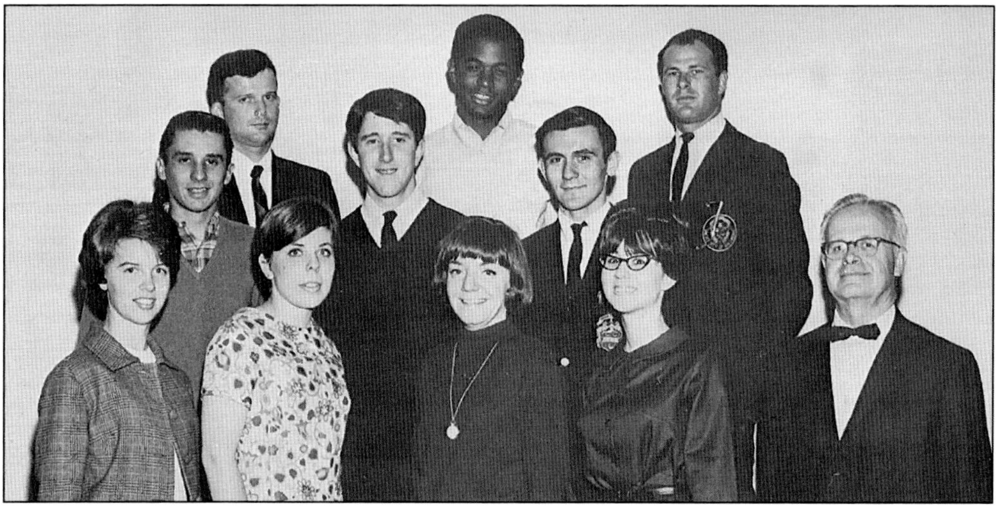

A New Cultural Awareness. Two organizations were formed to bring to UB students an appreciation of drama and the arts. The Literati (English club), formed in fall 1966, was supported by the members seen in the 1967 photograph above. From left to right are as follows: (first row) Judy Emgee, Carole Supp, Elaine Harrison, Betty Russell, and Dr. Al Rose, advisor; (second row) Alan Kratz, Harold Glazer, and Tom LeRoux; (third row) Bill Grove, Michael Lee, and Will Freeman. In 1970, the Council of Arts (below) was formed by Dr. Daniel Craig to visit local cultural institutions. The members pictured here are, from left to right, as follows: (first row) David Hume, Rosalie Marcus, Harold Heale, Peter Siriano (president), Molly Harrington, and Stefanie Bain; (second row) Emil Kobylecki, Dick Jacobs, Terry Callahan, and unidentified; (third row) Stuart Goldberg, unidentified, Edwina Allen, and James Teuscher; (fourth row) Rocco DeRosa, Dr. Craig (advisor), Richard Stutz, Donald Cosgrove, Gary Garnett, Jimmy Gilpin, and unidentified.

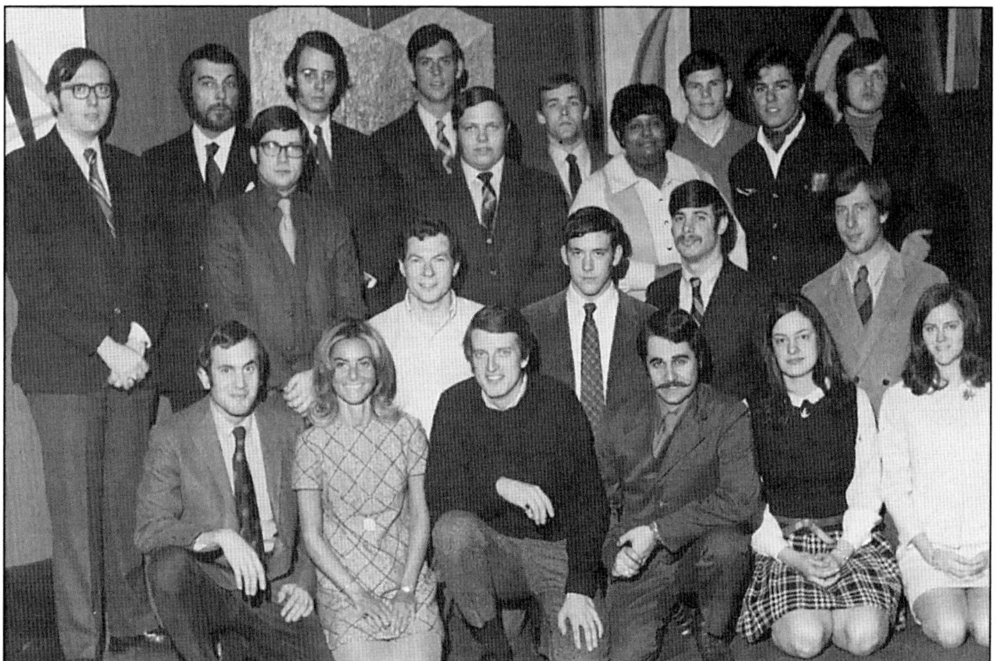

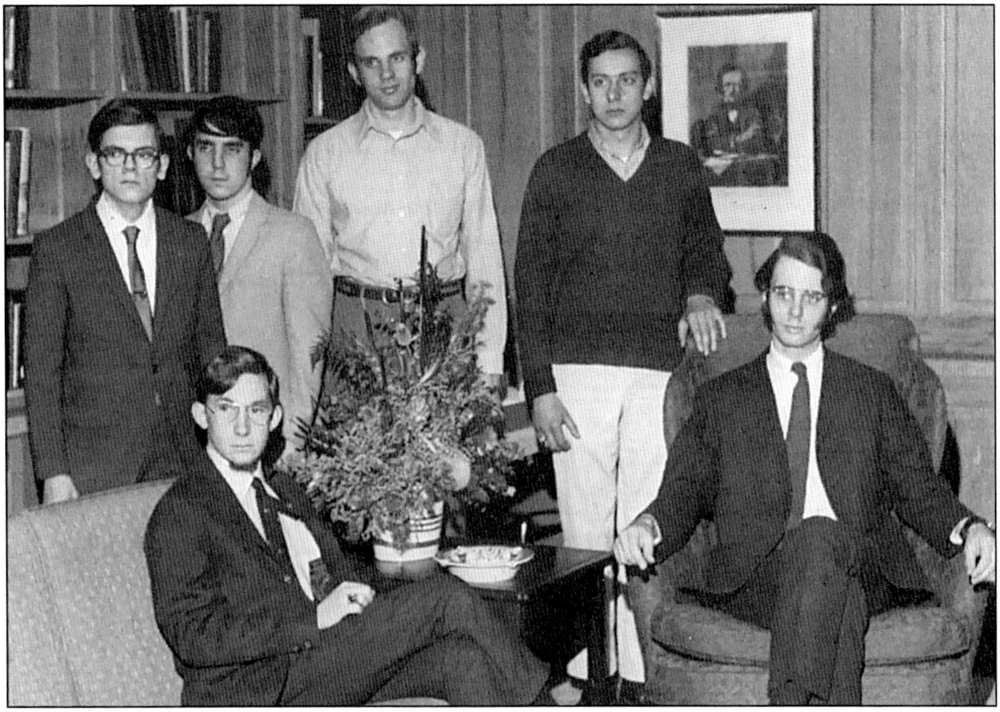

The Student Library Committee. The Student Library Committee meets with the librarian and serves as a liaison between students and the library. In this 1970 photograph, the members are as follows, from left to right: (seated) Bill Haroth (president) and Richard Stutz; (standing) Jerry Martin, Neil Posner, Jamie Blout, and Bruce Miller.

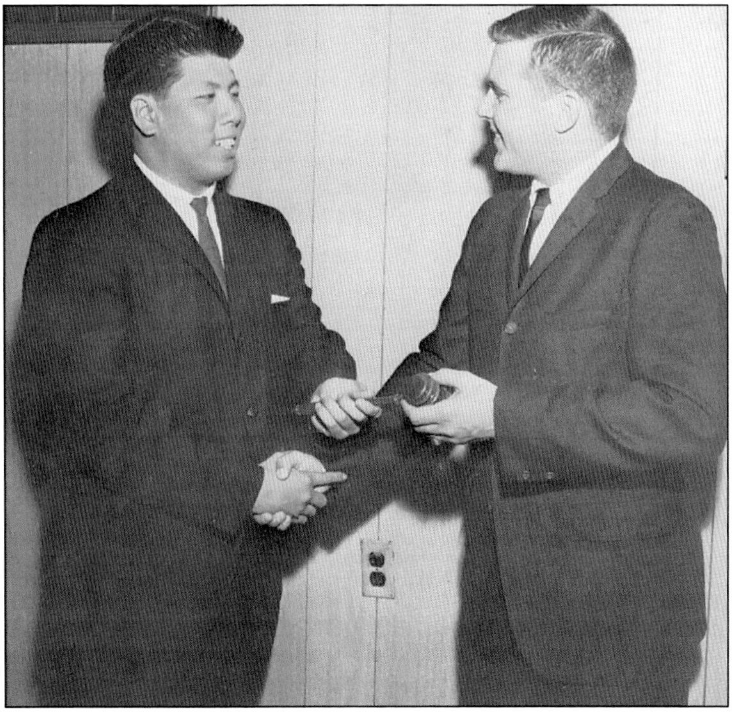

SGA Changing of the Guard. The incoming Student Government Association president, Duane Chen, receives the president's gavel from the outgoing president, Phil Heiner.

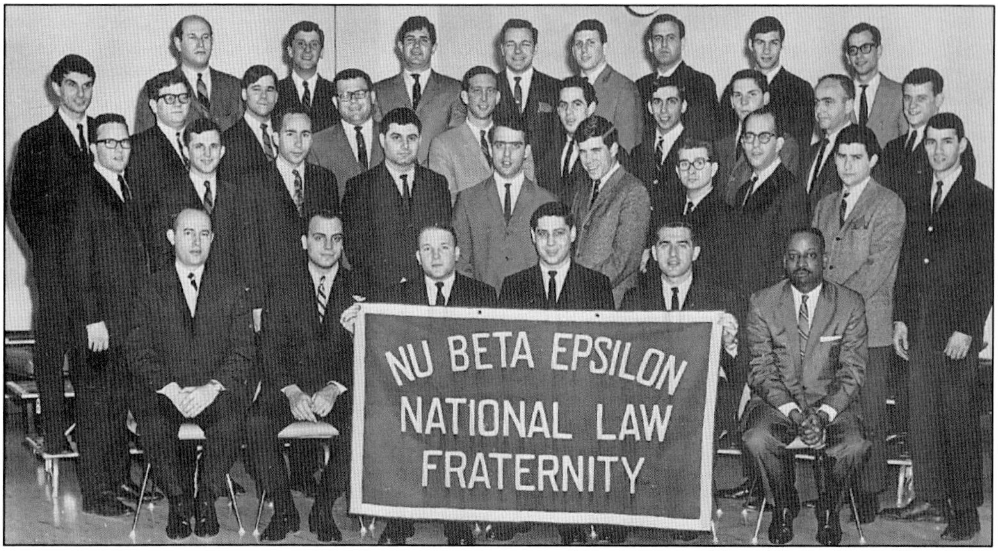

Nu Beta Epsilon. The Alpha Chapter, from left to right, are pictured as follows: (first row) the Honorable Charles E. Moylan (advisor), M. Dansicker, H. Kodeck, M. Glishakow, S. Blibaum, and the Honorable George L. Russell (advisor); (second row) N. Kodeck, M. Lessens, A. Luchinsky, J. Hyatt, A. Branch, R. Eskow, L. Luperini, H. Leibowitz, H. Davidson, and P. Klein; (third row) M. Scubla, M. Egoren, M. Resnick, S. Schuchalter, J. London, E. Feldman, J. Blumenthal, J. Dorner, E. Cadeux, and M. Jacob; (fourth row) E. Walman, R. Landsman, G. Berlin, D. Fletcher, M. Balser, J. Engelman, S. Wasserman, and A. Gersh. This 1967 group is comprised of members from the University of Baltimore, University of Maryland, and Eastern College, which later merged with UB.

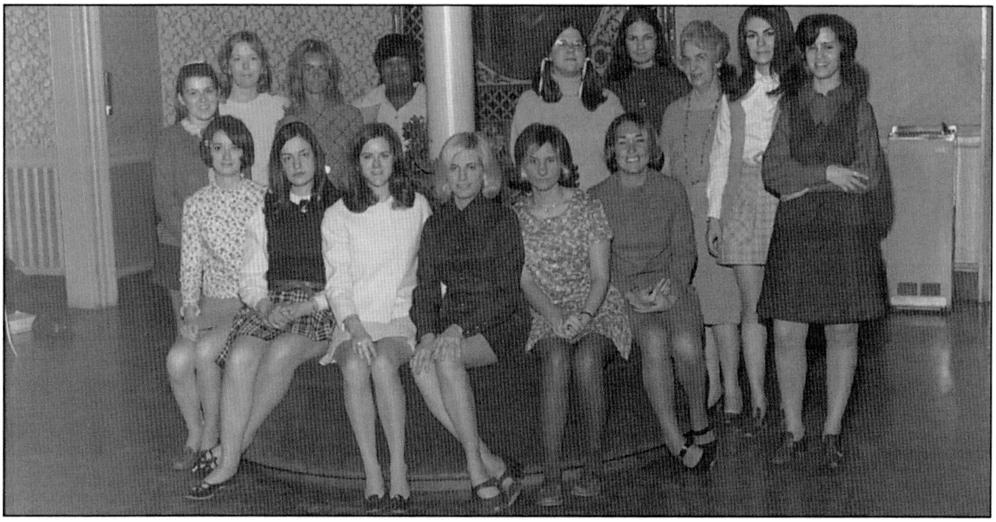

The Women's Association. The Women's Association is a reorganization of the Women's League, which started in 1936. The organization is devoted to furthering the special interests and aims of the coeds. The members seen here in 1970 are as follows, from left to right: (seated) Terry Musk (treasurer), Molly Harrington (historian), Stephanie Bain (president), Ronnie Portyraj (vice-president), Mary J. Posluszny, and Beverly Bull (secretary); (standing) Judy Jarrett, Charlotte Bedsole, Rosalie Marcus, Edwina Allen, Lyn Rabin, Sharon Karas, Mrs. Thomas (advisor), Laura D'Anna, and Mary Ellen Bauer.

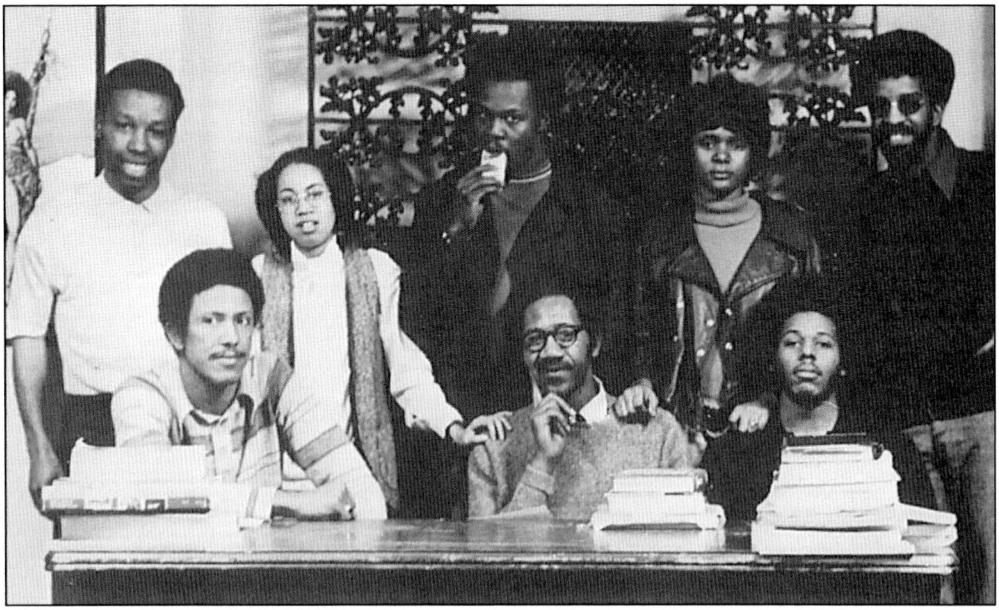

The Black Student Union. The BSU was the successor to the Cosmopolitans, who were organized on December 8, 1969, to stimulate black awareness both in and outside the university community. The members, pictured here in 1972, are as follows, from left to right: (standing) Kareen Shabazz, Rose Patterson, Charles R. Turner, Irma Morgan, and Rudy Hill; (seated) Lorn Hill, Booker T. Rush, and Dwight Reed.

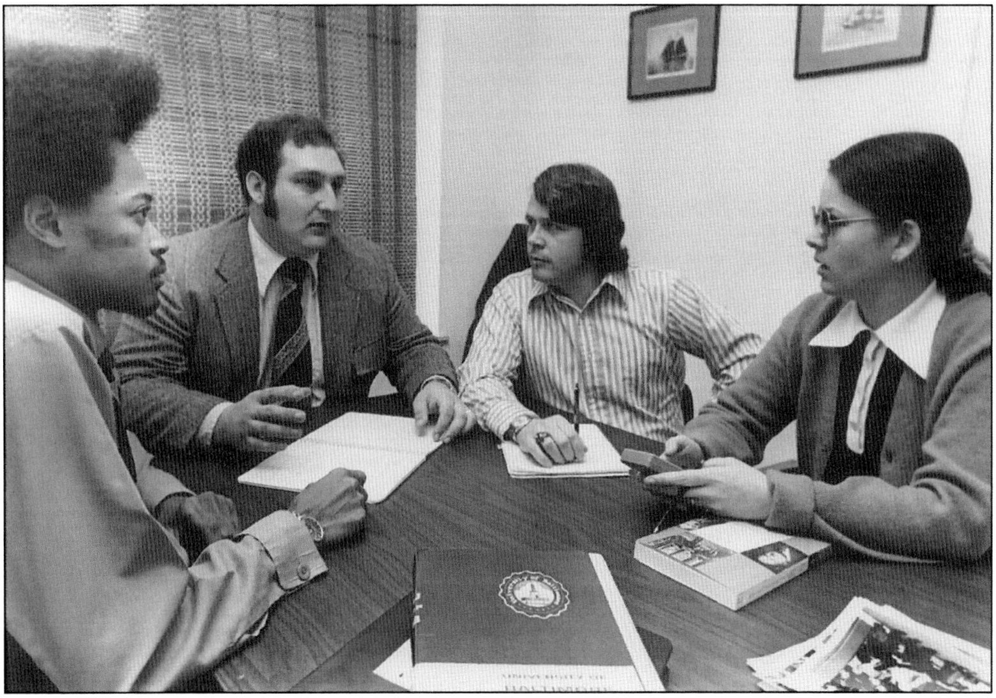

The Vietnam Veterans Club. In 1973, around 50 Vietnam veterans organized a club. Shown here, from left to right, are Orlando Yarborough, Gerry Donlon, Gary Phillips, and Jackie Kinnear as they discuss upcoming activities.

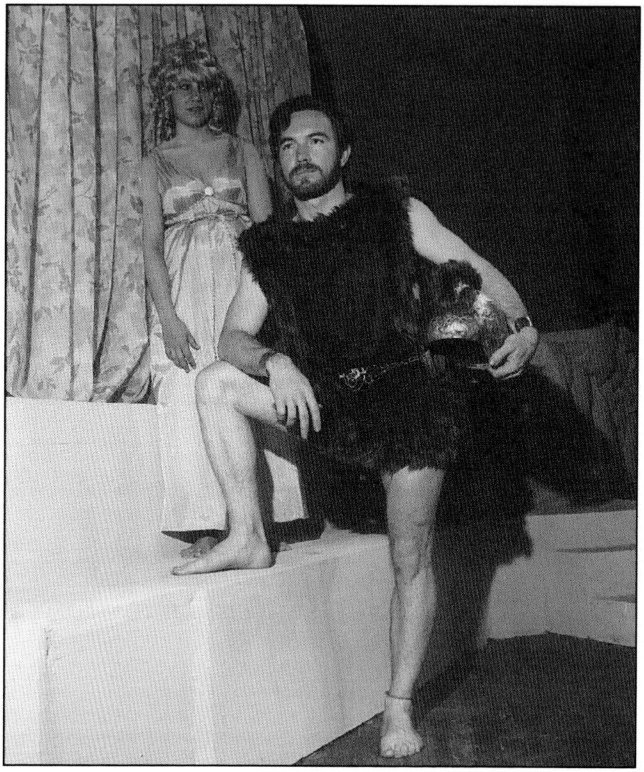

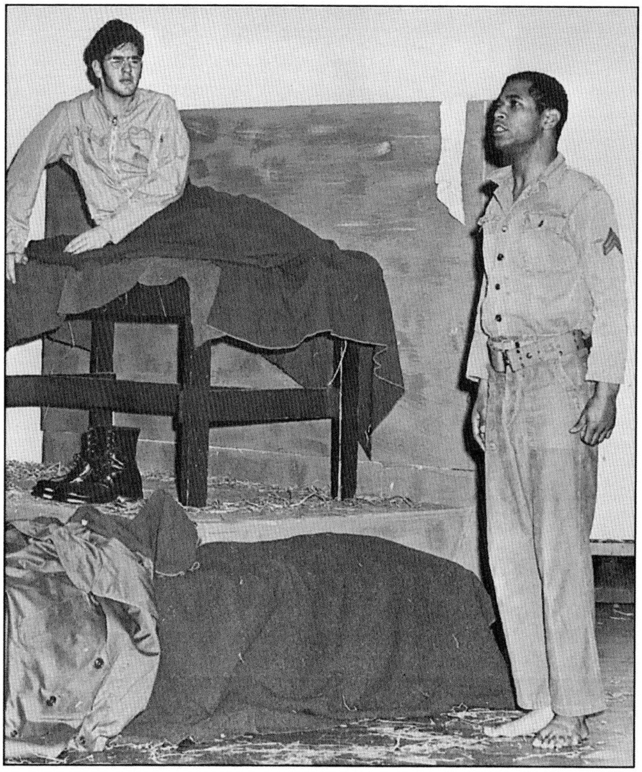

University Players. A drama production organization called University Players provides opportunities for UB students to increase their knowledge and appreciation of drama and gain practical experience in theater production. Pictured above is the 1972 production of *Amphitryon 38*, featuring Rene Ruggiero (left) as Alkemena and Martin Huebschman (right) as Amphitryon. Below, John Melnick (left) listens to Mike Lee (right) in the 1968 production of *A Sleep-of-Prisoners.*

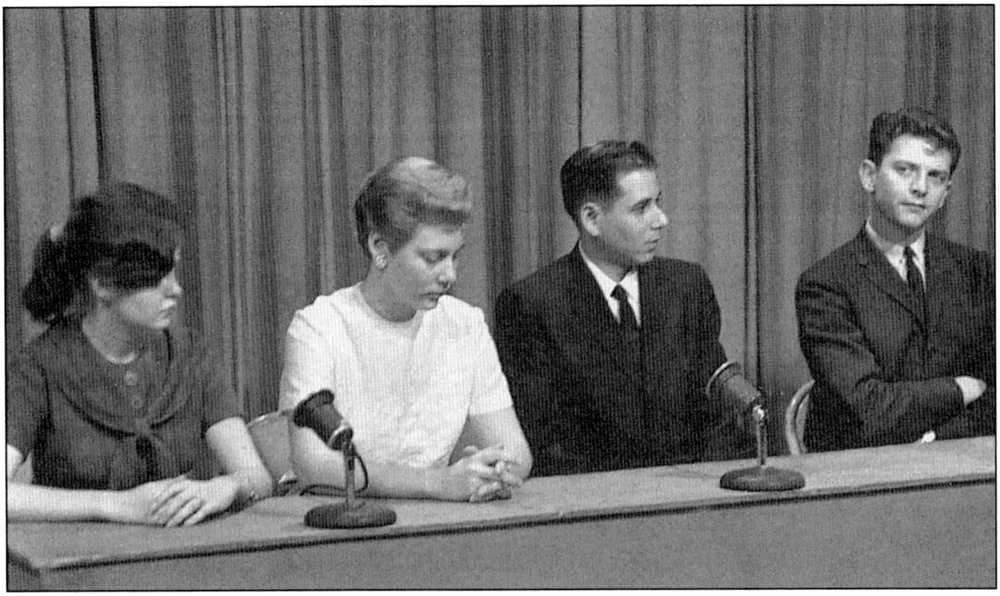

Television. The university has a strong attachment to local news. The Archives and Special Collections Department of the Langsdale Library is the repository for the first news station in Baltimore, WMAR-TV, whose footage dates from 1948. In 1960, for the second year in a row, the university sent a panel of students to appear on the American Legion program *To Promote Good Will.* The panel consisted of, from left to right, Pam Nicholson, secretary of the freshman class; Stephanie Crowley, president of the Women's Association; Warren Silverman, editor of *The Baloo*; and David Wiseman, president of the SGA. In the 1990s (below), two students interview Edgar Allan Poe shortly after he took up residence at the university's Gordon Plaza.

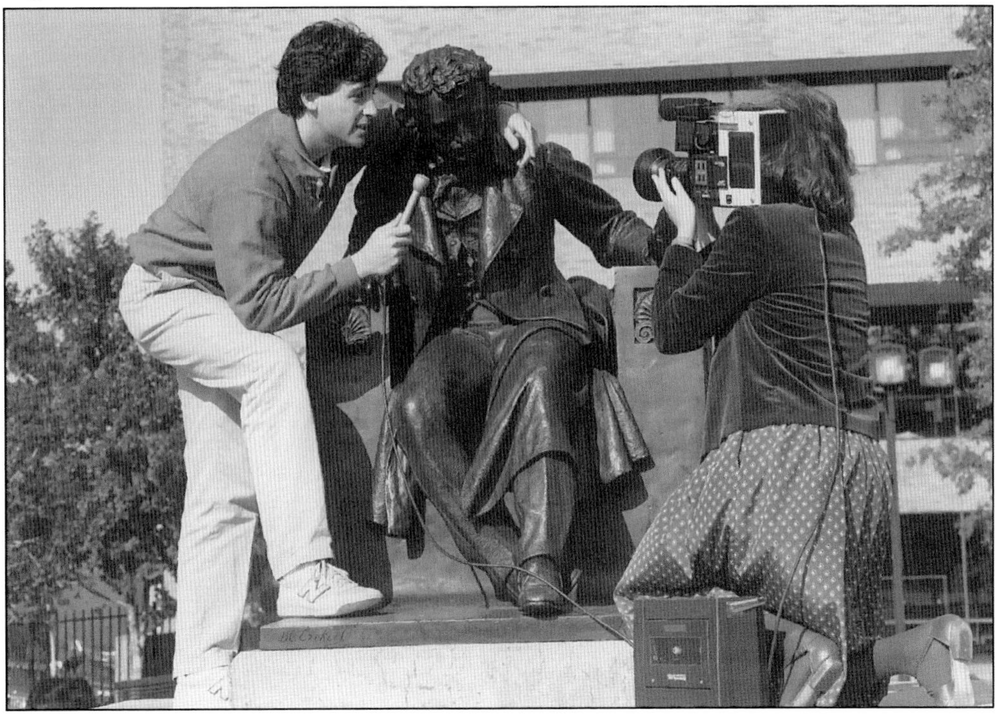

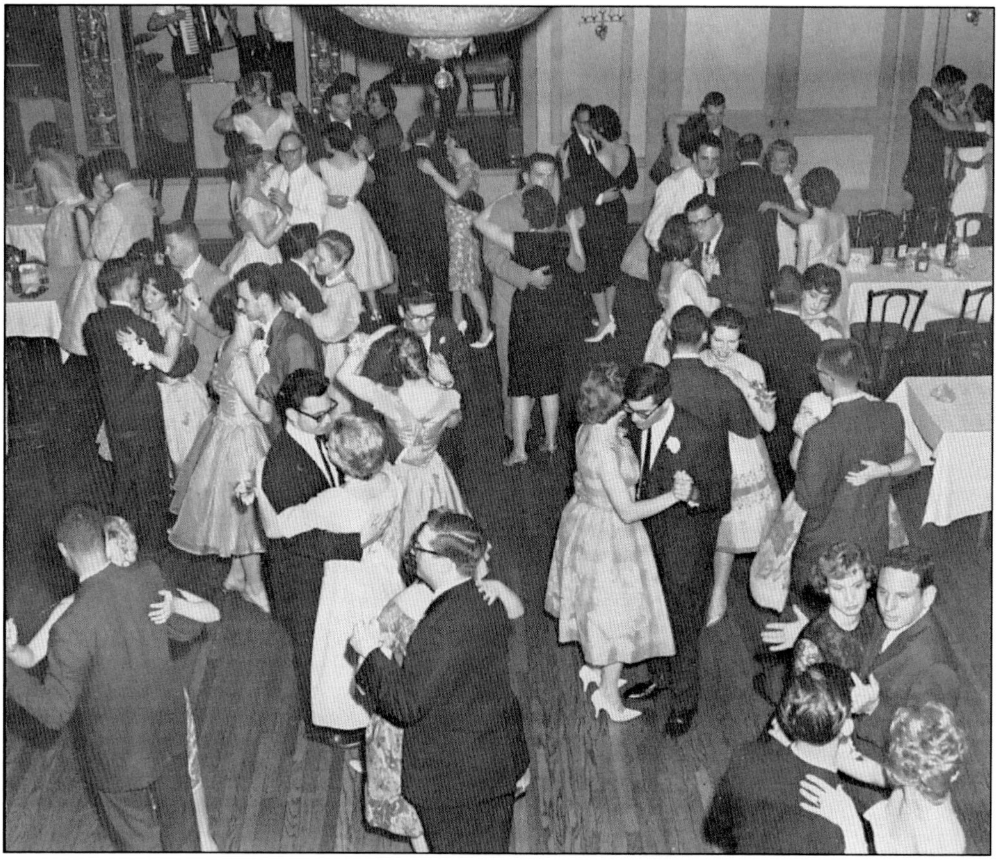

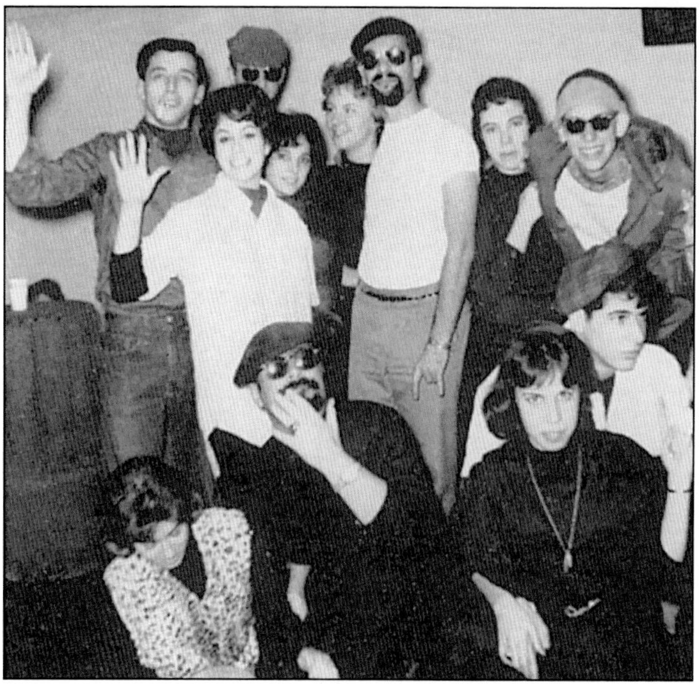

The Junior-Sophomore Prom. The first annual Junior-Sophomore Prom was held in 1961.

A Coffeehouse, 1961. Among the 1961 social activities in which the brothers of Alpha Omega Pi participated was a "Beatnik Bop," featuring a coffeehouse.

National Bohemian. In 1970, the university held a 72-hour football marathon to raise money for Santa Claus Anonymous. Among the activities was the Mr. Boh Look-A-Like Contest.

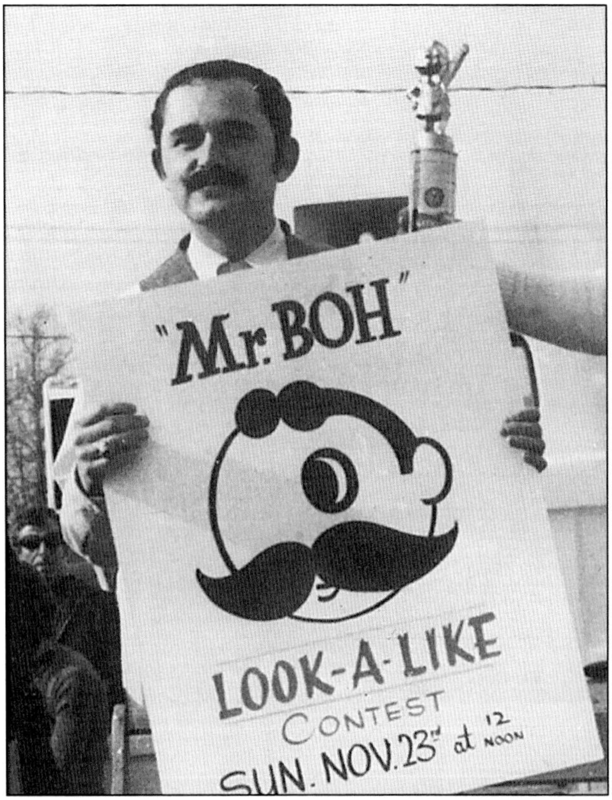

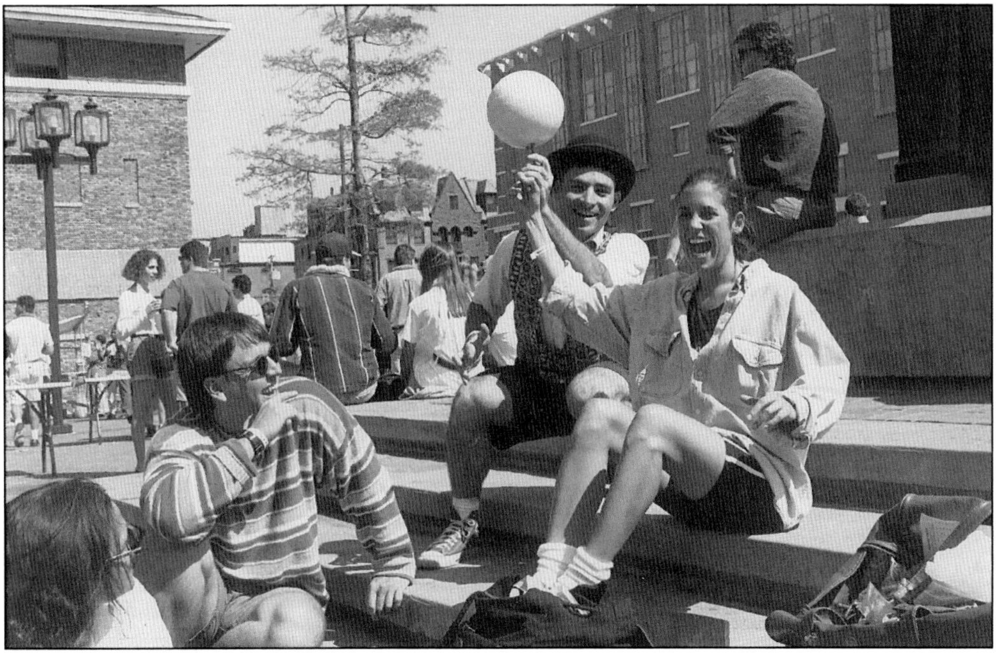

A Block Party. Students enjoy the warm spring weather by having fun while raising money for their clubs and organizations at the block party, held at the beginning of the fall and end of the spring semesters.

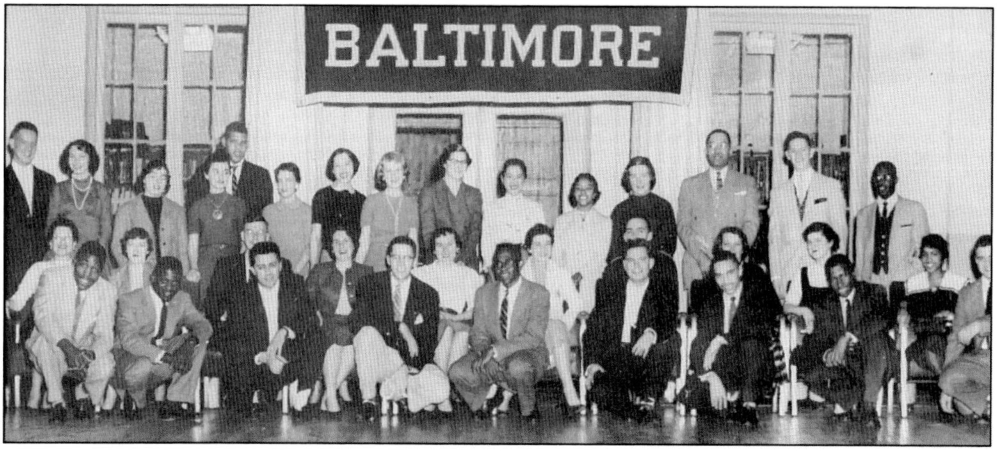

The National Student Association. In 1955, the university hosted the Mason-Dixon Regional Meeting. Among the delegates pictured are UB representatives Tom Pappas, Bob Doyle, and Tom Kemmer.

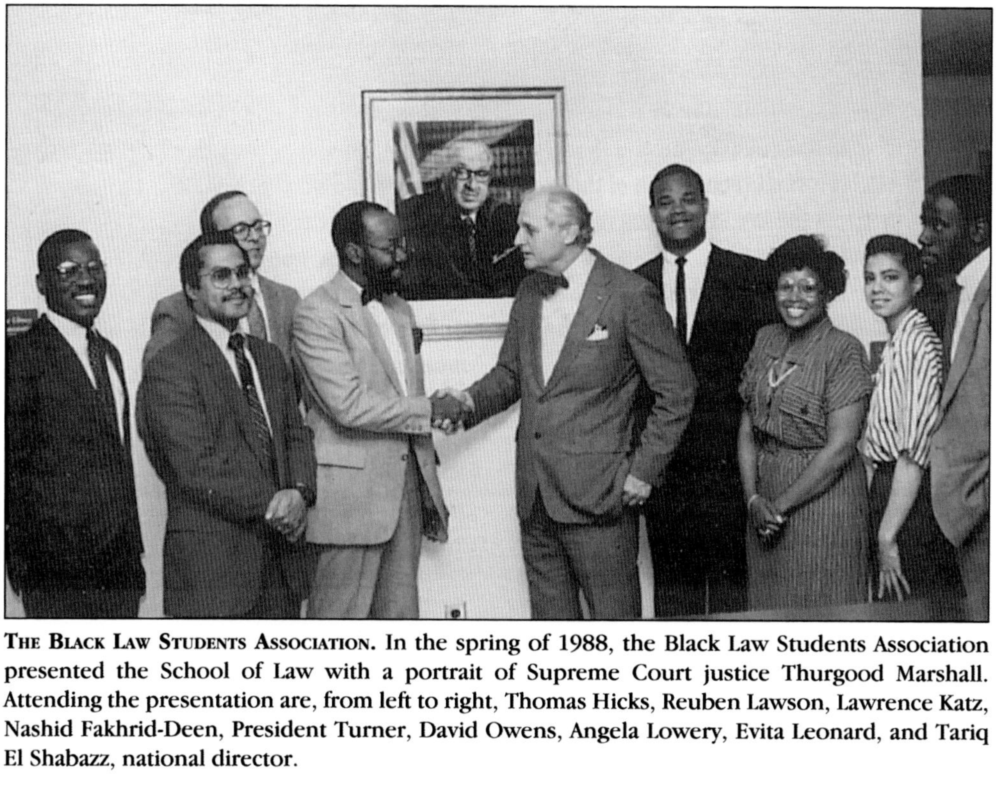

The Black Law Students Association. In the spring of 1988, the Black Law Students Association presented the School of Law with a portrait of Supreme Court justice Thurgood Marshall. Attending the presentation are, from left to right, Thomas Hicks, Reuben Lawson, Lawrence Katz, Nashid Fakhrid-Deen, President Turner, David Owens, Angela Lowery, Evita Leonard, and Tariq El Shabazz, national director.

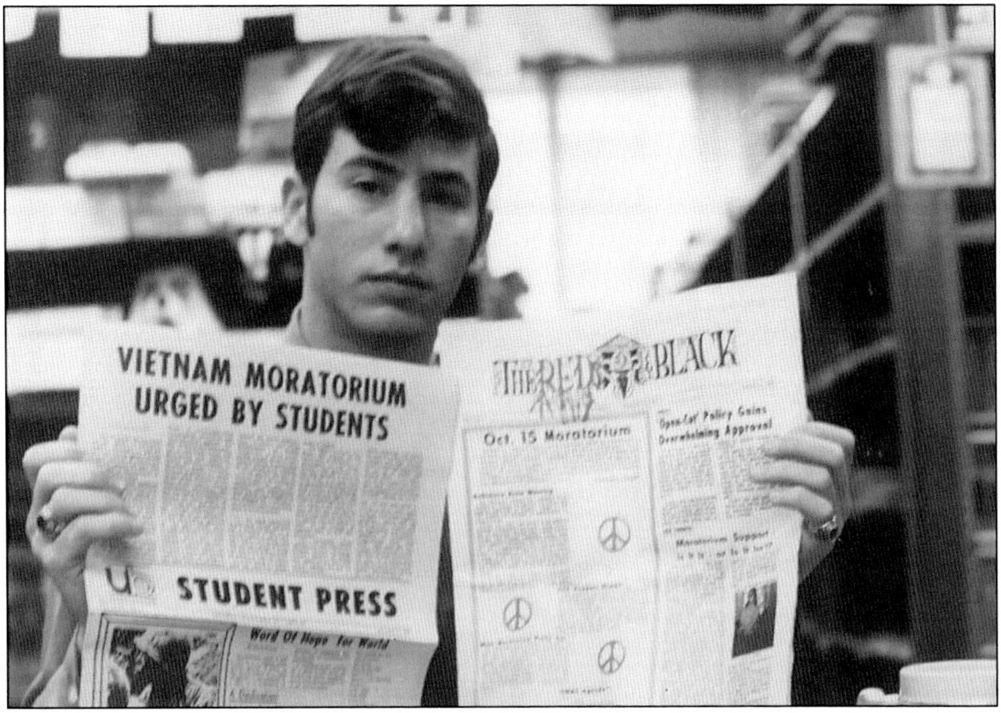

Vietnam War Protest. In 1970, a student strike was called after four students were killed by Ohio National Guardsmen at Kent State and a similar incident occurred at Mississippi's Jackson State. The strike also protested against the war in Vietnam and the Cambodian issue. In the photograph above, Richard Boruta displays the school paper urging students to take their protest to the streets. In the two photos below, protesters from UB block Charles Street and then join other protesters in a march to Charles Center, where a citywide protest rally was held.

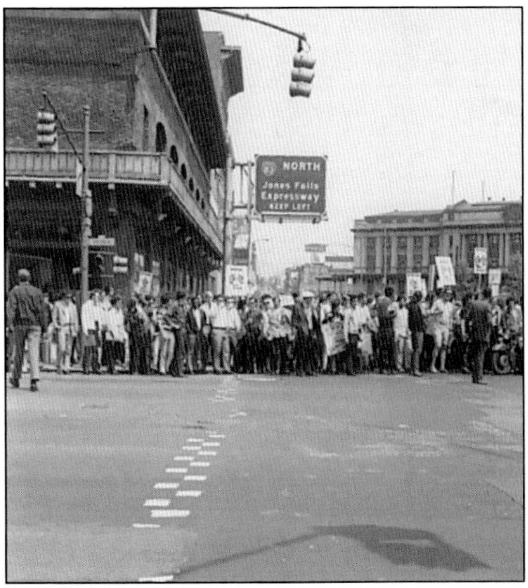

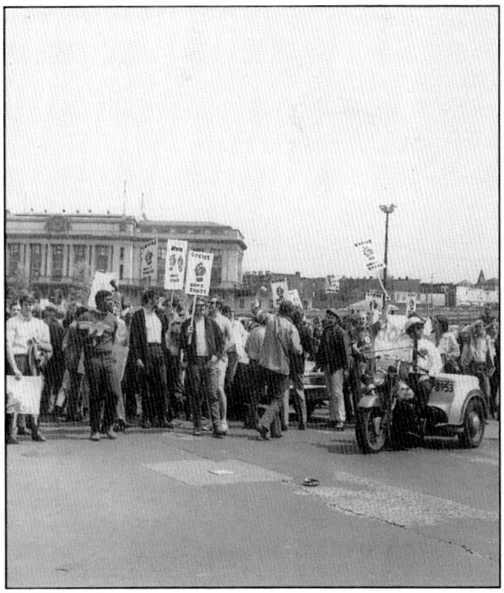

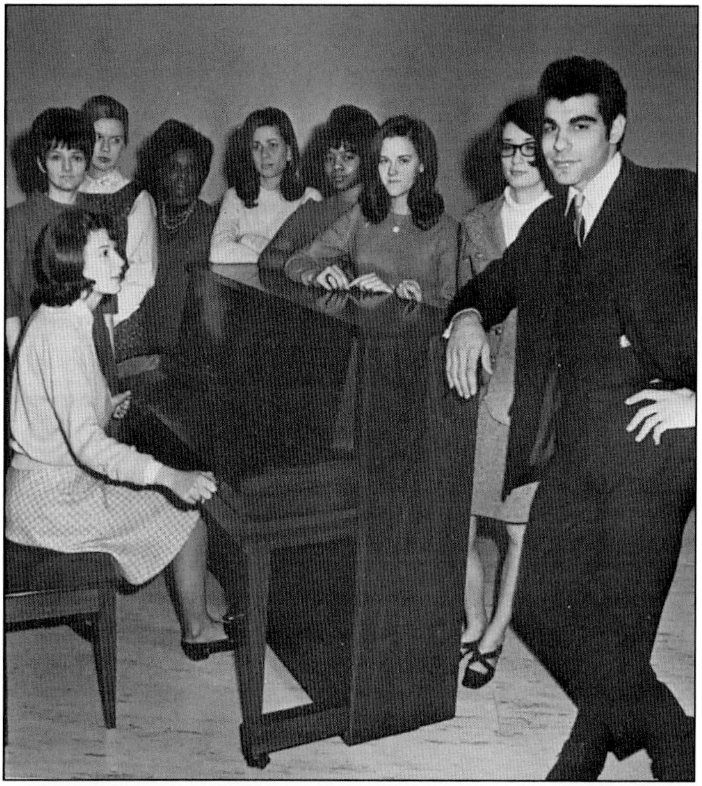

The Glee Club. The members of the glee club in this 1967 photograph are, from left to right, Joyce A. Heath, D. Schram, Patricia A. Crumbly, D. Clover, Vivienne E. Moritz, Stefanie Bain, Teresa Musk, and S. Darwin. The club served the school by entertaining at the interfaith services and musical programs, where they performed both traditional hymns and folk music.

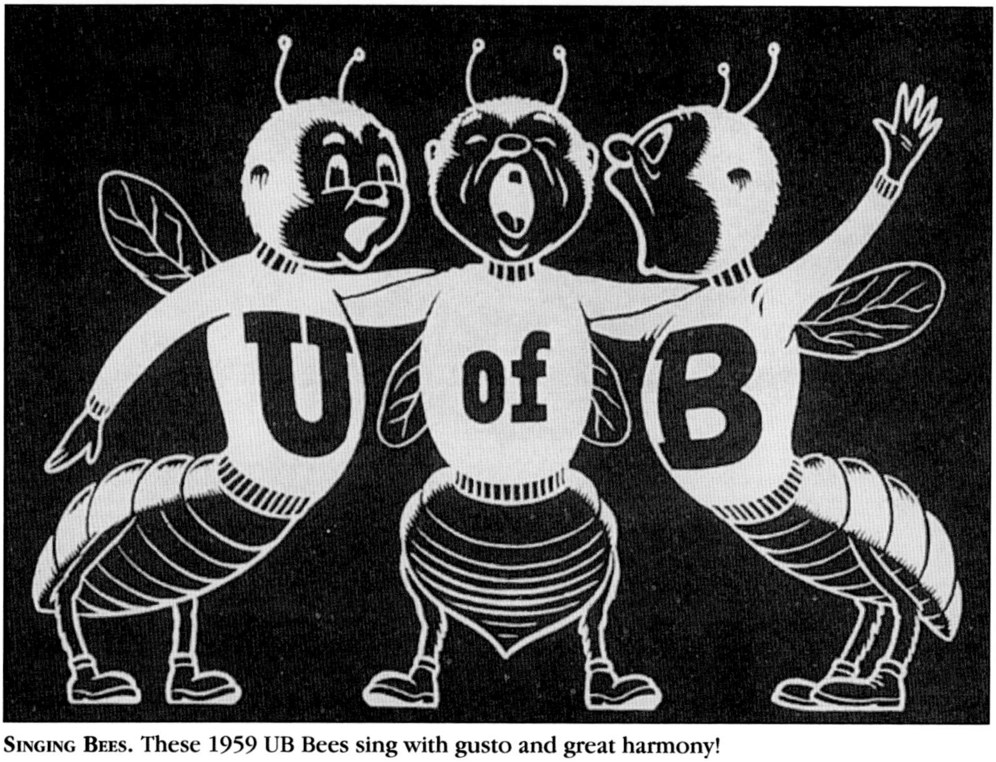

Singing Bees. These 1959 UB Bees sing with gusto and great harmony!

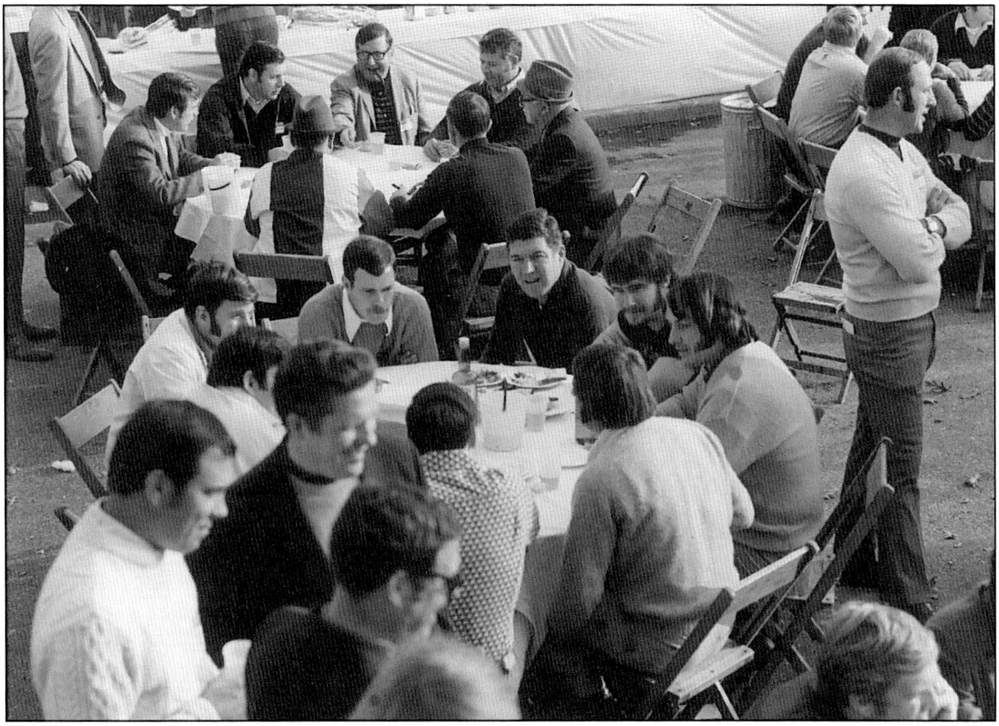

The Annual Bull Roast. In the early 1970s, the athletic department hosted annual bull roasts.

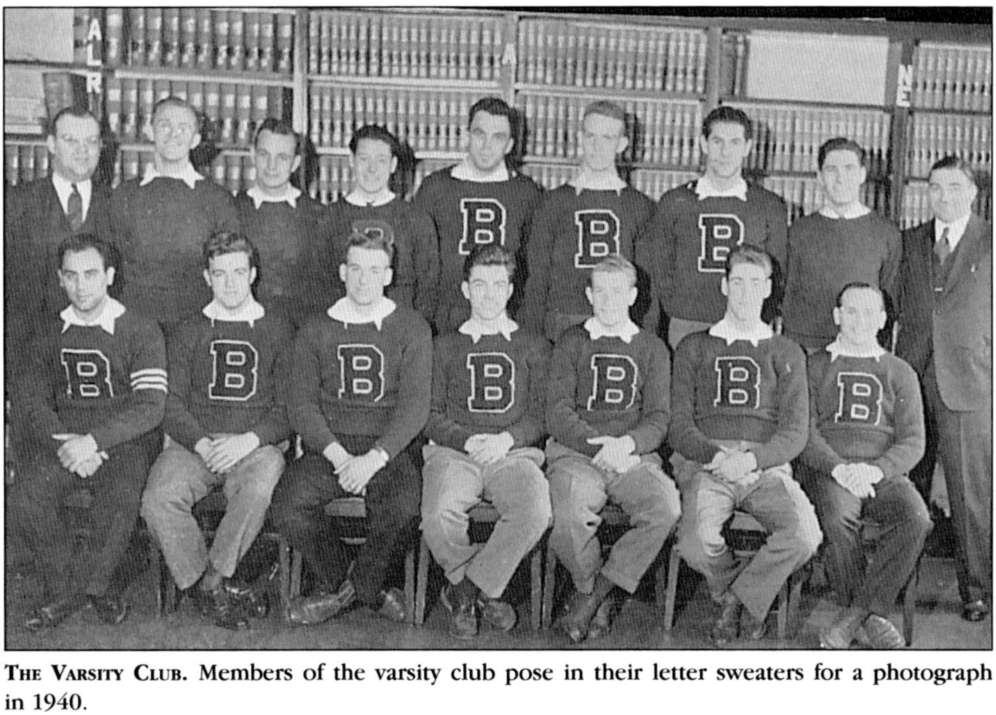

The Varsity Club. Members of the varsity club pose in their letter sweaters for a photograph in 1940.

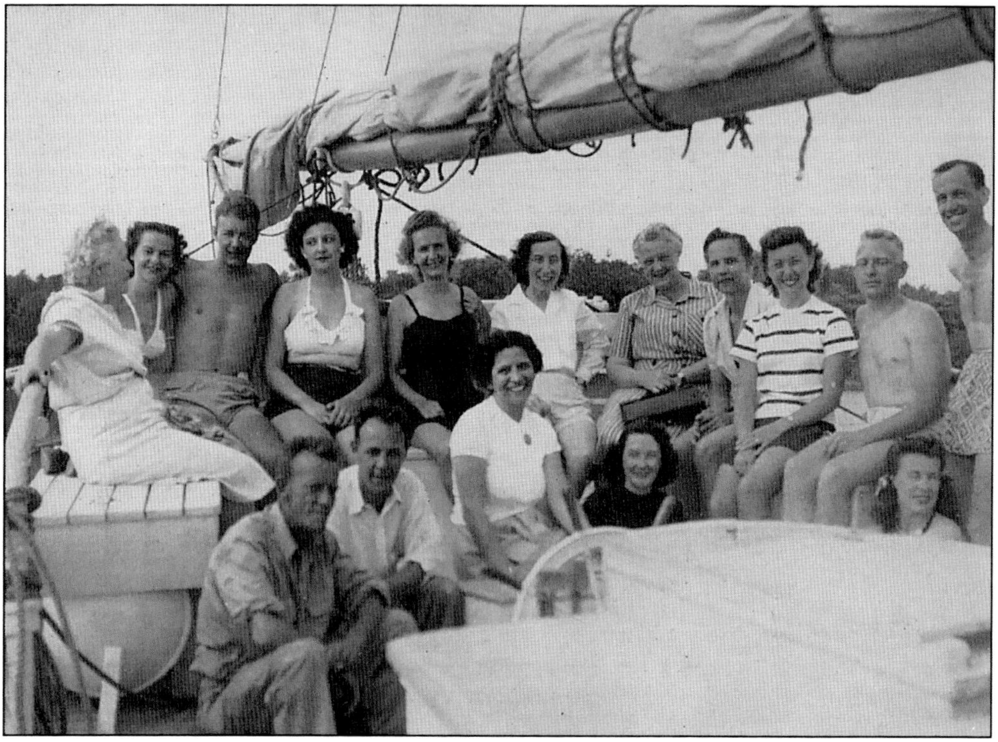

Iota Tau Tau. Seen here in this 1951 photograph are members and friends of the Lambda Chapter Sorority on the yacht of Judge J. Abner Saylor, legal sponsor of the group. The purpose of Iota Tau Tau is the advancement of women in the legal profession.

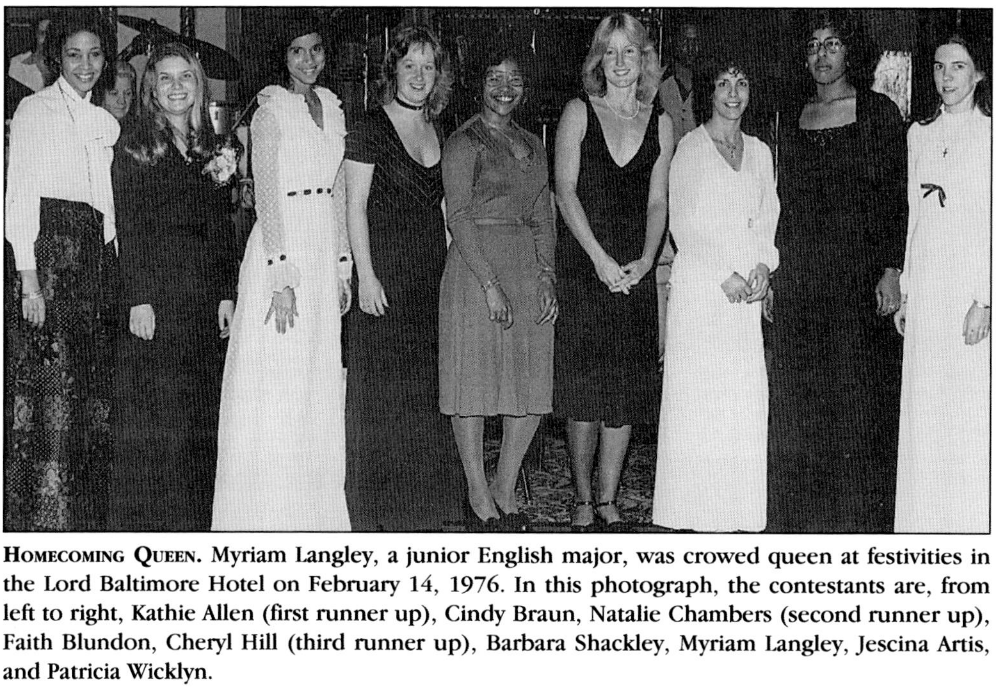

Homecoming Queen. Myriam Langley, a junior English major, was crowed queen at festivities in the Lord Baltimore Hotel on February 14, 1976. In this photograph, the contestants are, from left to right, Kathie Allen (first runner up), Cindy Braun, Natalie Chambers (second runner up), Faith Blundon, Cheryl Hill (third runner up), Barbara Shackley, Myriam Langley, Jescina Artis, and Patricia Wicklyn.

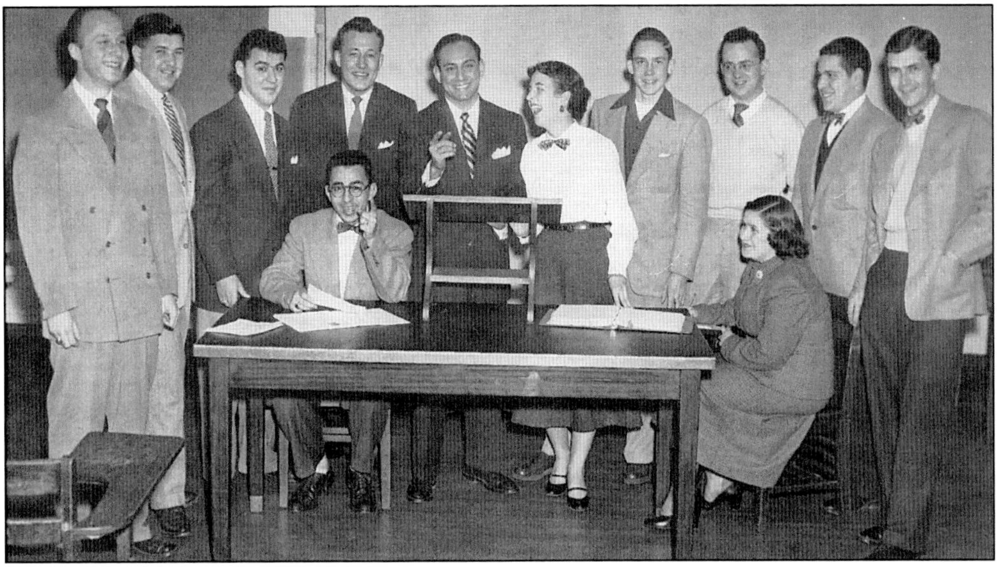

THE 1952 STUDENT COUNCIL. These student council members are as follows, from left to right: (seated) Mel Paul and Betty Eckhardt; (standing) Stuart Renbaum, Ken Glauber, Melvin Steinberg (future lieutenant governor of Maryland), Bill Hartje, Gene Silberman (president), Ruth Stansbury, Bob Todd, Russ Furness, Harry Fisher, and John Webb (faculty advisor).

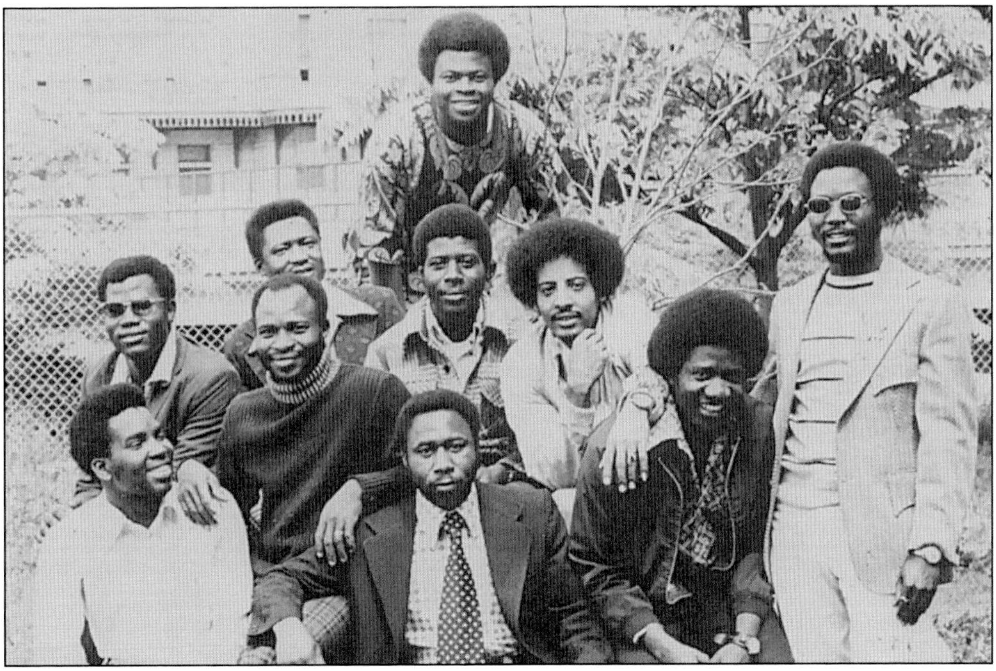

THE INTERNATIONAL STUDENTS ORGANIZATION. This 1975 photograph shows some of members of the organization. The university has a long history of attracting international students to its campus.

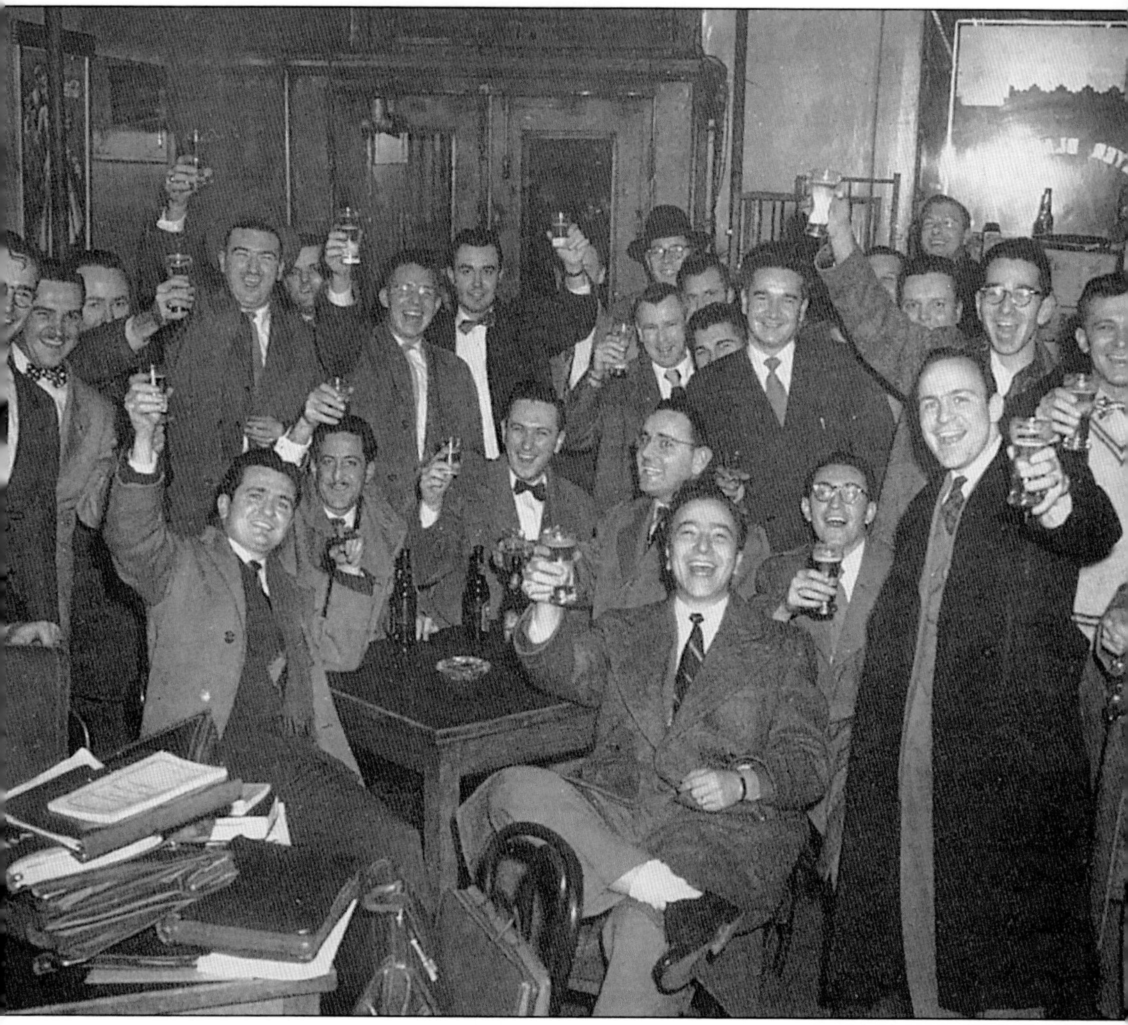

Down at Meyers, 1951. Located on Howard Street at Armory Place, Meyers' was the place where UB students gathered for conversation, good fellowship, and studious camaraderie. This group of UB students are raising their glasses and cheering their host, owner Maxie.

Five

Athletics

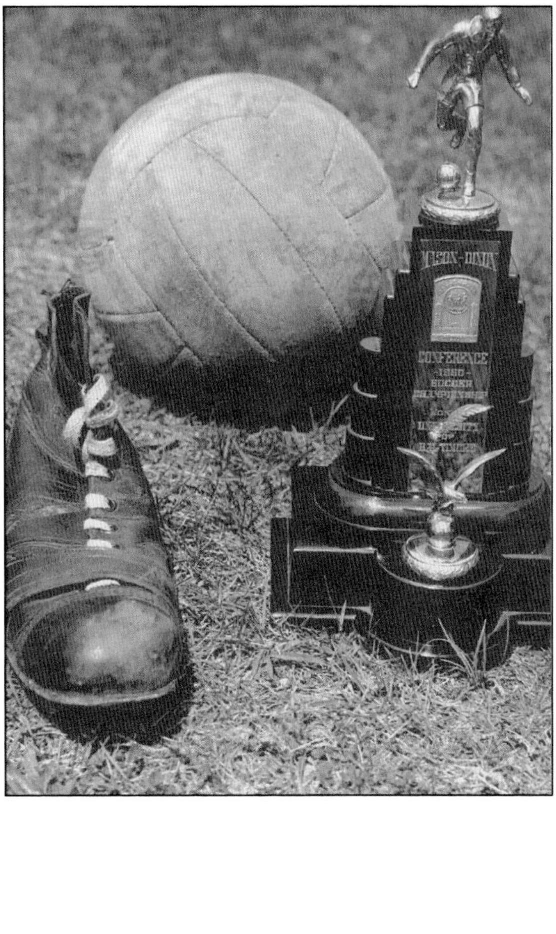

Intercollegiate Athletics. Shortly after the founding of the school in 1925, athletic and intramural sports were established. The rising cost and the small number of eligible students induced the university to withdraw from intercollegiate athletic competition at the end of the 1982–1983 academic year. In its place, the administration planned a new leisure activity program that would benefit all of the students.

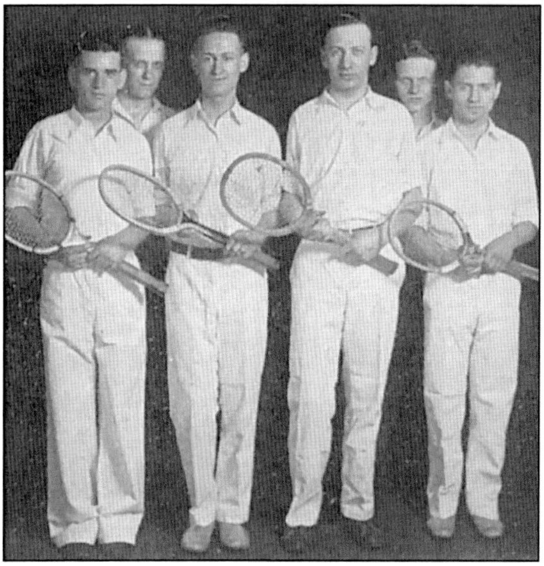

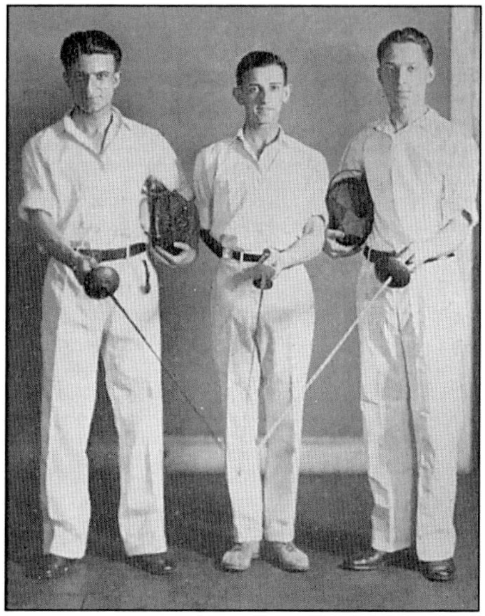

TENNIS AND FENCING, 1928. These two sports were among the first to be represented by athletic teams on campus. The tennis team members are, from left to right, Norman Salzman, Jules F. Diehl, Aaron Fagan, Sidney Salzman, Joseph M. Wyatt, and J. Paul Rocklin. The members of the fencing team are, from left to right, Milton Albert (captain), Leon Jarlow, and Ben Arbesman.

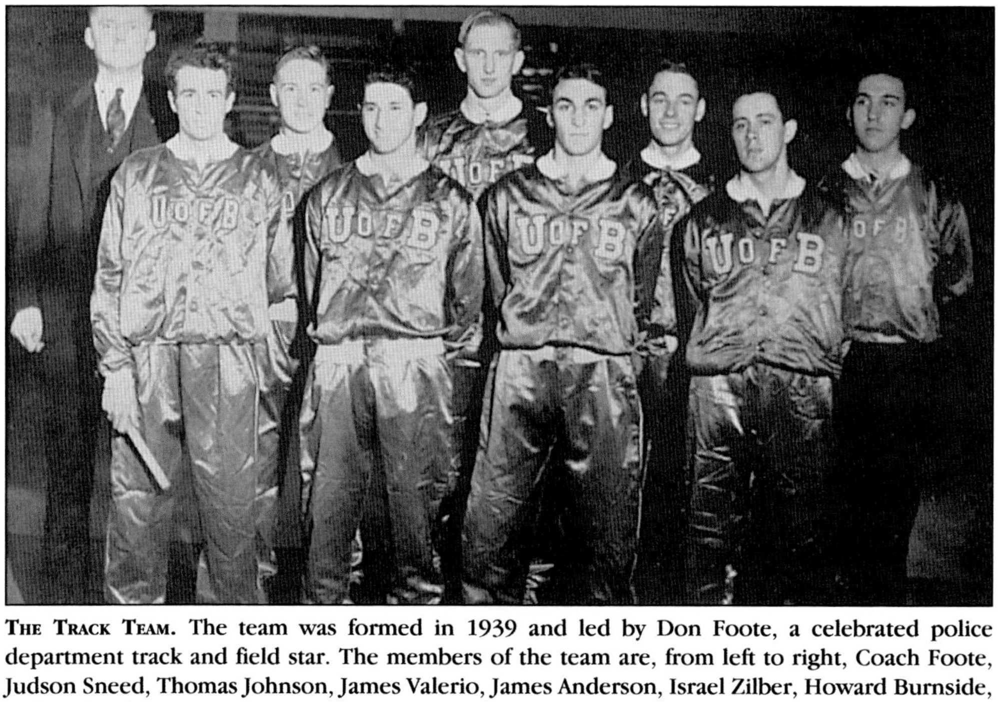

THE TRACK TEAM. The team was formed in 1939 and led by Don Foote, a celebrated police department track and field star. The members of the team are, from left to right, Coach Foote, Judson Sneed, Thomas Johnson, James Valerio, James Anderson, Israel Zilber, Howard Burnside, and Paul Rubin.

Queen Bees. Basketball has always held a special place at the university, with the first team being formed in 1928. However, it was a men's-only sport until 1938, when a coed team was formed. The team roster included Gertrude Layton, coach; Betty Sherwood, manager; Catherine Brooks; Grace Byrd; Minna Dietz; Natalie Hanson; Marie Kuechele; Margaret Schobel; and Ruth Turner. Several members of the team are shown here in an action shot.

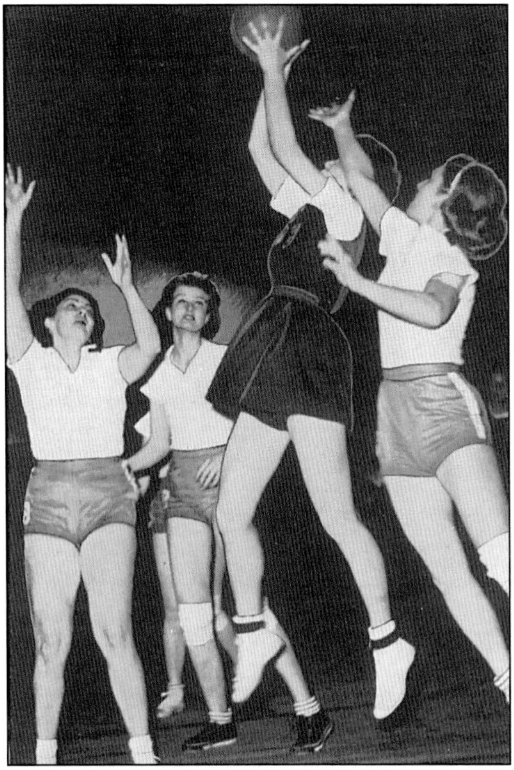

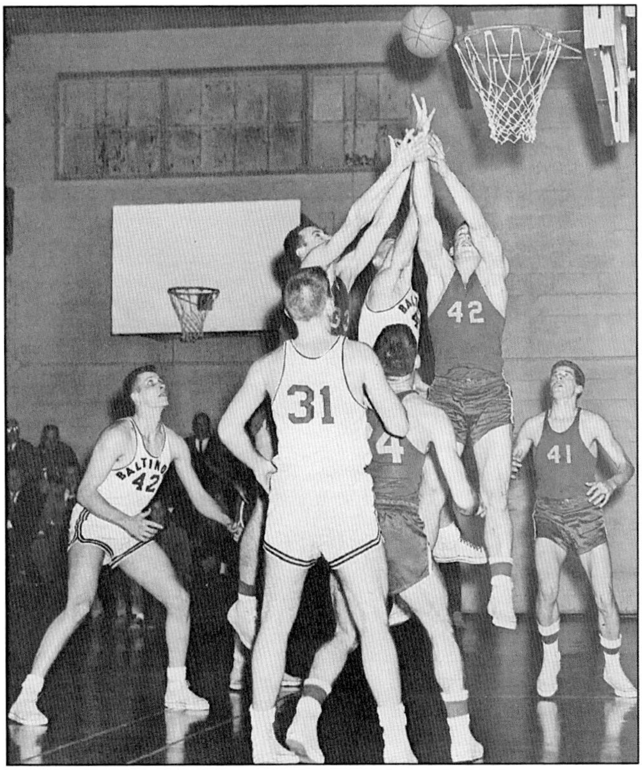

Men's Basketball. In this 1958 photograph, the Bees have the crowd holding their breath as everyone waits to see if this jump shot will score.

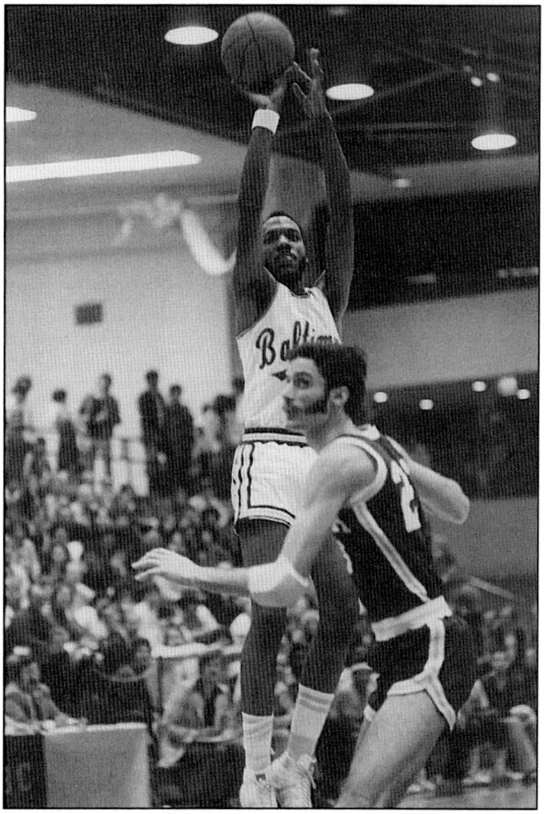

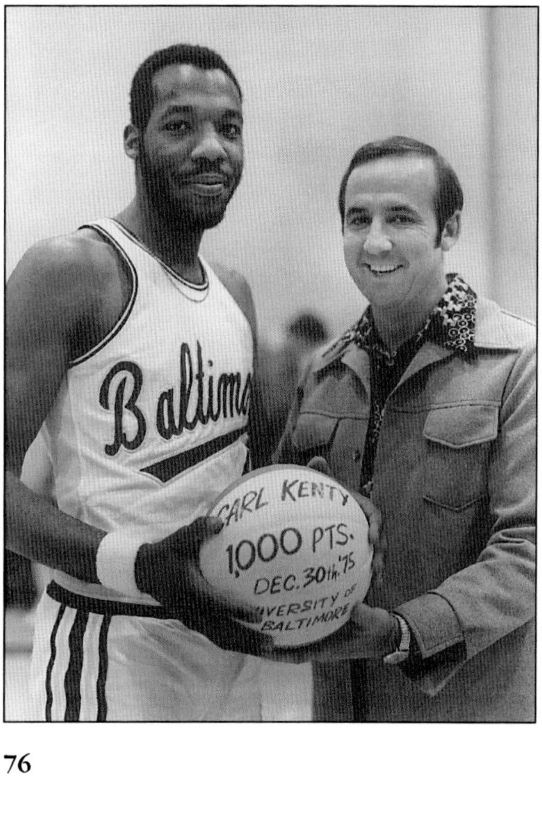

TWO KINGS OF THE COURT. In the top photograph, Carl Kenty is about to score another hoop shot. In the bottom picture, athletic director Frank Szymanski presents him with a souvenir basketball after he scored his 1,000th point on December 30, 1975.

Edward Petit. In this 1975 photograph, the other half of the university's athletic team—Ed Petit, the supply officer—is about to make a basket.

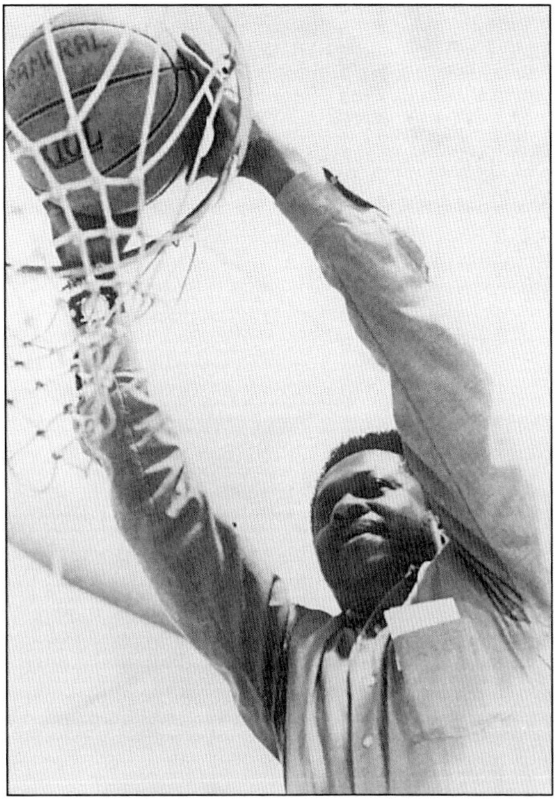

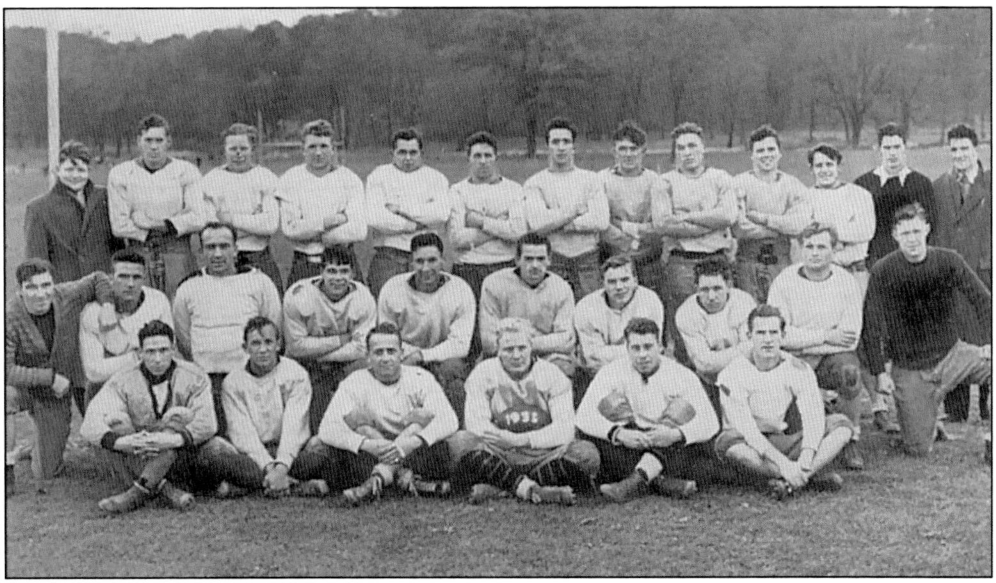

The Maroons. In 1930, a football team was organized, but by 1937, the university was no longer sporting a team. This photograph is from 1934.

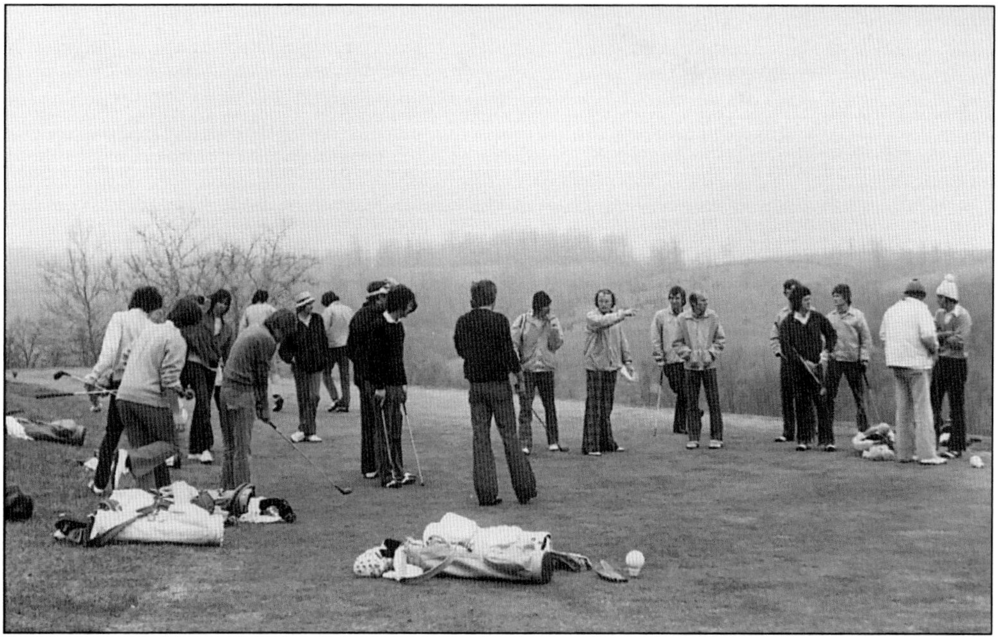

The Golf Team. Golf was added to the athletic program in 1938. In these two photographs from the mid-1970s, the team practices at the Mount Washington athletic facility.

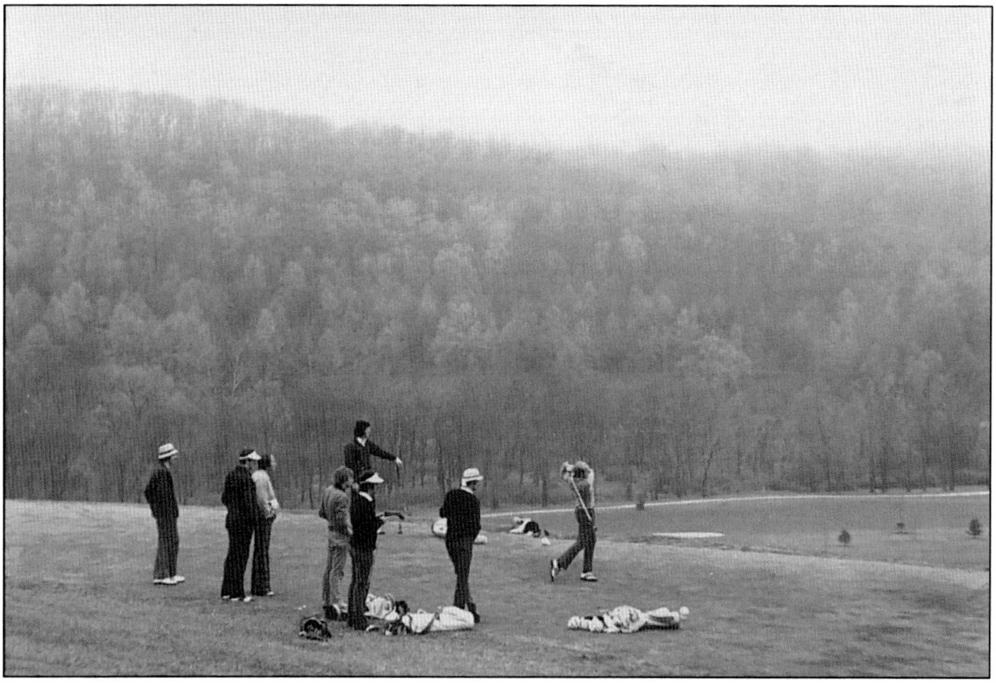

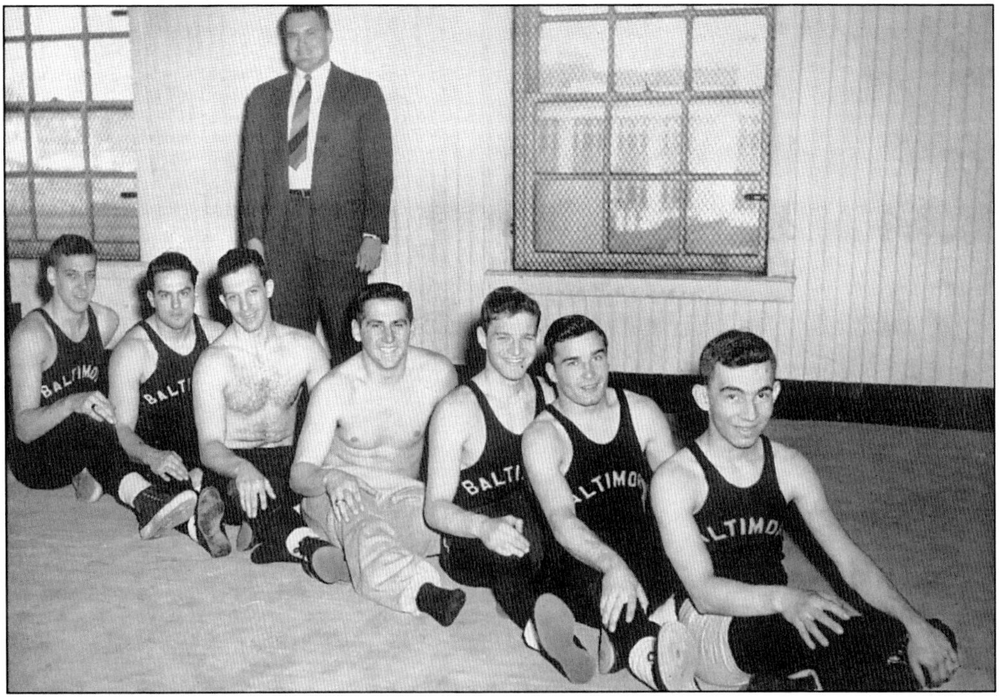

The Wrestling Team. This first wrestling team was organized in 1948 and coached by John Eareckson. It continued to be an integral part of the athletic program at the university until the intercollegiate program was disbanded in 1983. The 1951 team members are, from left to right, Bunky Wagner, Dave Palmer, (standing) Phil Lohrey (coach), Sid Goldin, Carol Waltemyer, Don Rhody, John Tolston, and John Hanges.

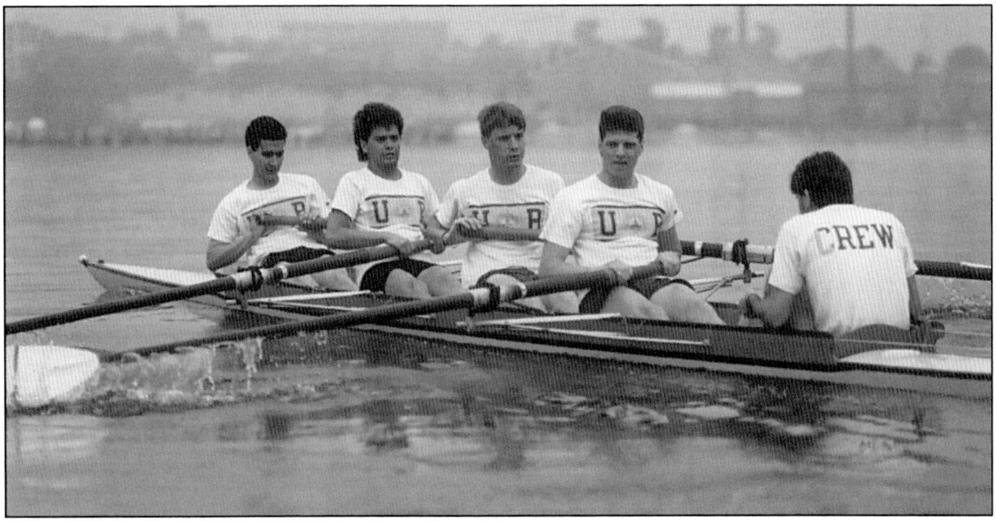

The Crew Club. Established in 1980, the team competes locally and nationally in meets sanctioned by the U.S. Rowing Association. In 1987, they had their best year, finishing first in the men's eight race and second for the mixed eight at the Baltimore Aerial Regatta. There are approximately 30 members, men and women, whose skills range from novice to advanced. The men's team is seen on the Middle Branch of the Patapsco River in this 1987 photograph; they are, from left to right, as Dave Munsma, Bob Buker, Joe Manning, Tom Mann, and Rob Santoni.

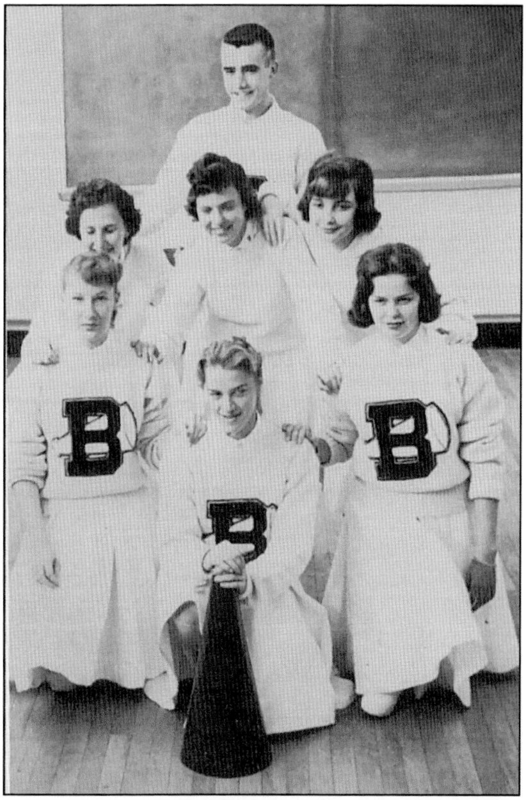

Cheerleaders. Whether leading the pep rally or encouraging players at game time, the cheerleading squads are at the forefront of school spirit. At left is the 1960 team; below is the "Junior Bees" cheerleading squad.

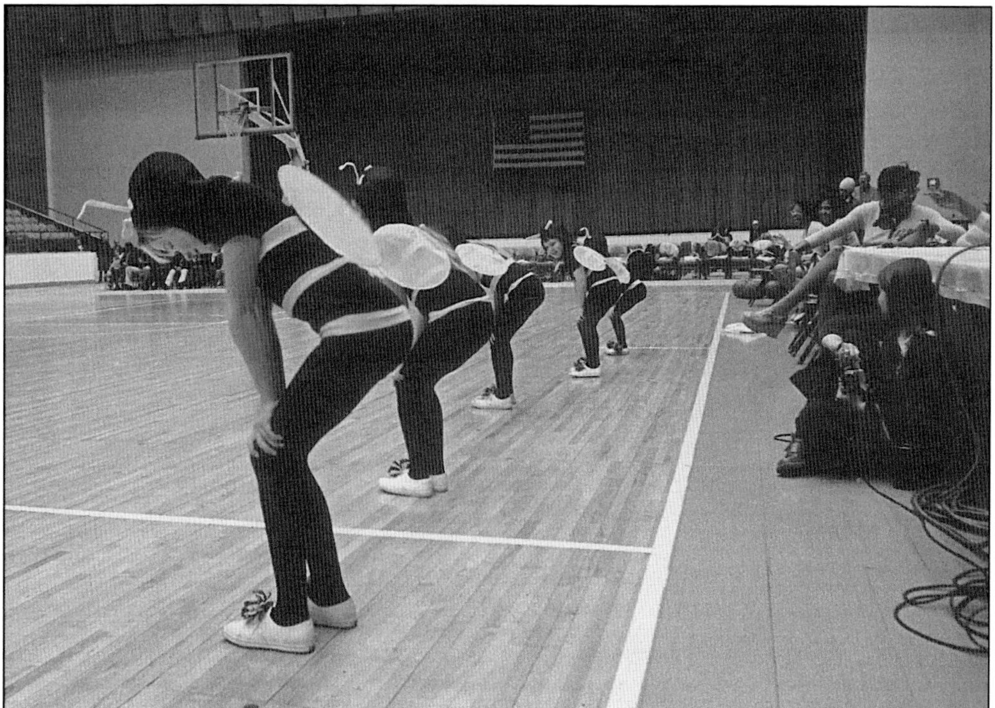

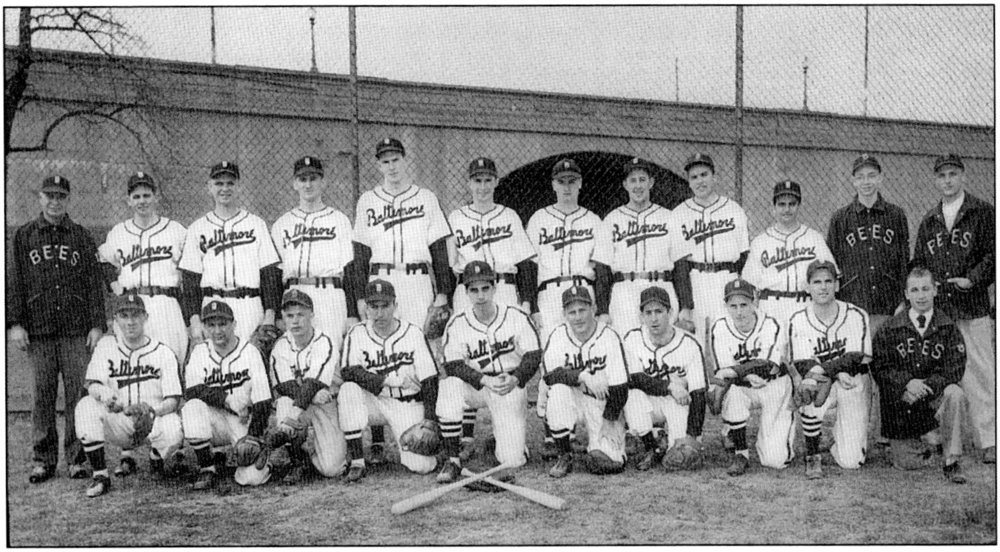

Baseball. A team was first established in 1941 as an intermural sport. In the photograph above, the 1950 team members are as follows, from left to right: (kneeling) Ressin, Bellusci, Kenny Miller, Woelper, Cohen, Deppish, Petrovich, Jackson, Tomassi, and D'Ambrosio, manager; (standing) Gottshall (coach), Ed Plitt, J. Miller, Mummert, MacPherson, Buttermore, Hart, Faulstich, Diffenbaugh, Giaraffa, Krafft (manager) and Hesse. Below, a team from the 1970s plays at the Mt. Washington facility.

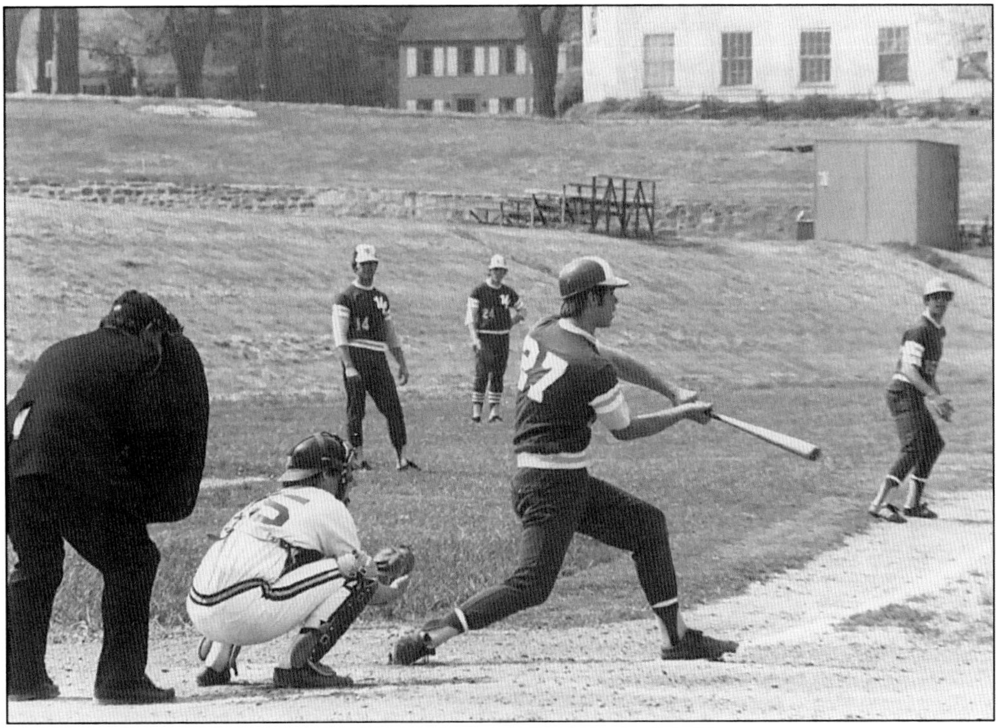

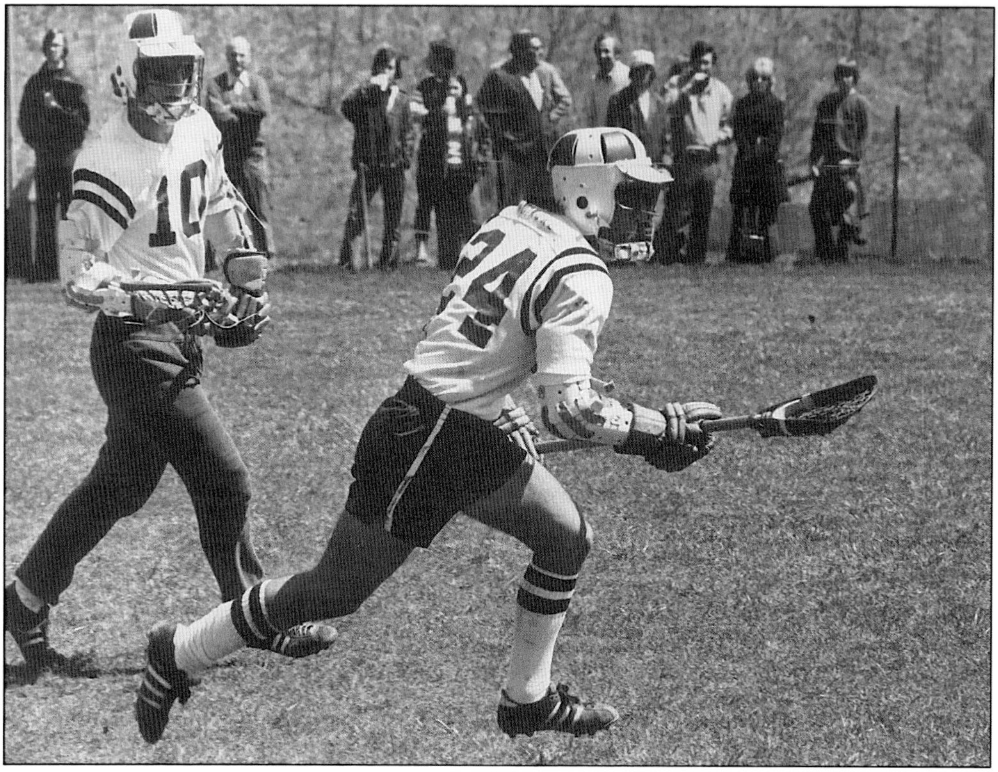

LACROSSE. The first lacrosse team was established in 1929. In these two photographs, the 1973 team takes on the Air Force at Mt. Washington Athletic Center. In the photograph below, Rick Cwalinski (center) is caught between two opposing team members.

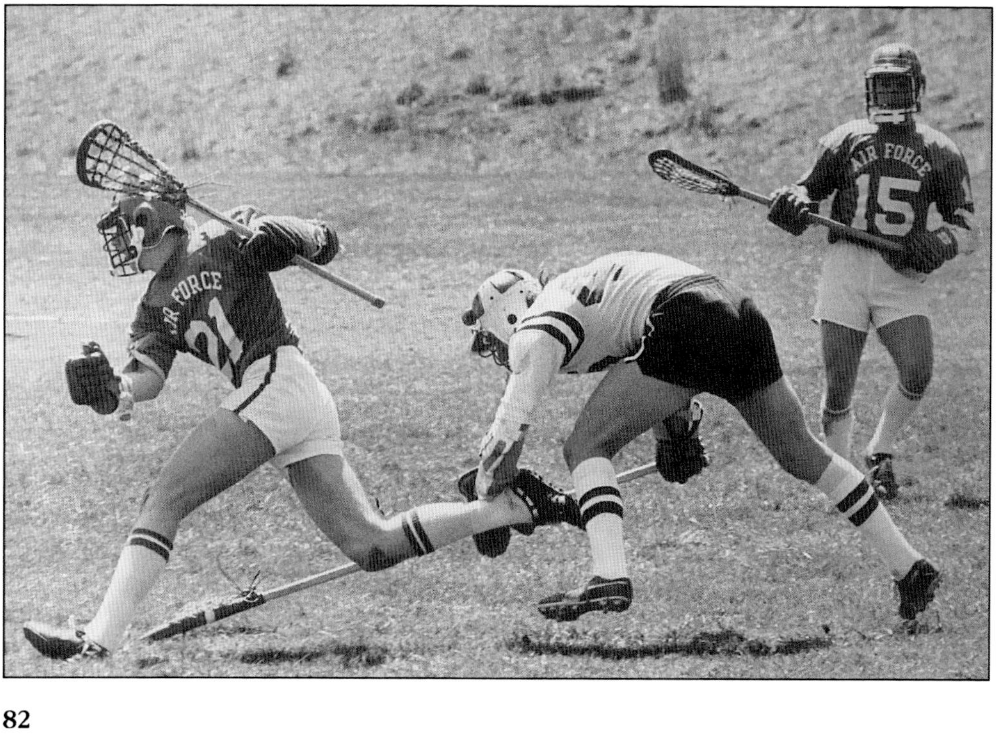

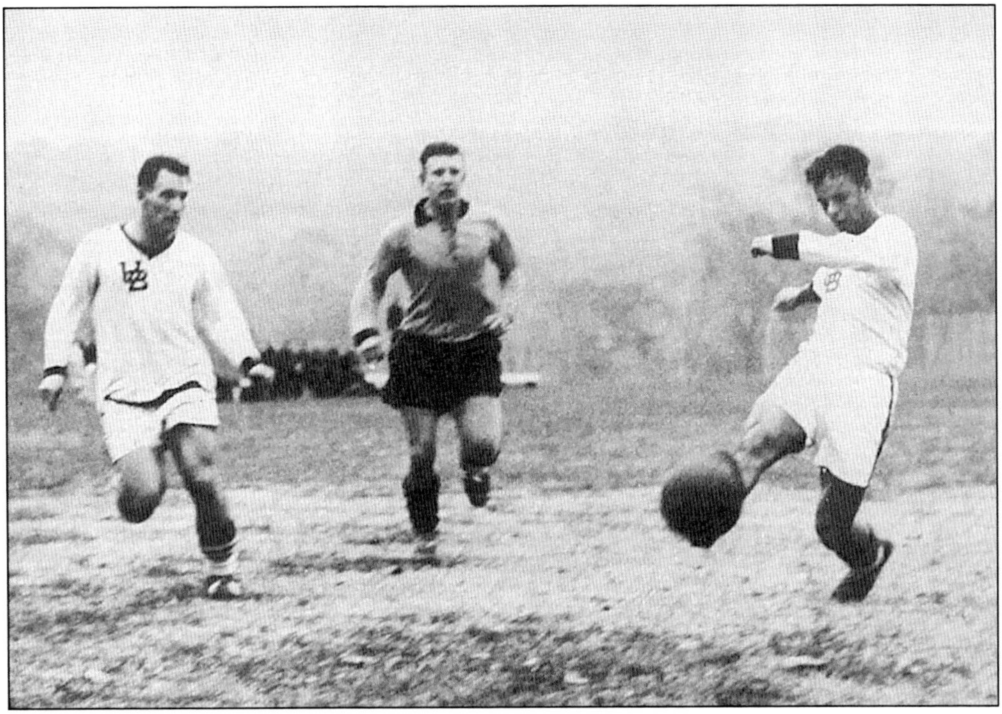

The Soccer Squad. The sport was first played in 1948. In 1958, the team was coached by ? Surock, a former Olympic champion. In the above photograph from 1958, freshman Al Velivona (right) connects for a goal. Below, C. Myers heads the ball toward the goal, but the goalie makes a save.

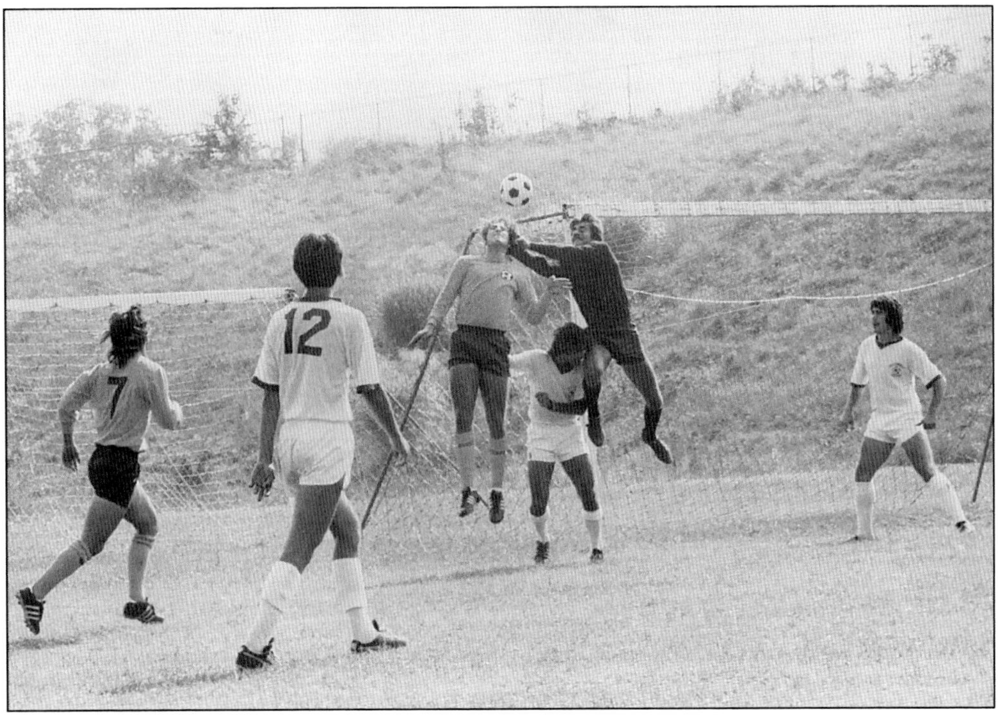

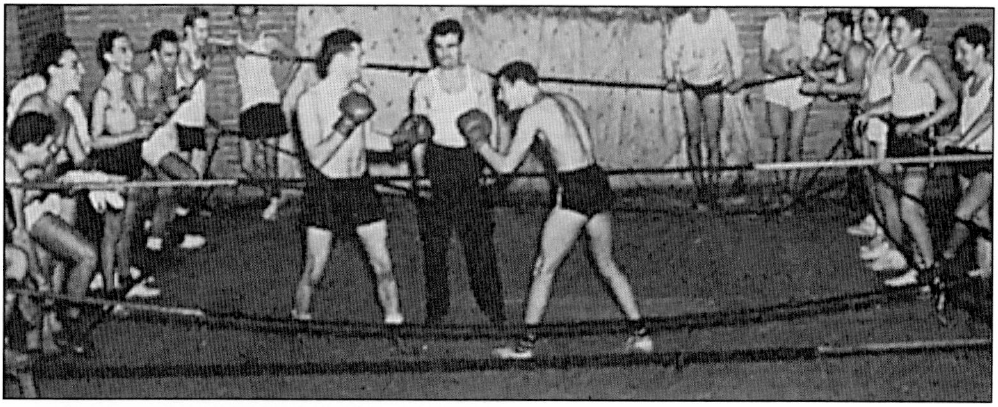

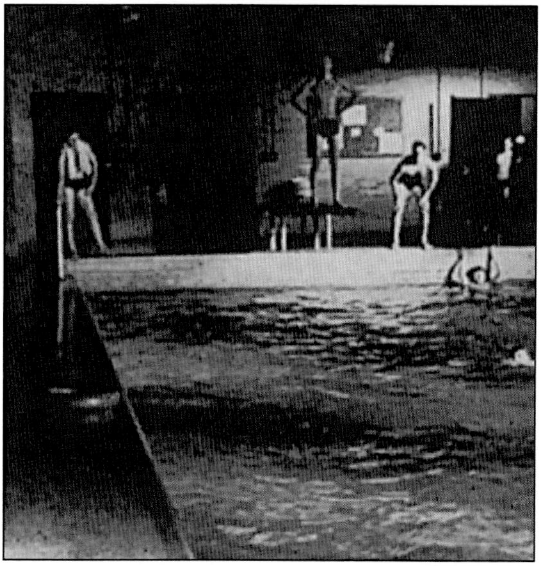

Above and left: **Intramurals.** Among the various sports that did not compete in NCAA sports were ping-pong, bowling, and the two that are pictured here, boxing and swimming. The school made use of the pool at the central YMCA.

Below: **The Athletic Club.** The athletic club serves the sports, health, fitness, and leisure needs of the university community, including students, faculty, staff, alumni, athletic club members, and the community surrounding the campus. Among the offerings are five racquetball/handball courts.

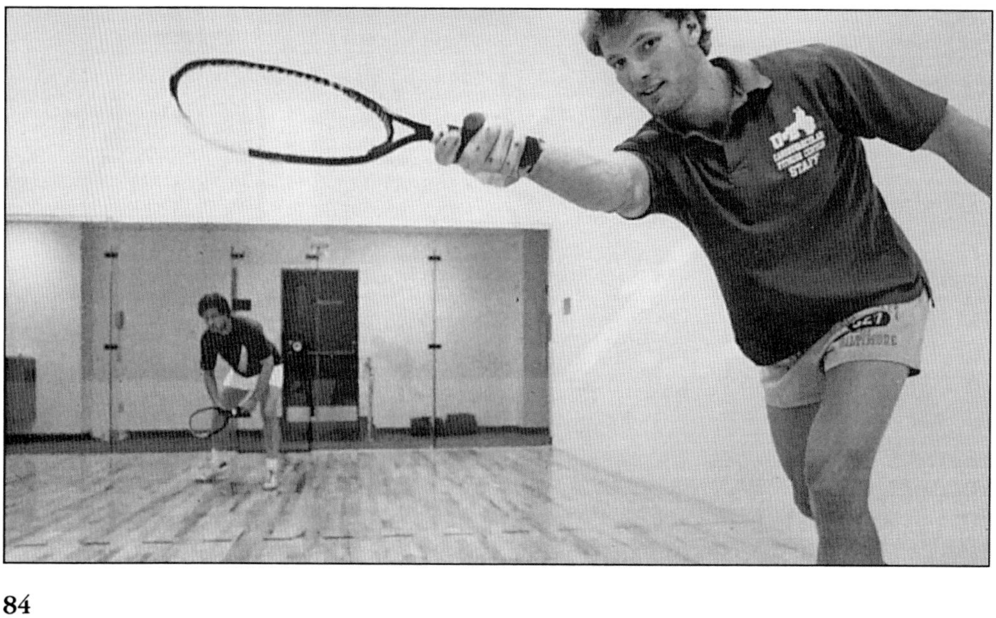

Six

ALUMNI

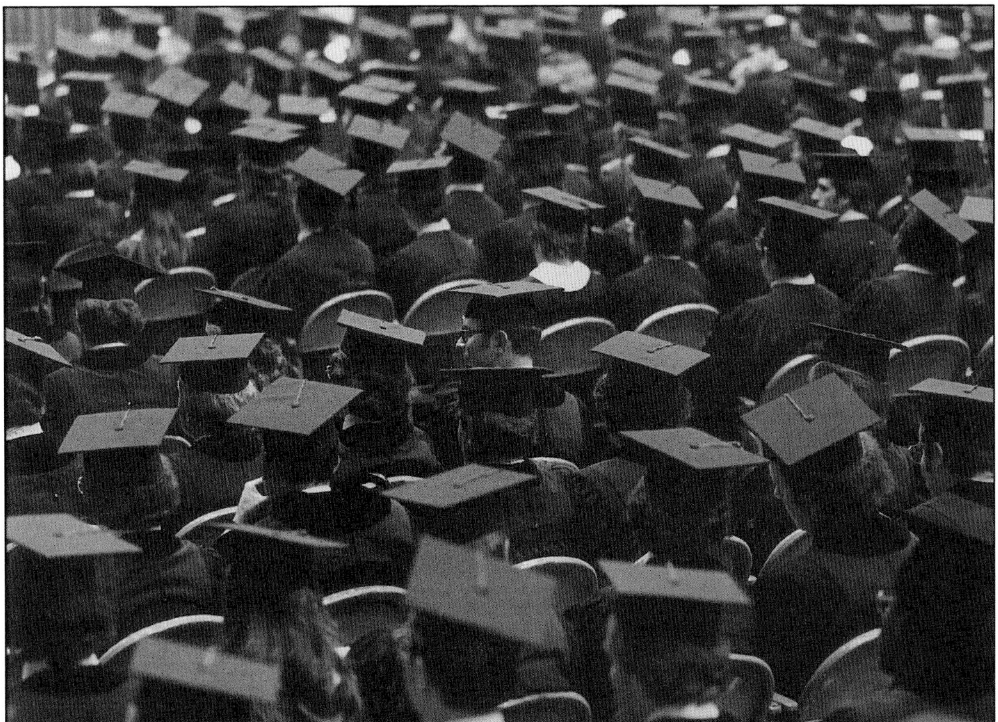

GRADUATION DAY. On graduation day, students celebrate the past, embrace the future, and become a part of the University of Baltimore's legacy.

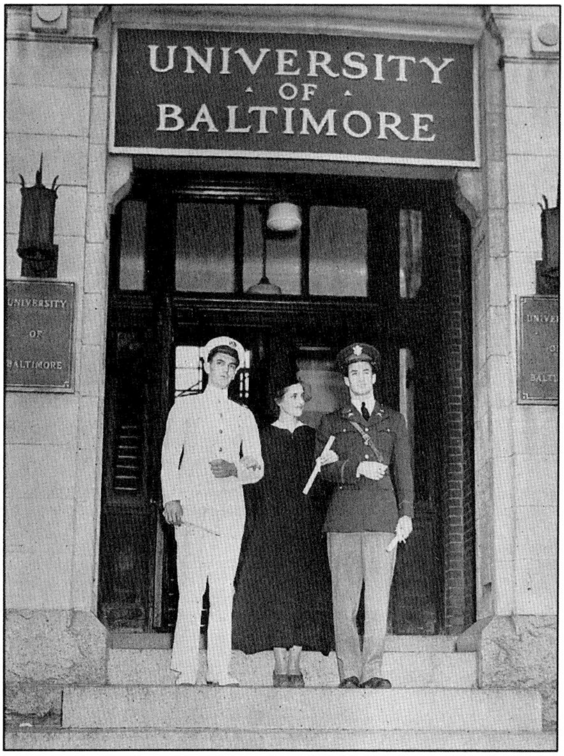

Graduation 1941. With war heavy on their minds, the editorial staff of *The Reporter* selected this as their "photograph of the year." By the time the yearbook went to press, four members of the class had already been appointed to the Flying Cadets.

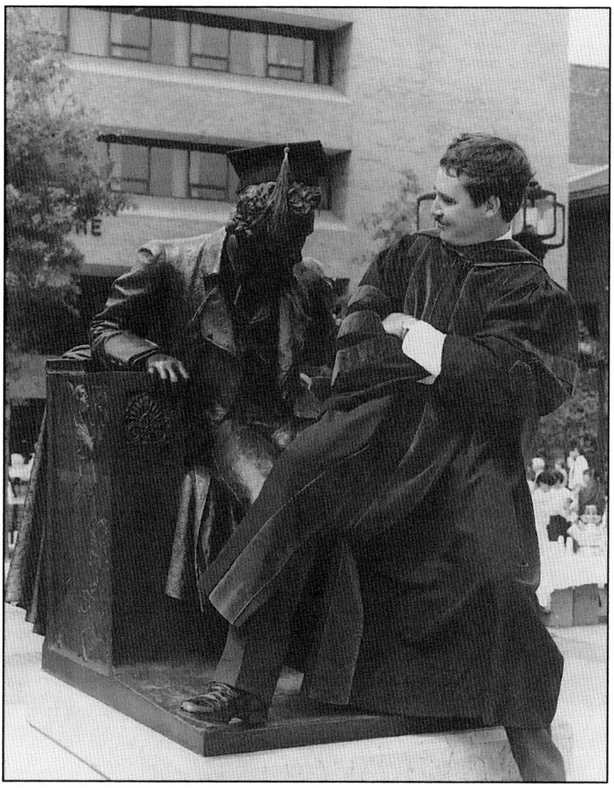

A New Tradition. On October 7, 1983, this statue of Edgar Allan Poe, sculpted by Sir Moses Ezekiel, was moved from Wyman Park to the new plaza at the university. It serves as a focal point and symbolic centerpiece for the emerging Mount Royal Center area of cultural and educational organizations. It has become a tradition to pose with the bard during the reception in Gordon Plaza held after the commencement exercise.

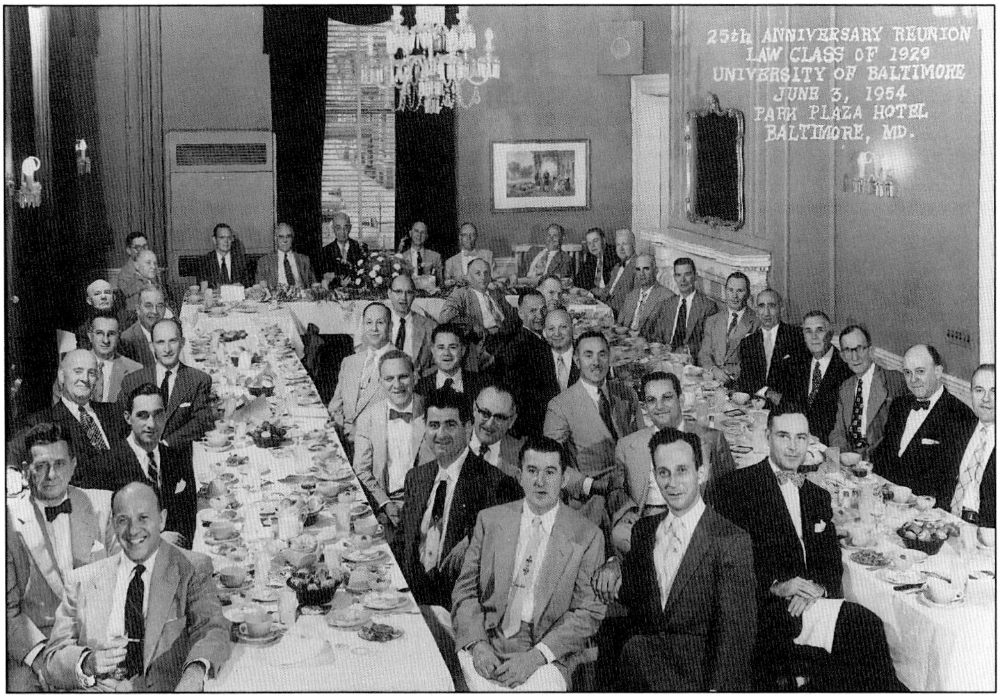

The 1929 Law Class Reunion. The 25th anniversary reunion was held on June 3, 1954, at the Park Plaza Hotel.

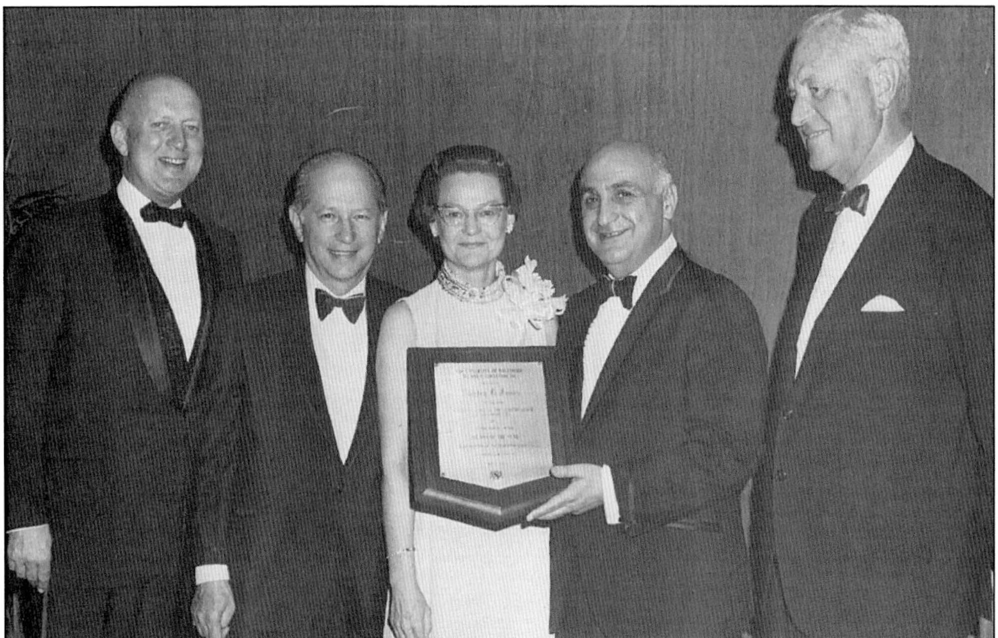

Alumnus of the Year. In 1970, Judge Shirley B. Jones, School of Law Class of 1946, was named the Alumnus of the Year. At the presentation were fellow members of the bench and UB alumni, from left to right, Chief Judge Dulany Foster, Judge Albert L. Sklar (president of the Alumni Association), Judge Jones, Chief Judge Daniel Friedman, and Chief Judge Hall Hammond.

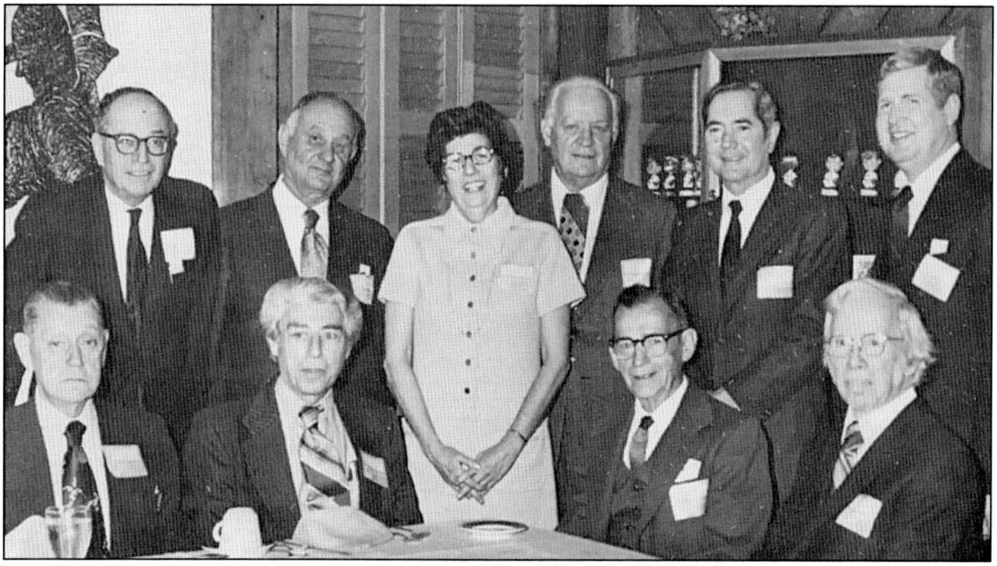

CLASS REPRESENTATIVES. A luncheon meeting was held in November 1973 for the class representatives of the first five graduating classes who worked with the Development Office to ensure participation in the annual fund drives. After lunch, the group posed with the Alumni Association executive secretary Ava Johnston. From left to right are as follows: (standing) Harry B. Wolf, '37; John Demyan, '34; Ava Johnston; Edward Baney, '35; Joseph Bognanni, '36; and Ed Gresham, director of development; (seated) Tillman J. Hicks, '33; Gilbert Bulmash, '37; Virgil Scott, '36; and George Copes, '33.

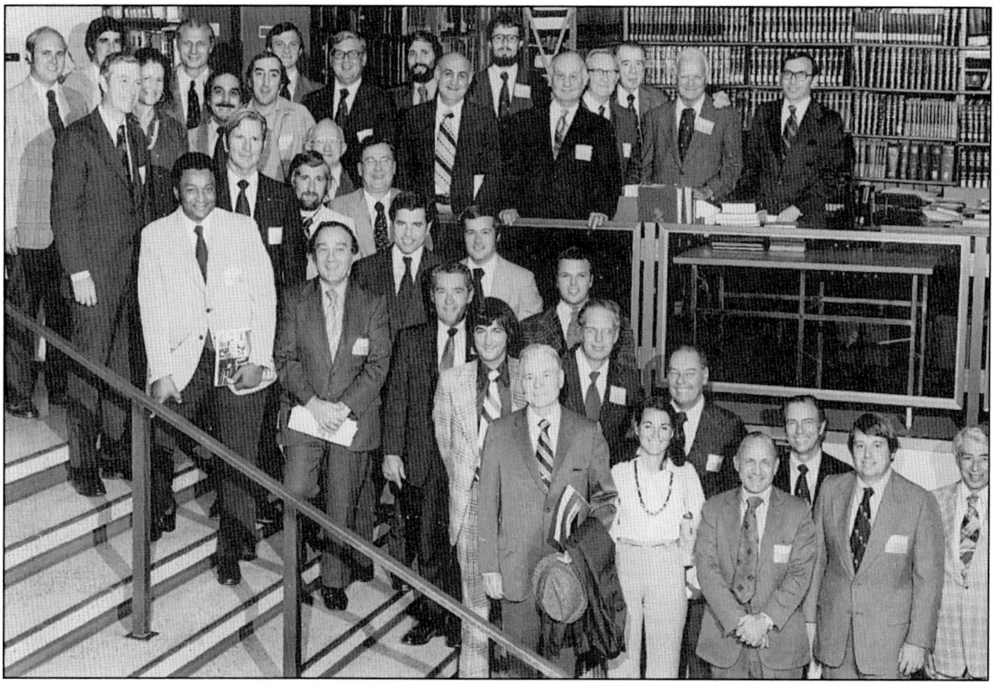

THE ALUMNI BOARD. Edward A. Johnston, president of the Alumni Association, welcomed the members of the board of governors to the first meeting of the 1975–1976 year on Tuesday evening, September 16, 1975. The meeting was held in the lower level of the Langsdale Library.

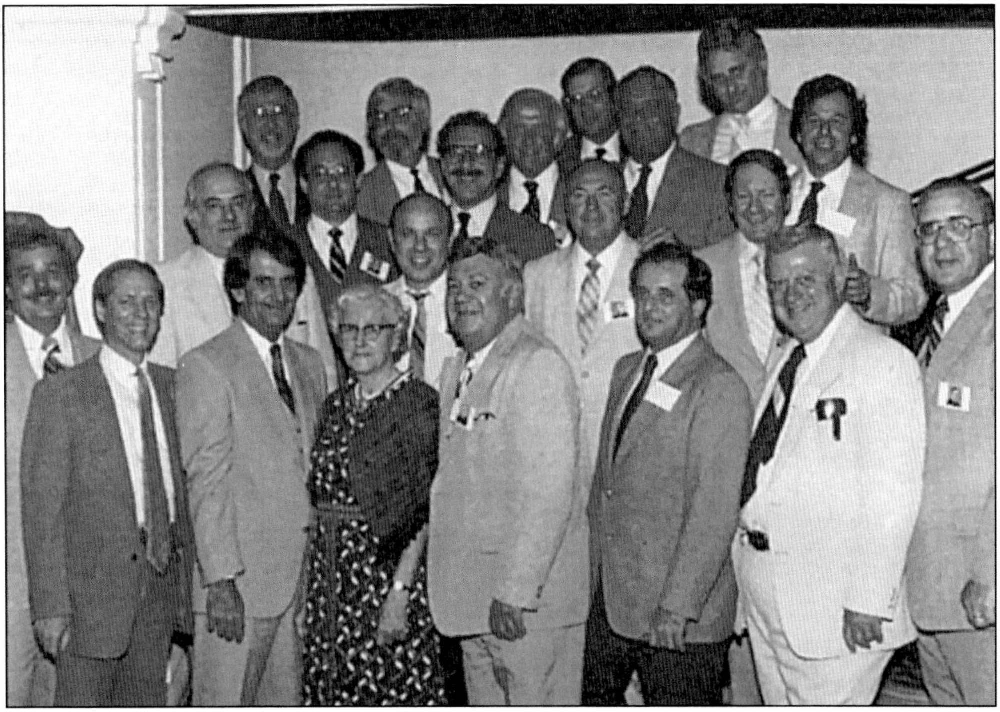

The Class of 1958. The Class of 1958 smiled happily for this group photograph taken in conjunction with their 25th reunion on June 6, 1983.

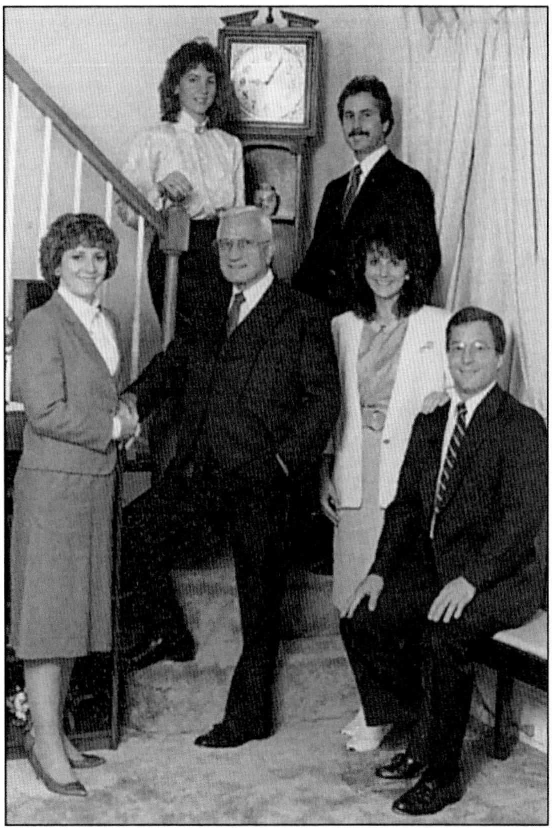

Alumni Family. The university has over 35,000 alumni and, therefore, it is not surprising that the sons and daughters of alumni have attended and become alumni, as well. One of these families is that of Judge Richard Motsay, whose family consists of, from left to right, Rosemary Motsay Ranier, Judge Motsay, Lucy, Patrick, Sharon, and James.

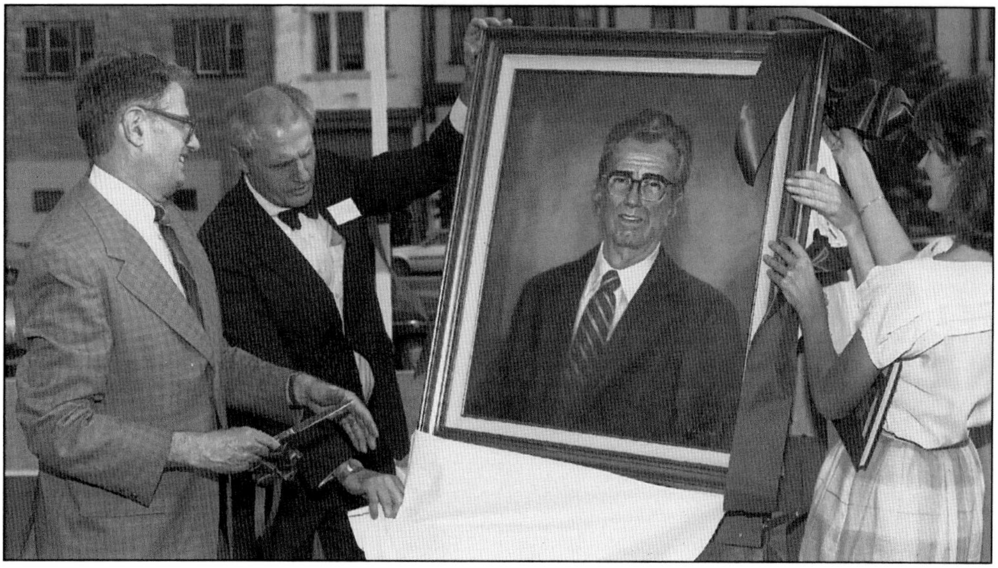

Yale Gordon. On May 22, 1984, the university officially dedicated the new plaza at Maryland and Mt. Royal Avenues in honor of Peggy and Yale Gordon. It was a posthumous honor for the Gordons, who were well known throughout Baltimore's civic and philanthropic communities for their of the city's arts, humanities, and education. At the ceremony, a portrait of Yale Gordon was unveiled by his brother, Raymond Gordon (left). Beside him are President Turner (middle) and Kate Peterson (right). The portrait was painted by Elizabeth Boyd and hangs in the Academic Center.

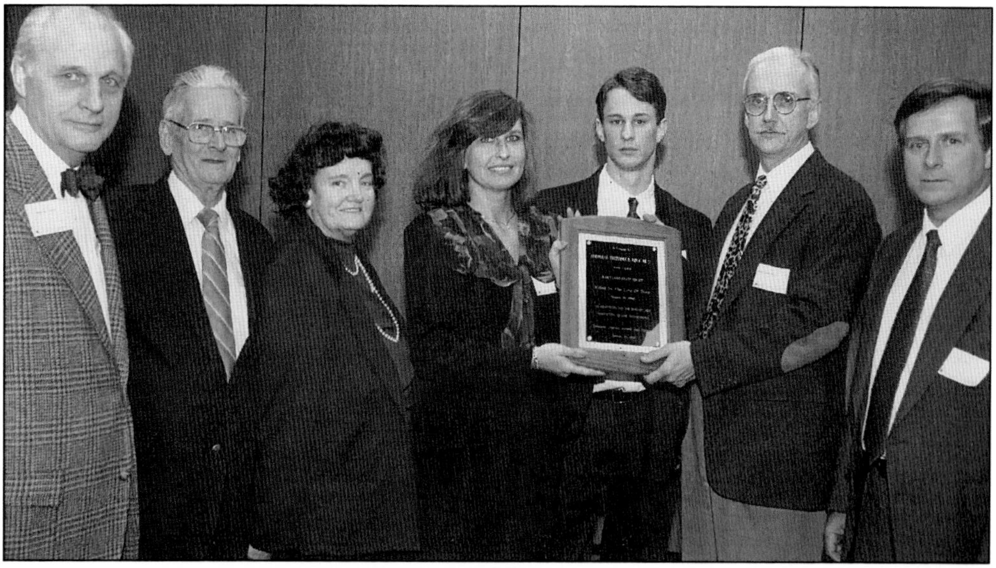

The Trooper Wolf Scholarship. In 1993, the Criminal Justice Alumni Group announced the establishment of the Corporal Theodore D. Wolf Scholarship. Maryland State Trooper Wolf was killed in the line of duty on November 29, 1990. He was a 1997 graduate of the Criminal Justice Program. Pictured at the presentation are, from left to right, President Turner; Mr. and Mrs. LeRoy Wolf; Mrs. Virginia Wolf, a former Langsdale Library employee; Ted Wolf Jr.; Dr. Deral Cheatwood, Criminal Justice Department; and Deputy Chief Edward Koch, Anne Arundel County Police Department.

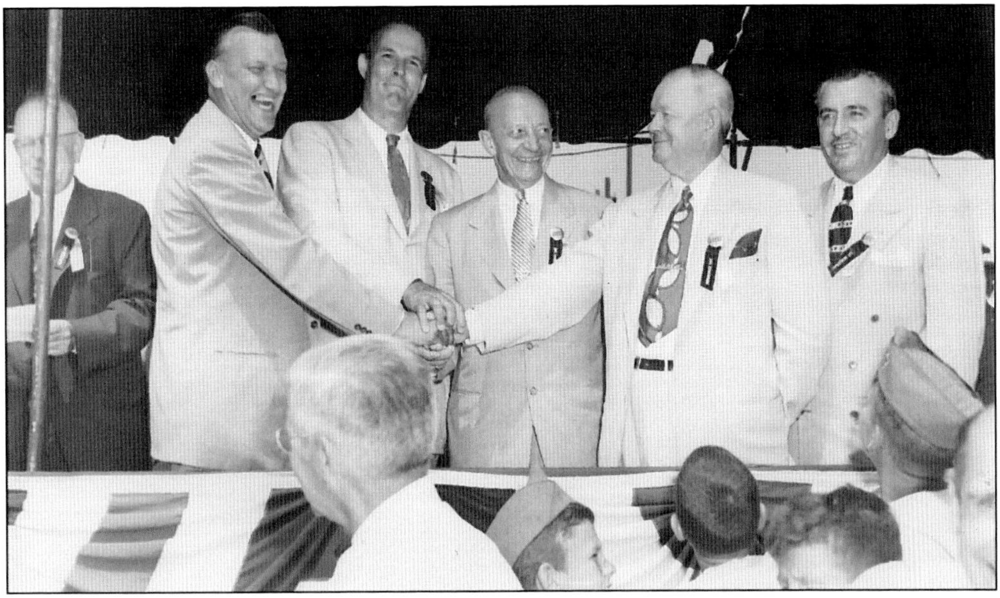

The Governor's Club. Among the participants of the dedication of the Chesapeake Bay Bridge are former Baltimore mayor and Maryland governor, Theodore R. McKeldin, who taught in the School of Law during the 1940s, and Governor Elbert N. Carville of Delaware, a 1931 graduate of the School of Law and member of the board of trustees. The group pictured, from left to right, are unidentified, Governor McKeldin, Governor Carvel, Governor Preston Lane, Governor Millard Tawes, and former congressman and Baltimore mayor Thomas D'Alesandro Jr., whose papers are in the university's archives.

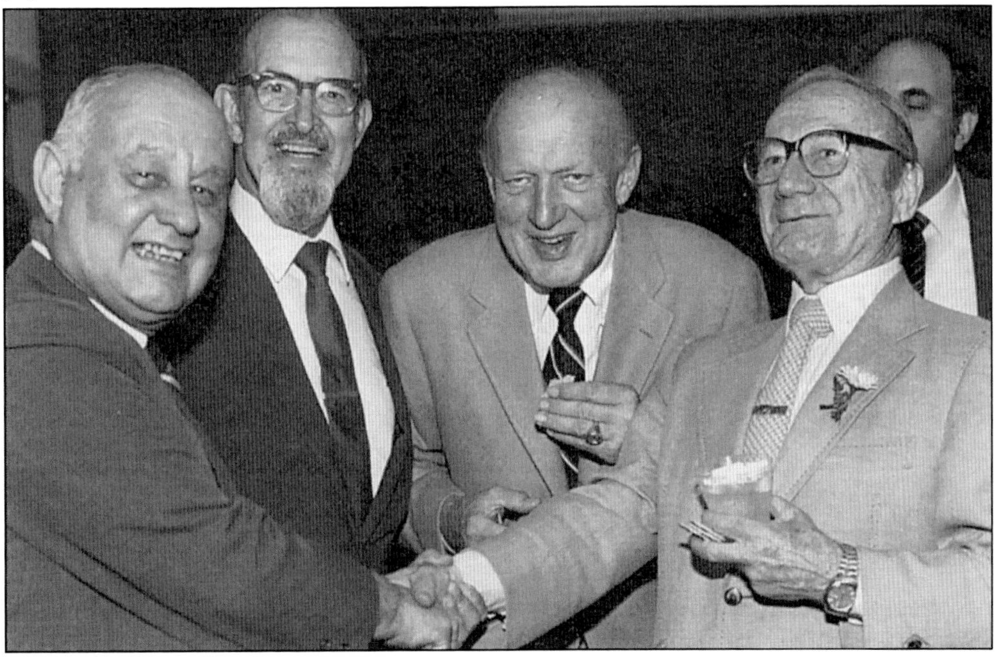

A Law Alumni Reunion. Law alumni reunions are the perfect occasion for old friends to get together. Shown here are, from left to right, John Demyan, Judge George Sachse, Judge Dulany Foster, and Baltimore City comptroller Hyman Pressman.

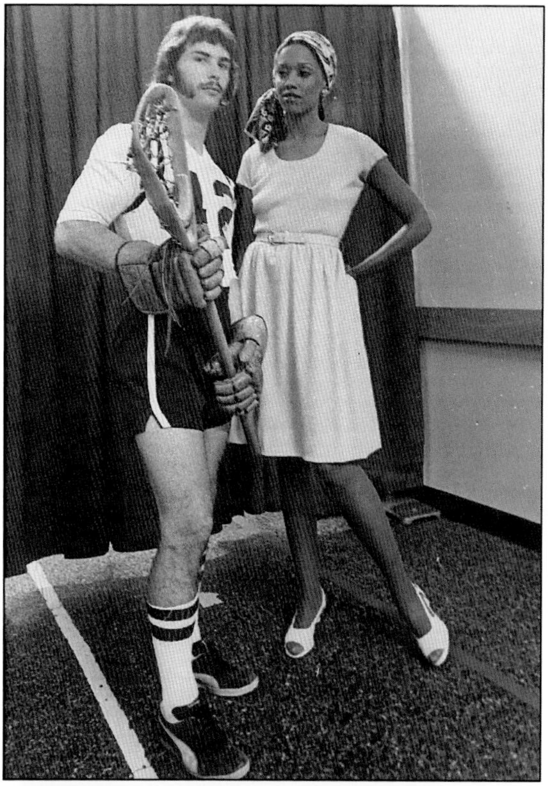

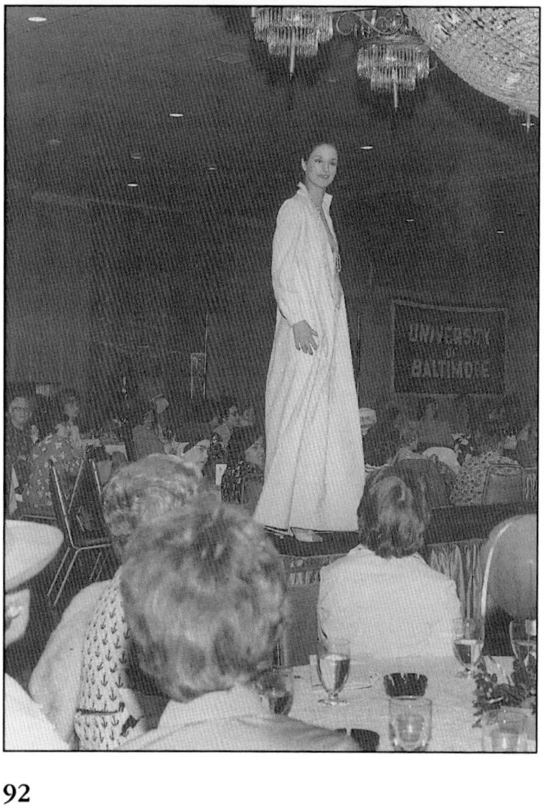

A 1975 Fashion Show and Luncheon. To benefit the Educational Foundation Scholarship Fund, this fashion show and luncheon was held at Martin's West and sponsored by the University Women. In the top photograph, a Patricia Stevens model gets a little help from a member of the lacrosse team. Among the fashions by designers Bill Blass, Halston, and Trigere was this elegant gown (bottom photograph) from Hutzler's dress salon.

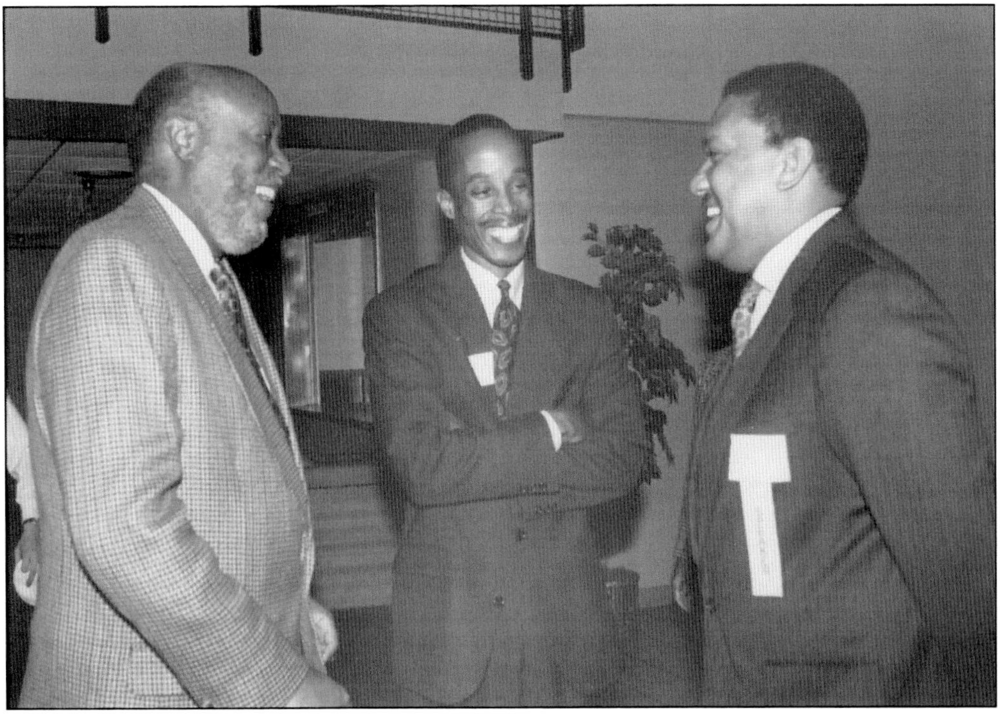

Sharing a Few Words. At the 1996 African-American Student, Alumni, Faculty, and Staff Reception are, from left to right, Robert Greene, Ronald Graham, and Anthony Fugate.

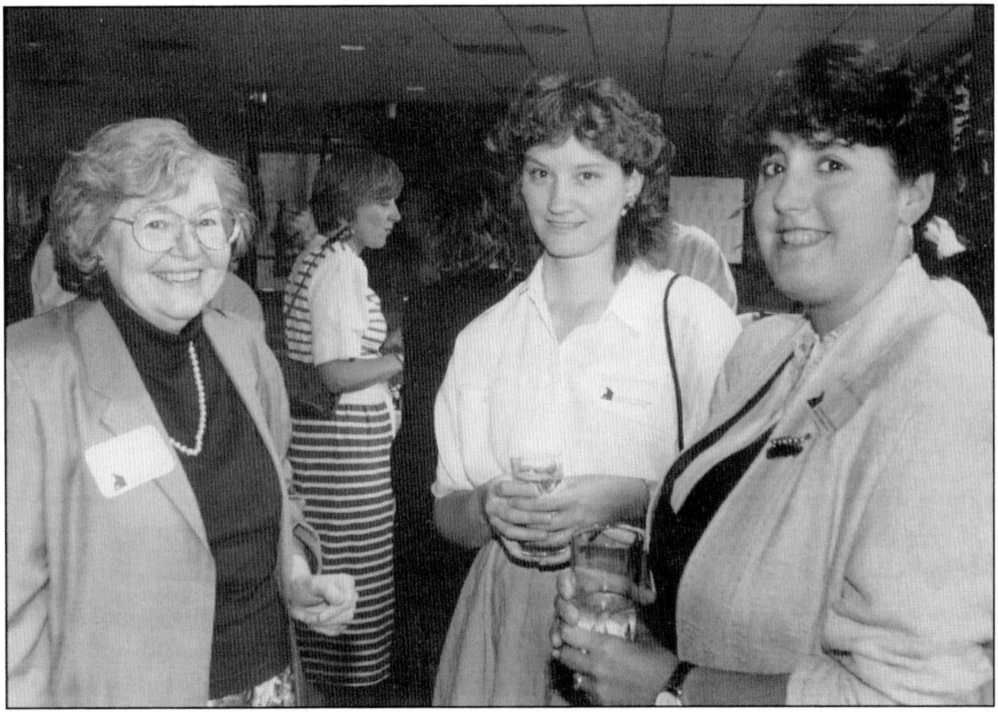

The 1991 Liberal Arts Reunion. Shown here are, from left to right, Dr. Carol Peirce, Angela Schwarzkopf, and Rita Baker-Schmidt.

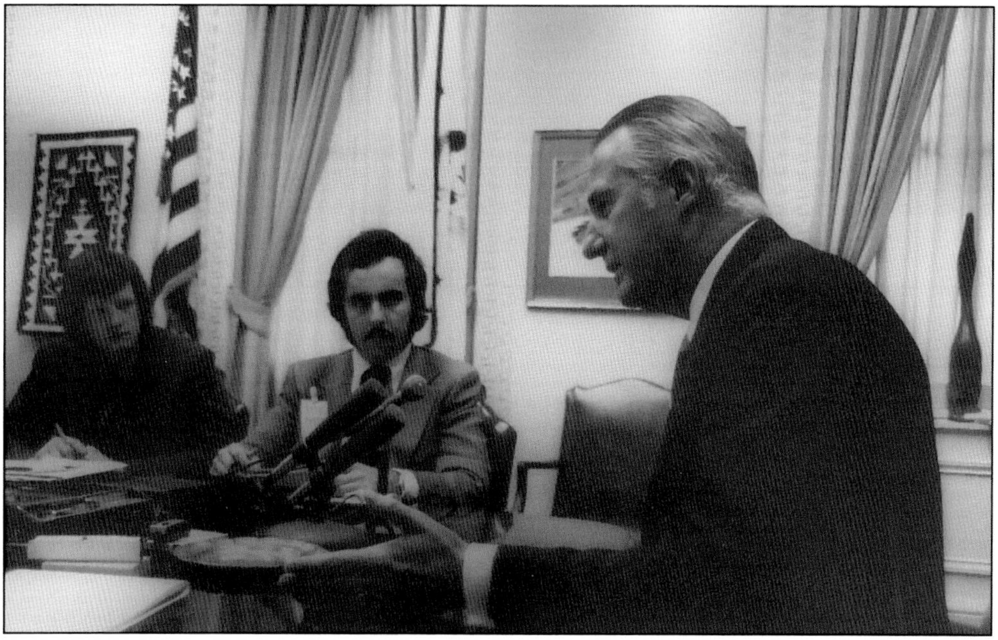

The Vice President of the United States. In September 1972, Spiro Agnew (right) granted an interview to three college students, including UB student senate president Edward McCauley (left). Agnew was a 1947 graduate of the School of Law, received the first Alumnus of the Year Award in 1967, and was an adjunct law professor during the 1960s.

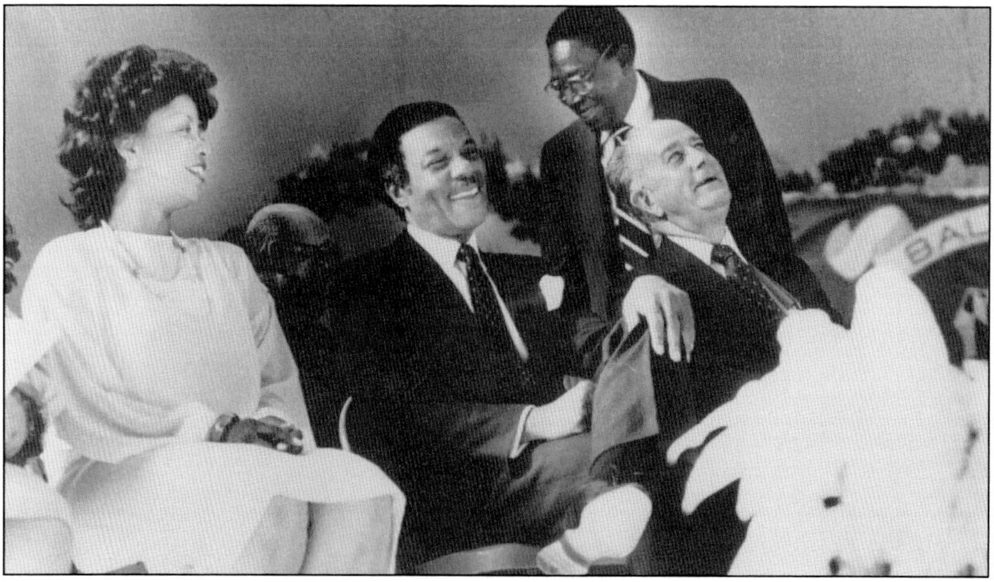

Alumni of the Year. Baltimore mayor, Maryland governor, and now state comptroller William Donald Schaefer, Class of 1951, and fellow alum Bishop Robinson, Class of 1971, have a long working relationship, as well as share Alumni of the Year distinctions. In this 1984 photograph, from left to right, Rhonda Robinson, Bishop Robinson, Mayor Schaefer, and his successor, Clarence "Du" Burns, attend the swearing-in ceremony for Robinson as police commissioner of Baltimore City. After his election to the office of governor, Robinson became the secretary of Public Safety in 1987.

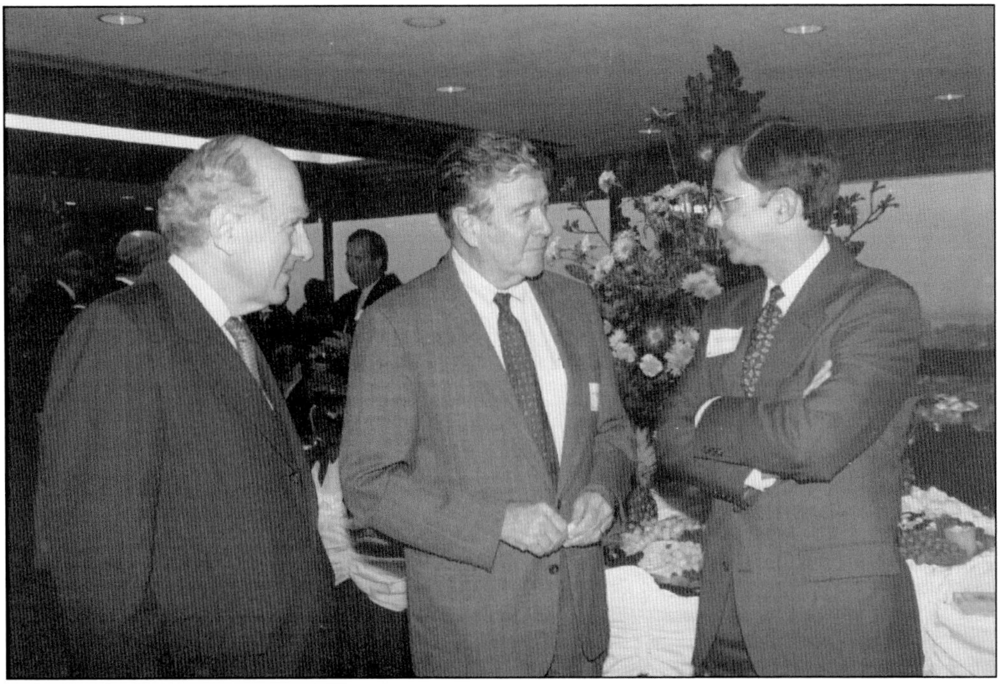

The 1993 Sebert Reception. At the reception to welcome John Sebert, the new dean of the School of Law, are, from left to right, Shale Stiller, School of Law Advisory Committee; Joseph Curran, attorney general of Maryland and School of Law graduate; and Dean Sebert.

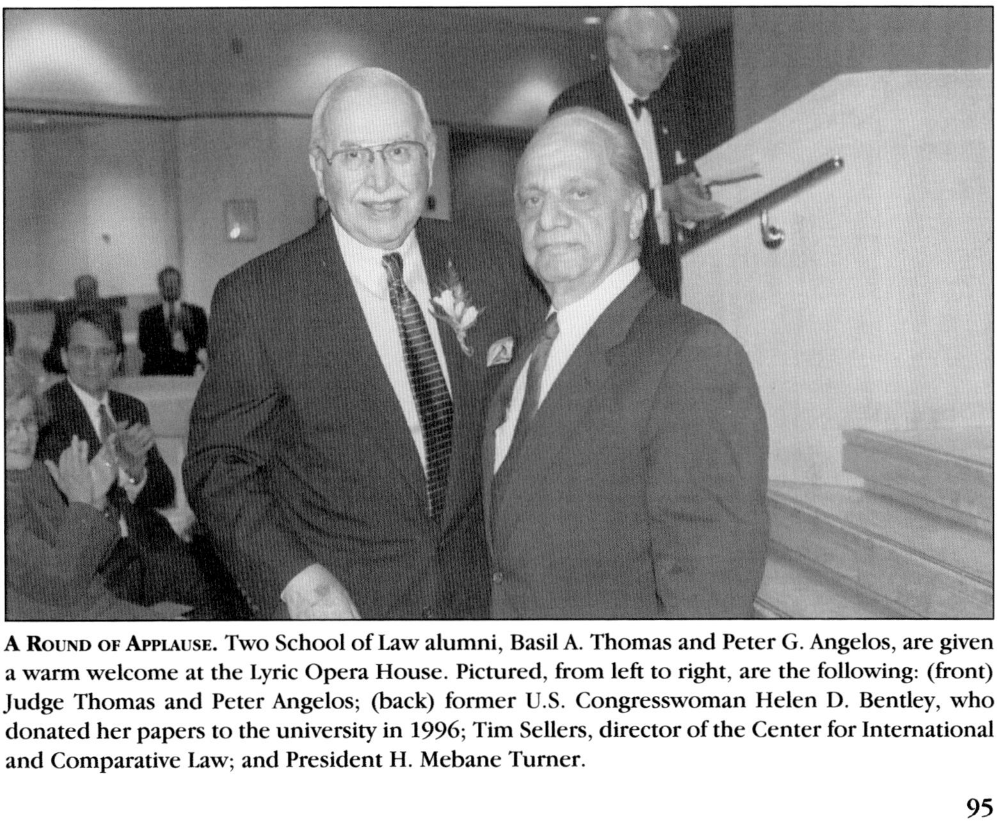

A Round of Applause. Two School of Law alumni, Basil A. Thomas and Peter G. Angelos, are given a warm welcome at the Lyric Opera House. Pictured, from left to right, are the following: (front) Judge Thomas and Peter Angelos; (back) former U.S. Congresswoman Helen D. Bentley, who donated her papers to the university in 1996; Tim Sellers, director of the Center for International and Comparative Law; and President H. Mebane Turner.

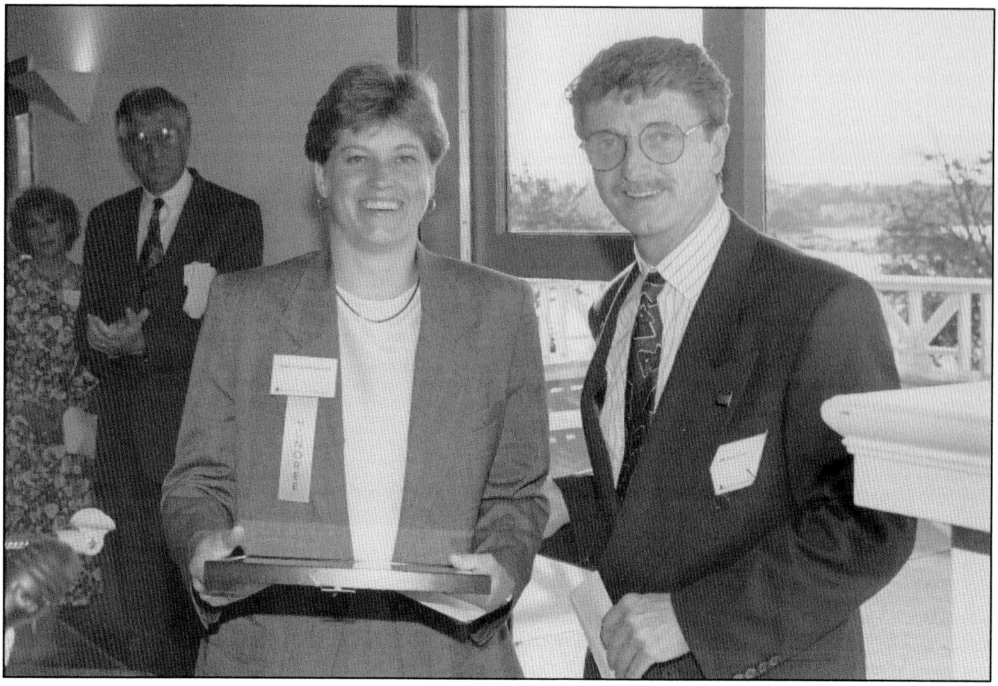

Spirit of Excellence. The Alumni Association's Spirit of Excellence awards recognize achievements among faculty and staff who have had a unique impact outside of the university or community activity that has brought recognition to the university. The 1992 recipient of the faculty award was School of Law professor Marla Hollandsworth. Seen in this photograph at the presentation are, from left to right, an unidentified woman; Charles E. Siegmann, School of Business Advisory Council; Professor Hollandsworth; and James P. Sullivan, alumni president.

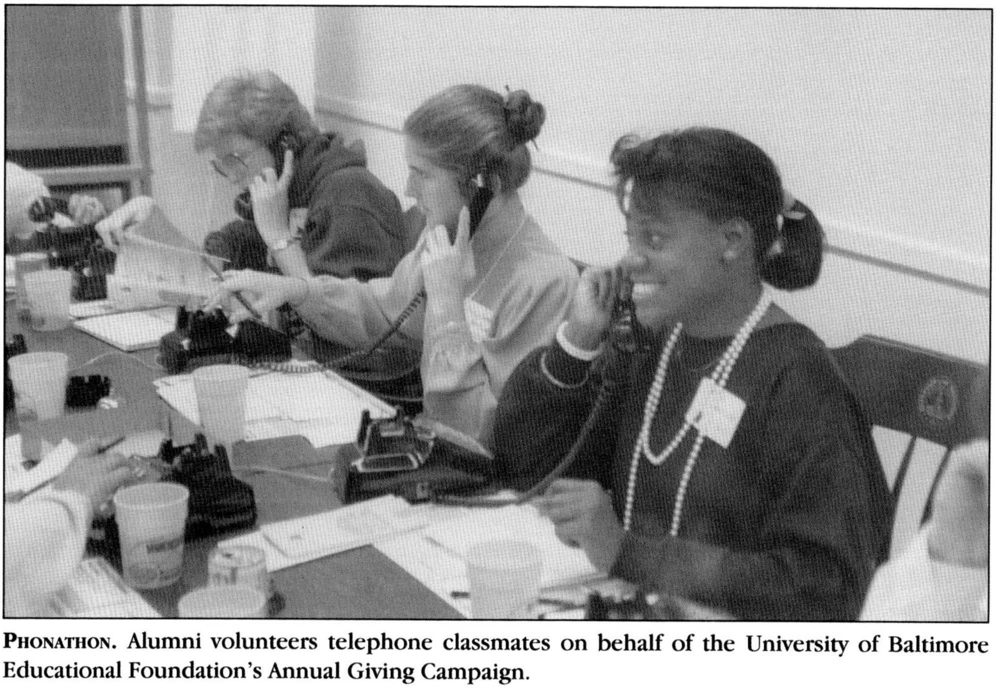

Phonathon. Alumni volunteers telephone classmates on behalf of the University of Baltimore Educational Foundation's Annual Giving Campaign.

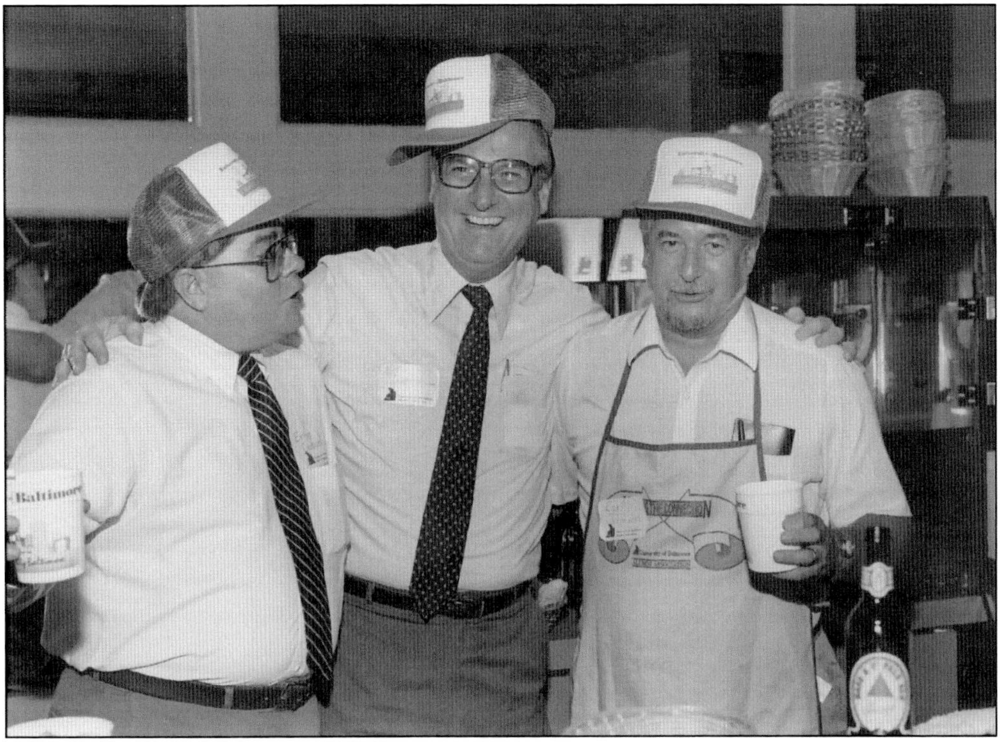

AN ALUMNI CELEBRATION. These three alumni gathering in good cheer are, from left to right, Ernie Crofoot, Bill Lavasseur, and Earl Johnson.

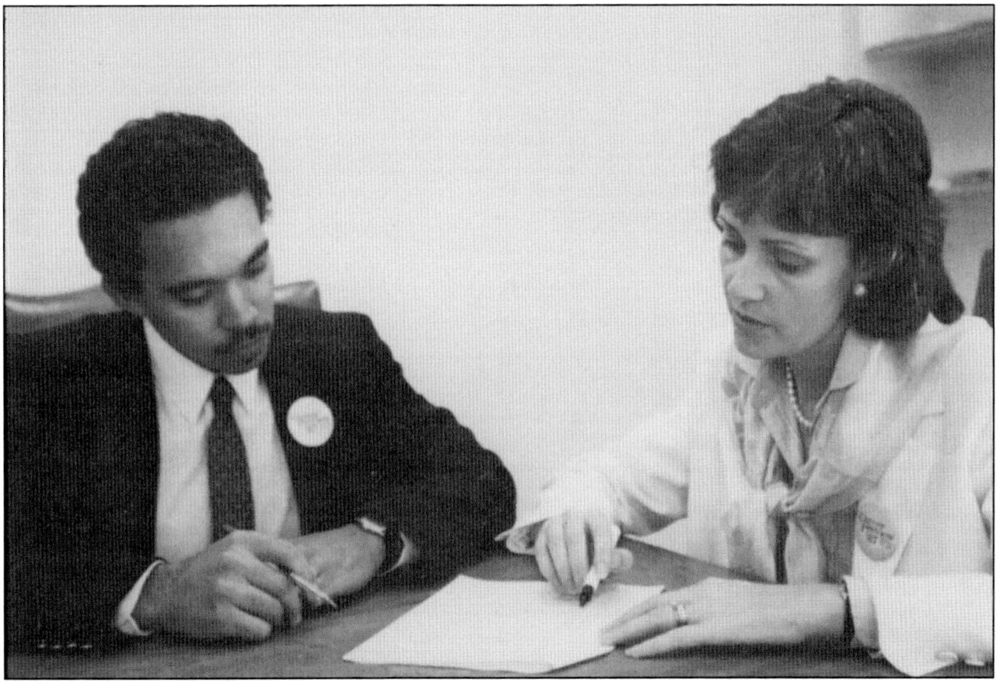

CAREER PREVIEW '87. Pictured are Student Alumni Connection member Bryant Anderson (left), chair of the event, and Ann Kenderdine (right), coordinator of Career Preview Week.

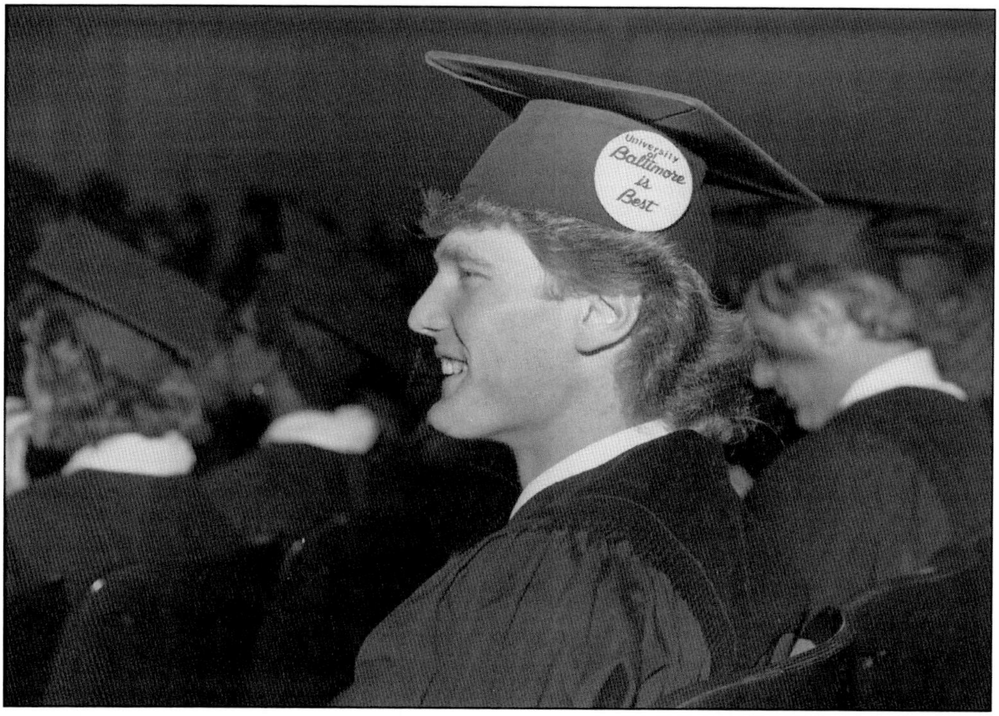

UNIVERSITY OF BALTIMORE IS BEST. In the photograph above, the button on this graduate's mortarboard says it all. Below, another commencement ends the academic year.

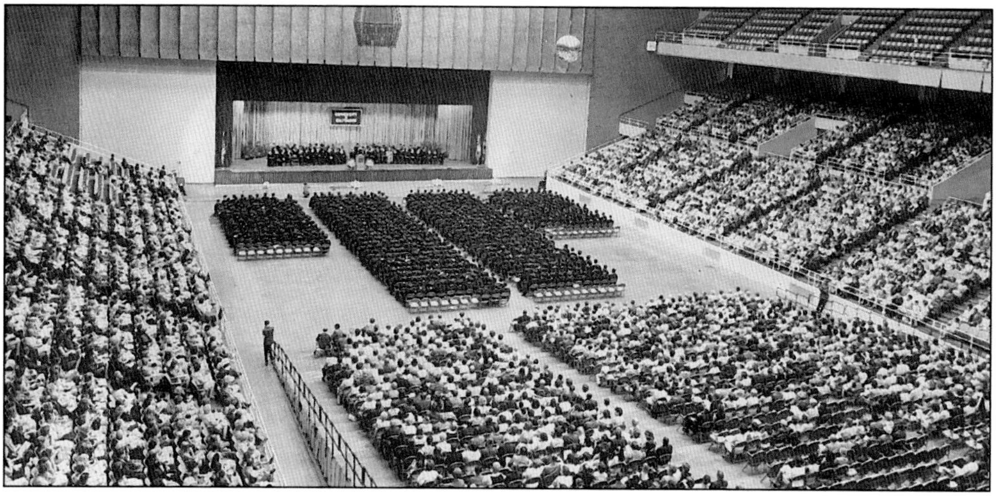

Seven

FRIENDS AND VISITORS

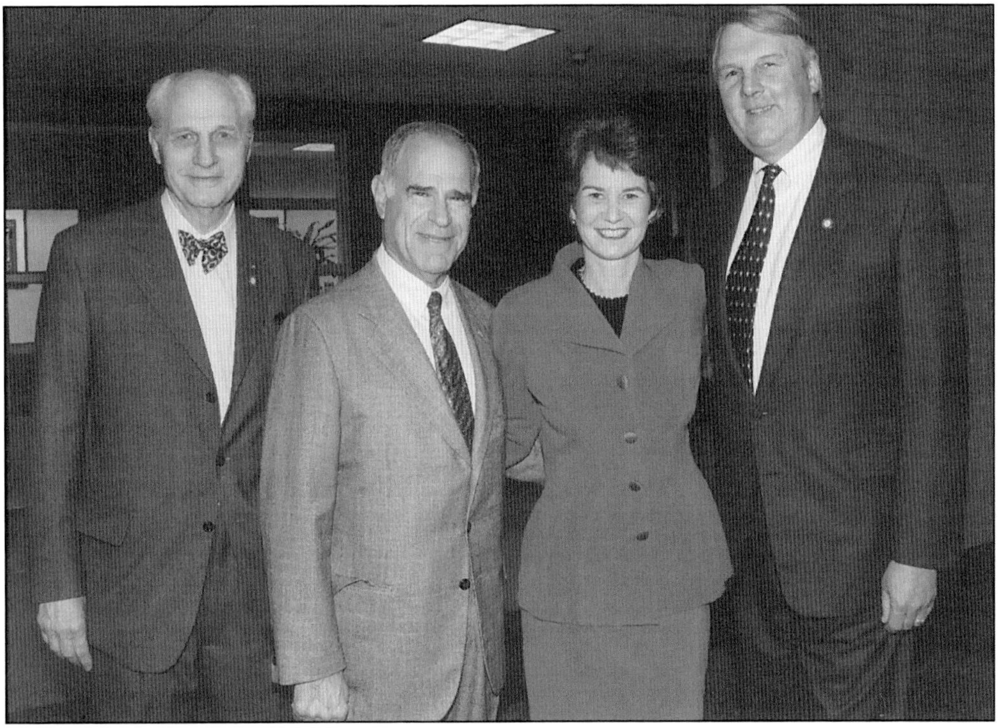

THE FIRST ROSENBERG LECTURE. In 1999, Henry A. Rosenberg established an endowment within the university's School of Public Affairs. As part of this generous gift an annual lecture series and symposia was established. On April 18, 2000, the first lecture was delivered by Maryland's lieutenant governor Kathleen Kennedy Townsend. Pictured here are, from left to right, President Turner, Henry A. Rosenberg, Kathleen Kennedy Townsend, and Carl Sternberg, dean College of Liberal Arts.

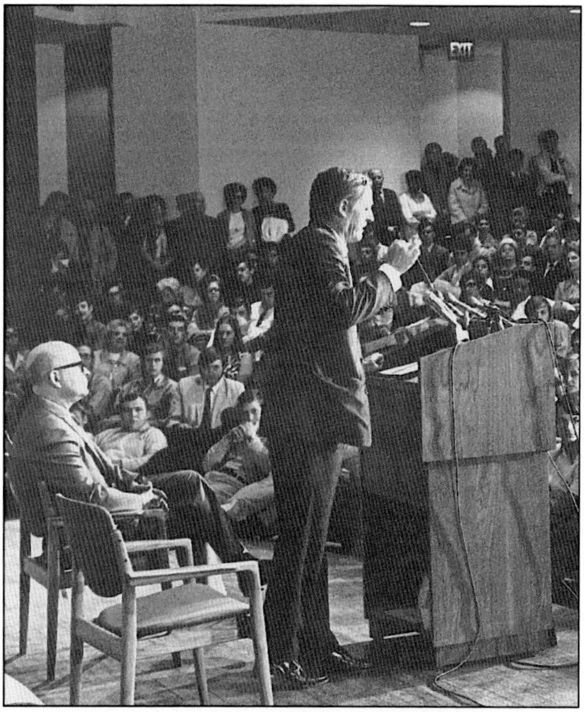

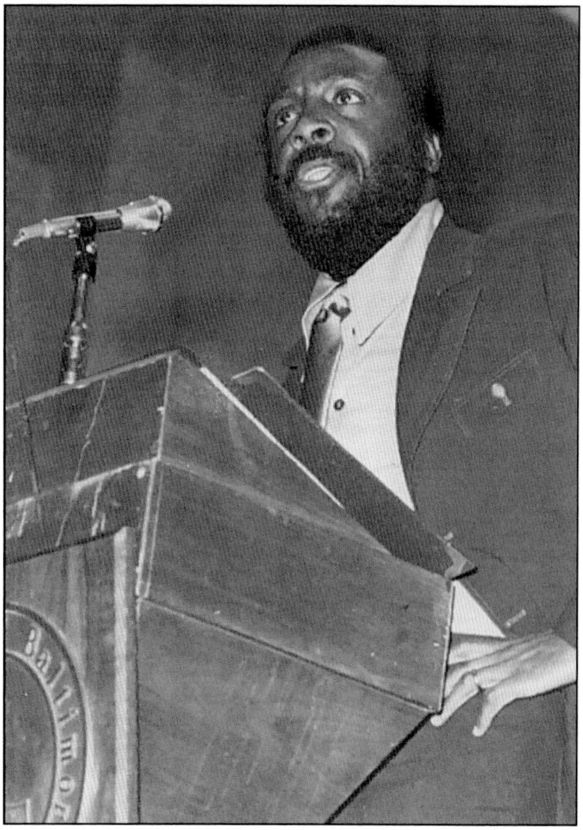

Right and Left. In the 1970s, the university sponsored a speaker series that brought a wide range of speakers from conservative commentator William F. Buckley (top photograph) to Dick Gregory, the noted American Civil Rights advocate (bottom photograph).

RALPH NADER. In March 1971, Ralph Nader visited the campus to speak about his fight for consumer's rights.

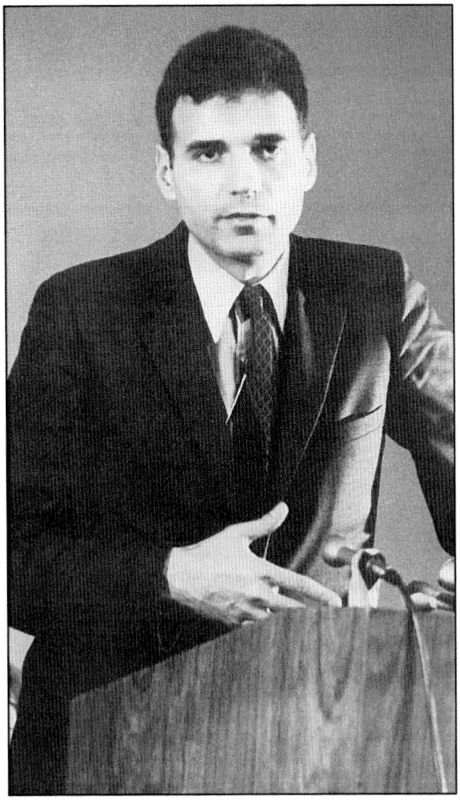

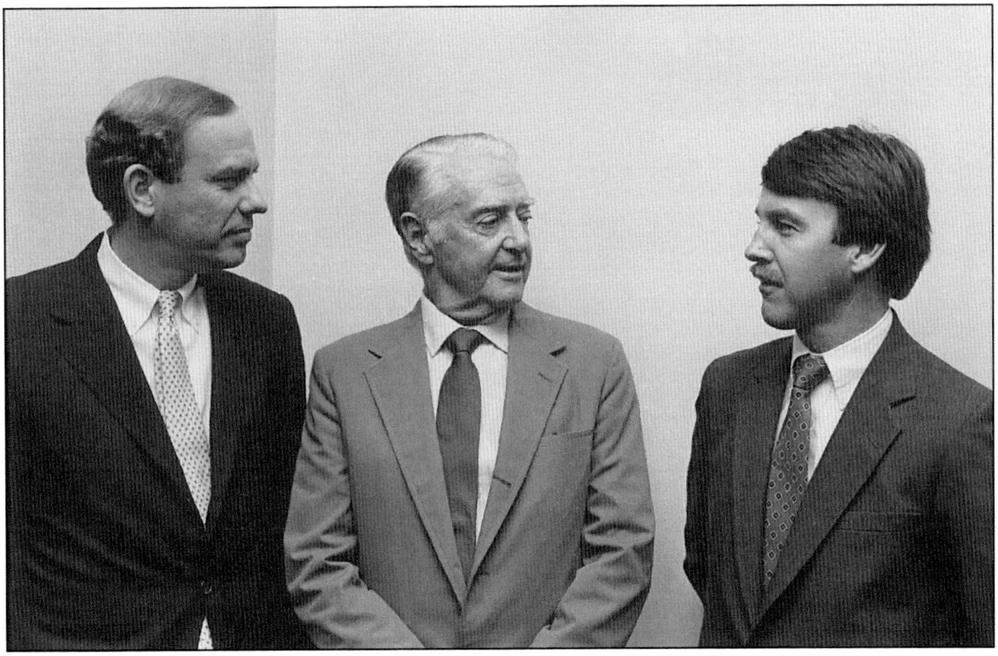

CAREER PREVIEW '85. NBC television news reporter Howard K. Smith was the keynote speaker at this alumni event. In the photograph are, from left to right, an unidentified man, Howard K. Smith, and Warner S. Waters Jr.

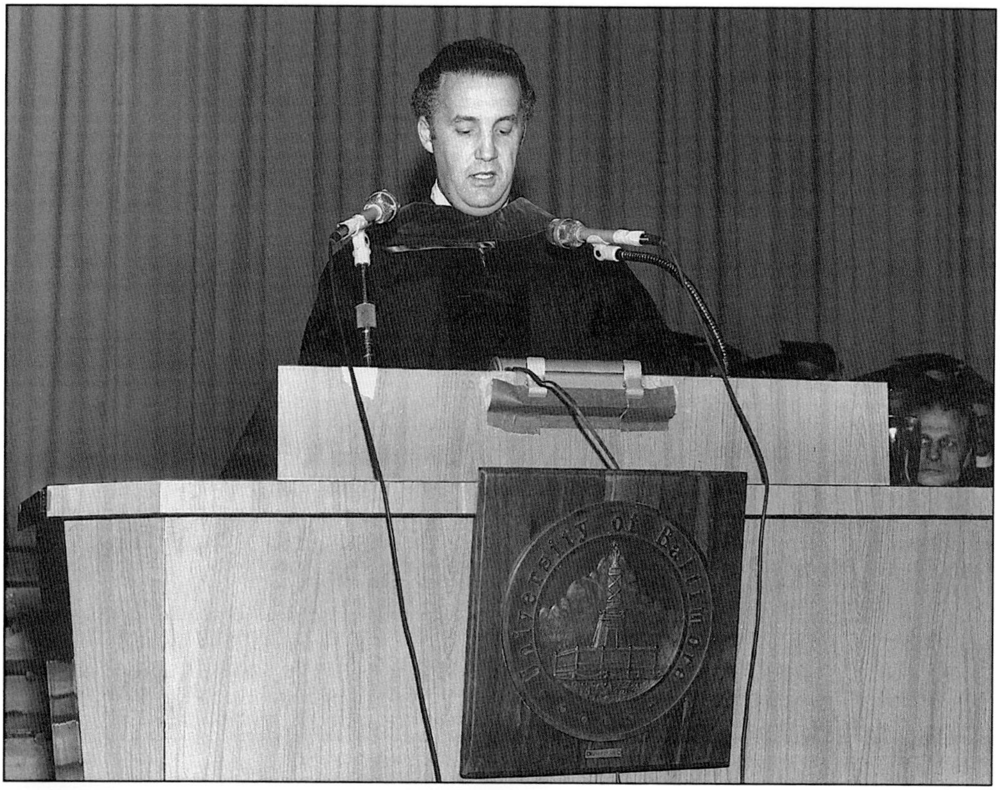

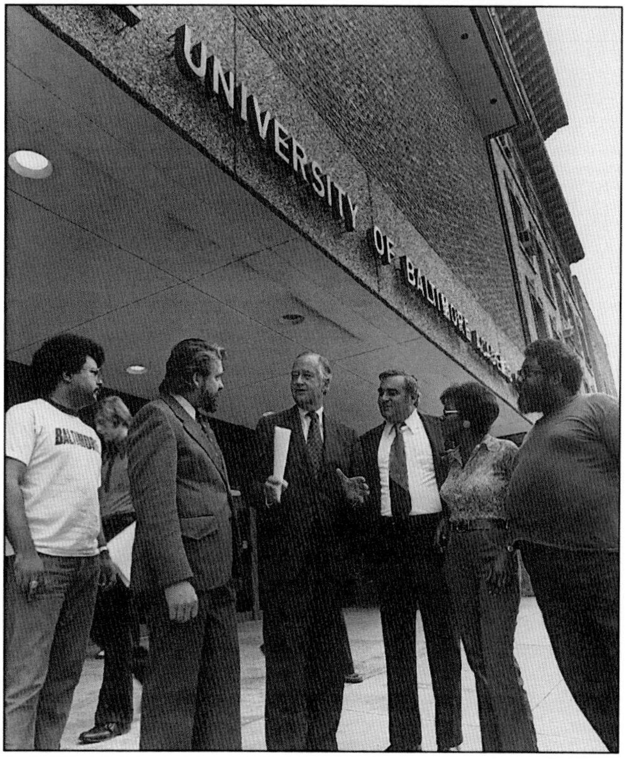

MARYLAND SENATORS. U.S. Senator Paul Sarbanes (then a congressman) addresses the 1975 commencement after being awarded an honorary doctor of laws degree in the photograph above. In the undated photograph at left are, from left to right, David Thaniel, George McDevitt (dean of students), Senator Charles "Mac" Mathias, Ralph Cannon, Marsha Fisher, and Gerald Pitts. Senator Mathias was the main speaker at a Conference on the Elimination of Barriers for the Handicapped.

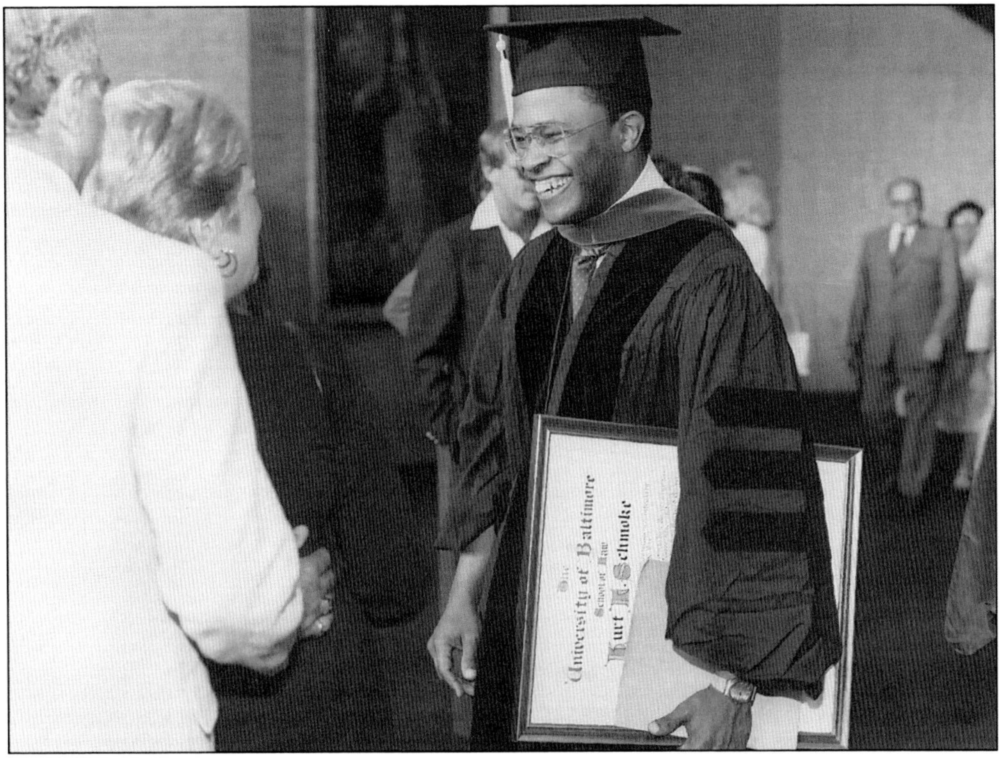

Baltimore Mayors. Kurt L. Schmoke, who was state's attorney for Baltimore at the time and later became the city's mayor, received an honorary doctor of laws degree at the 1985 commencement. In the photograph above, he is being congratulated in the lobby of the Lyric Opera House after the ceremony. In the photograph below, Mayor Thomas D'Alesandro III dedicates the university's Academic Center on December 9, 1971.

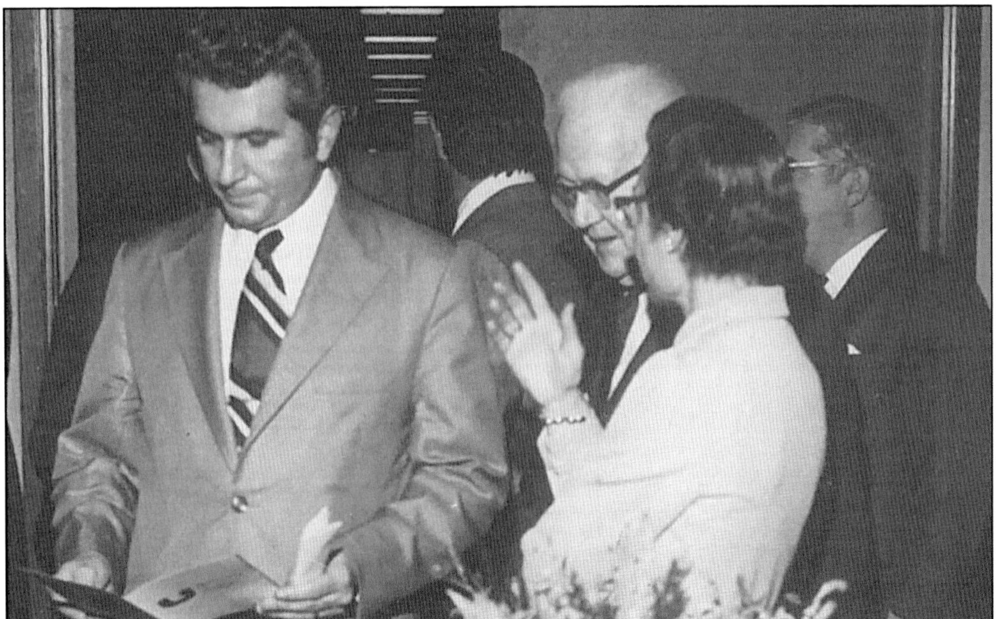

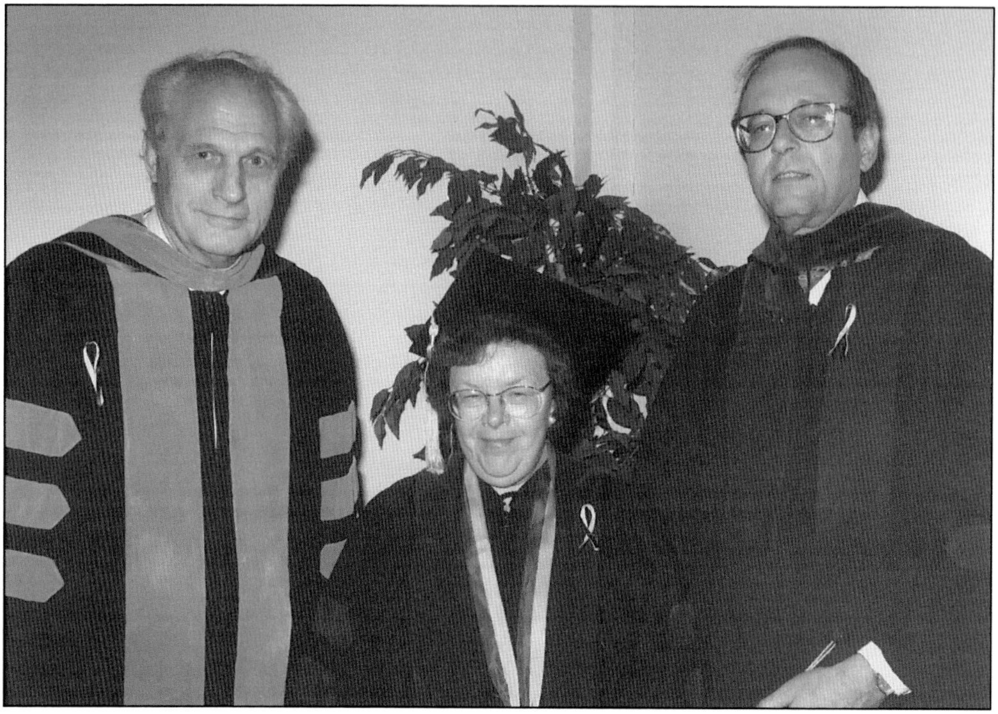

HONORARY DEGREES. In the photograph above, from left to right, President Turner, Senator Barbara Mikulski, and Lawrence Katz (dean of the School of Law) are seen after the 1992 commencement. In the photograph below, Maryland comptroller Louis L. Goldstein addresses the graduates in 1977.

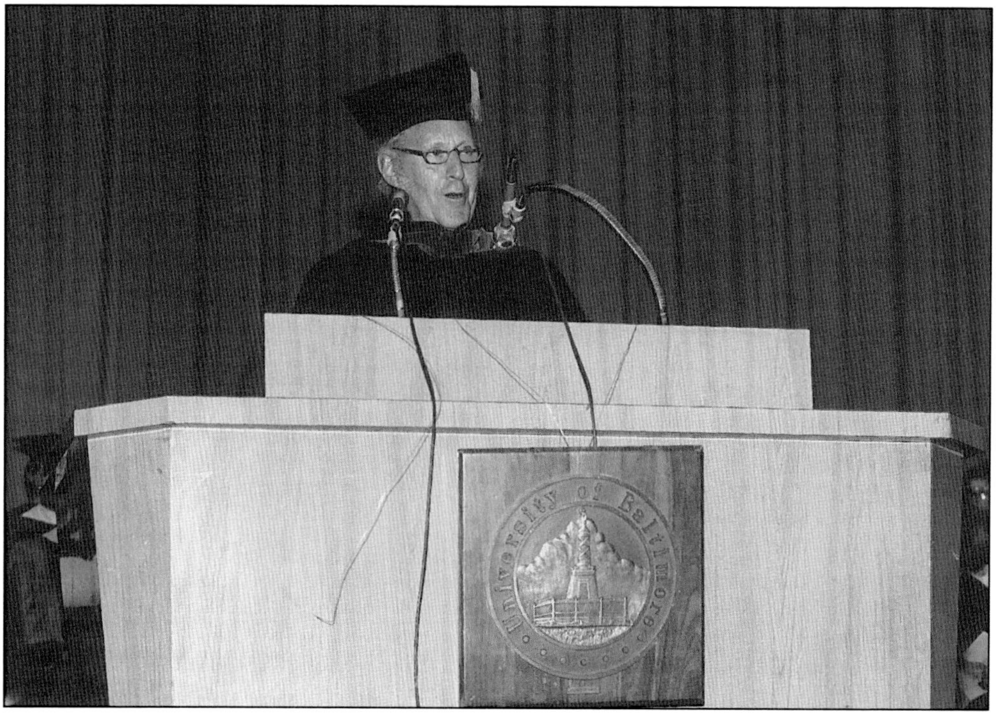

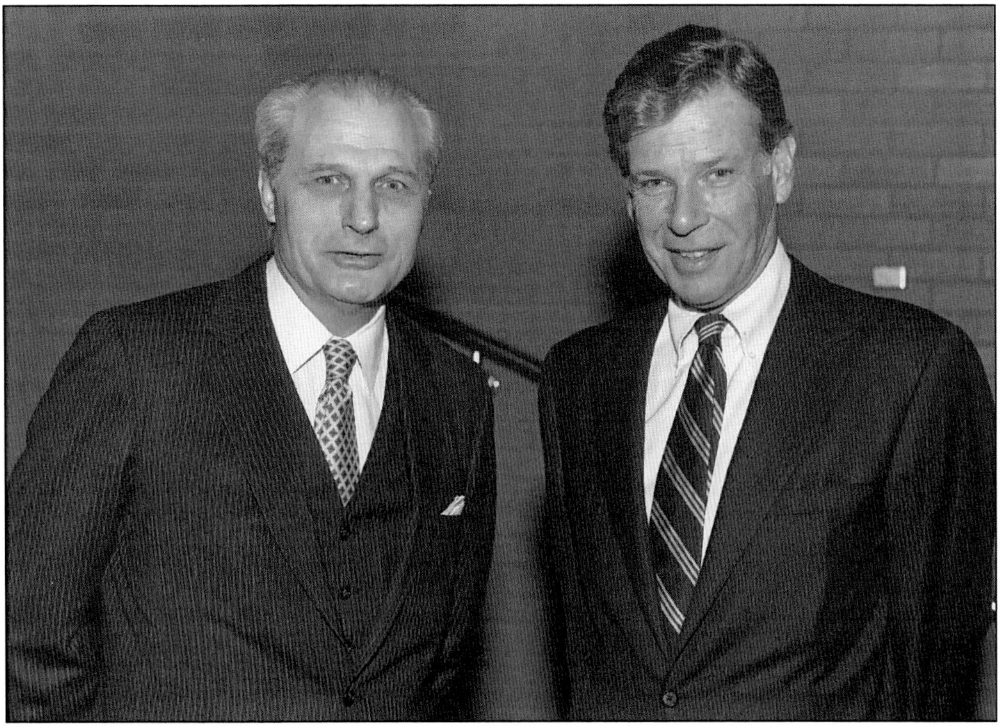

Harry R. Hughes. In this 1986 photograph, H. Mebane Turner (left) is paid a visit by Governor Harry R. Hughes (right).

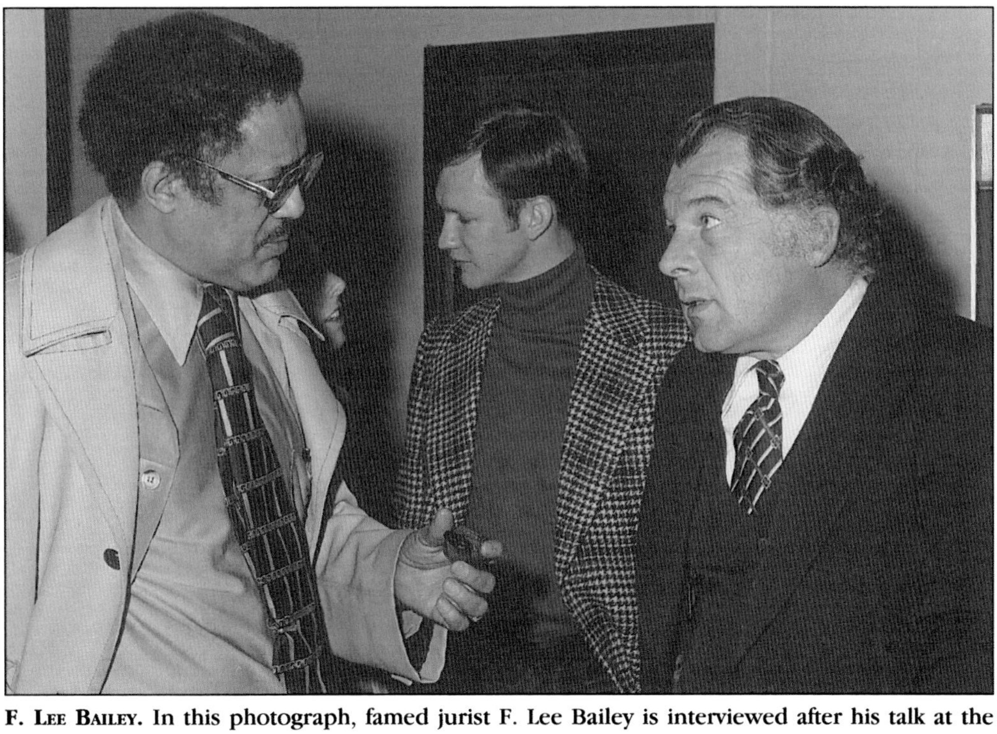

F. Lee Bailey. In this photograph, famed jurist F. Lee Bailey is interviewed after his talk at the School of Law.

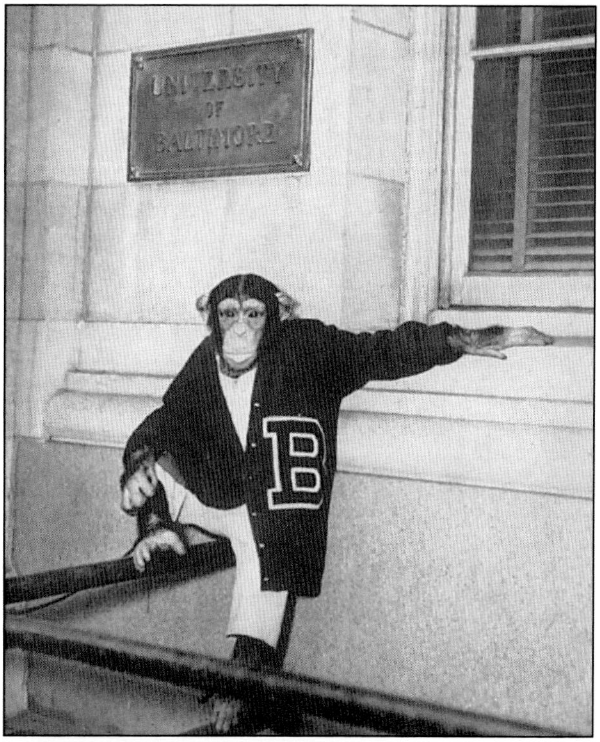

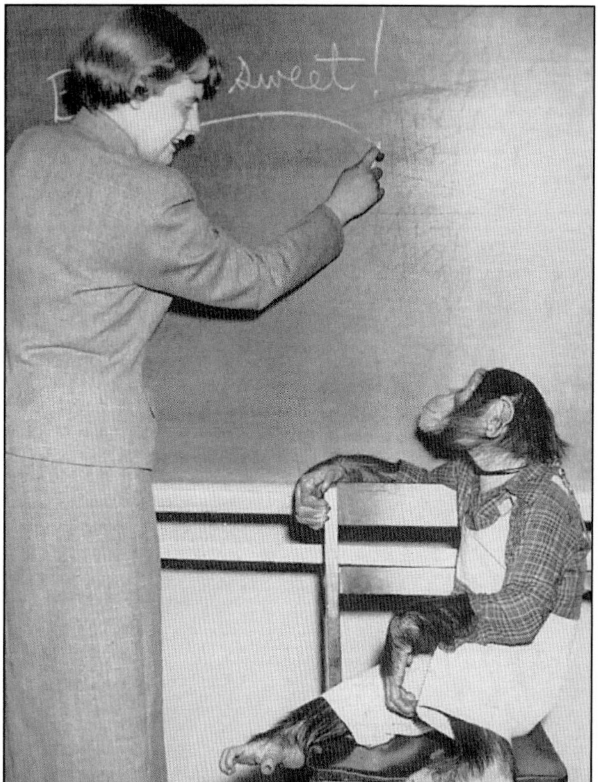

Schooltime for Bonzo. Realizing that his movie career would not last forever, Ronald Regan's co-star visited the university in 1951. He is seen in the top photograph wearing his letterman's sweater, and in the bottom photograph taking an English class.

Eight

The Campus

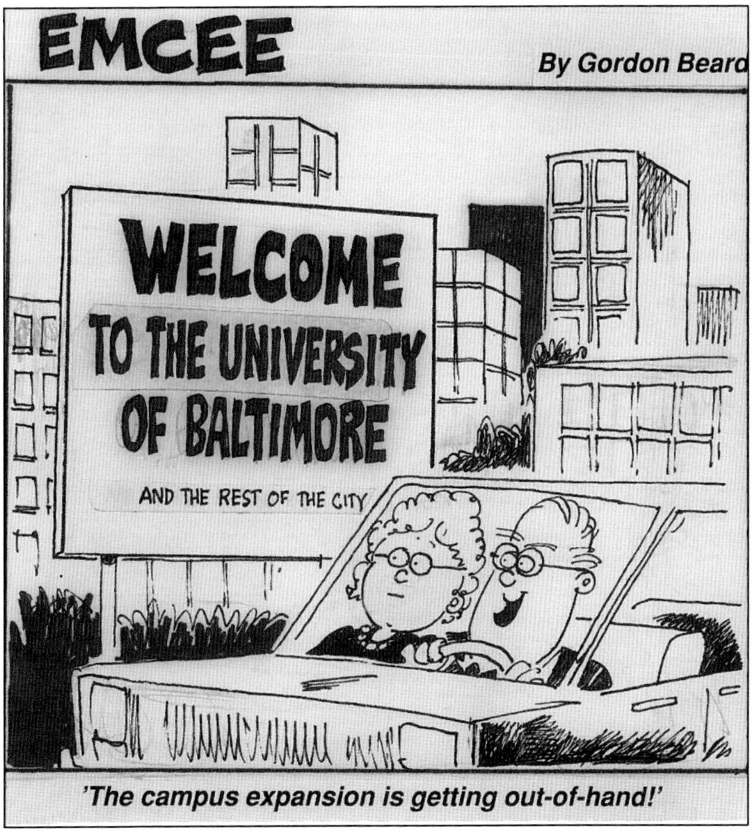

Welcome to UB. This 1991 editorial cartoon appeared in the "Other Voices" page of the *Baltimore Evening Sun* newspaper, wryly commenting on the growth of the university's urban campus since its founding in 1925.

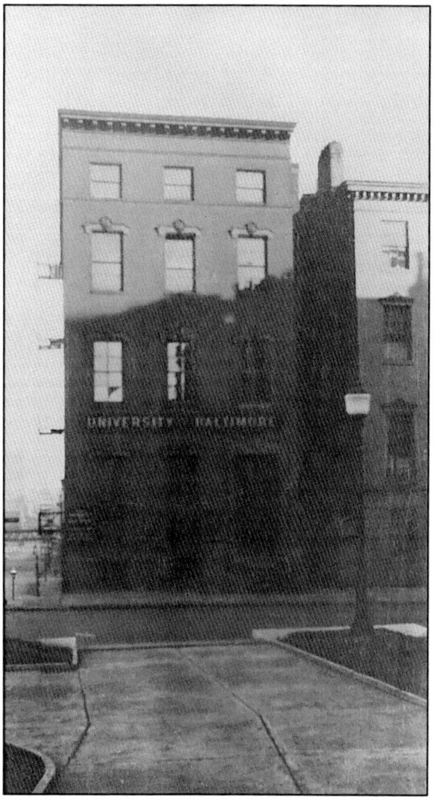

UB Opens its Doors. On October 1, 1925, the first classes were held in this four-story, red brick building on St. Paul Street, overlooking Mount Vernon Square. The building along with the other row houses on the block were torn down in 1960 for a proposed development that never took place. The Waterloo Row Apartments are now located on this site.

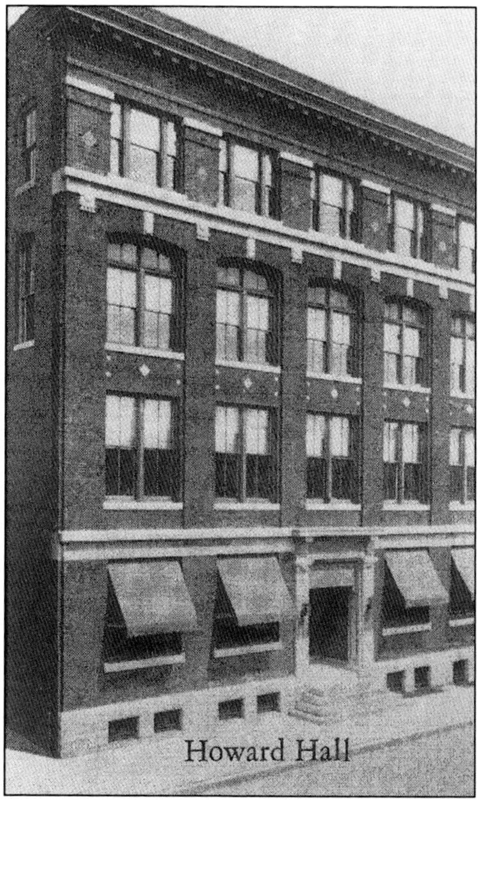

Howard Hall. By 1926, the St. Paul Street site had become too small, and an annex was acquired on the corner of St. Paul and Centre Streets to house the freshman law class. At the end of the 1929 academic year, the trustees decided that a larger building was needed, so the school purchased the former College of Dentistry Building at 840 North Howard Street. Known as Howard Hall, it was a large brick building with lecture rooms large enough to accommodate as many as 200 students.

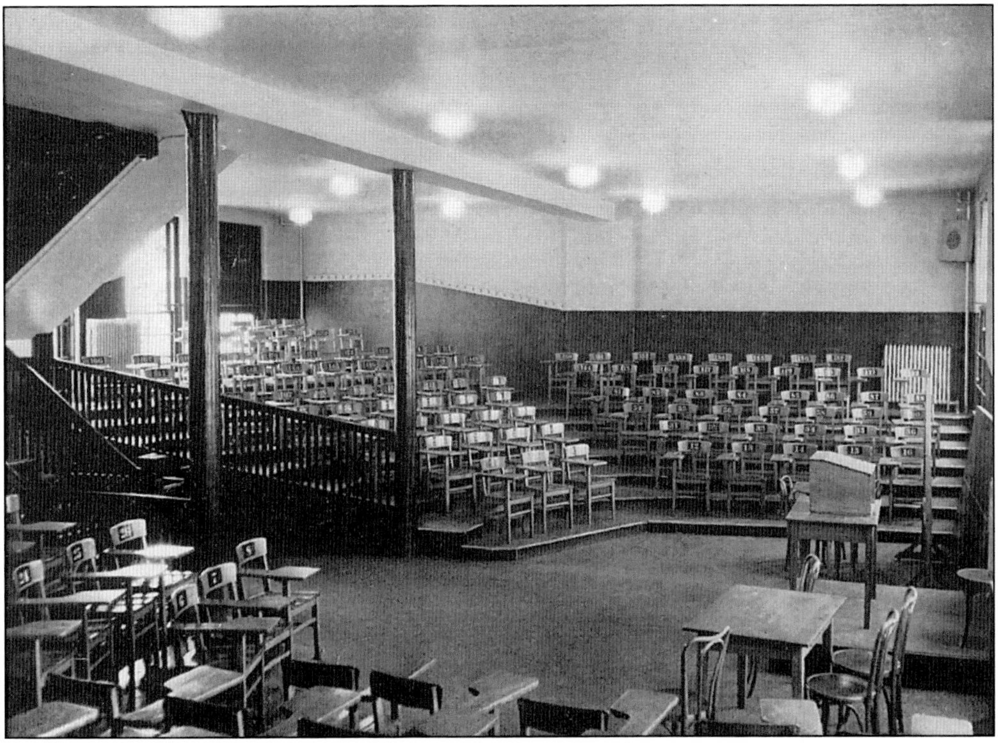

Interior Views. These two 1938 photographs show, above, the largest lecture hall in Howard Hall and, below, the library.

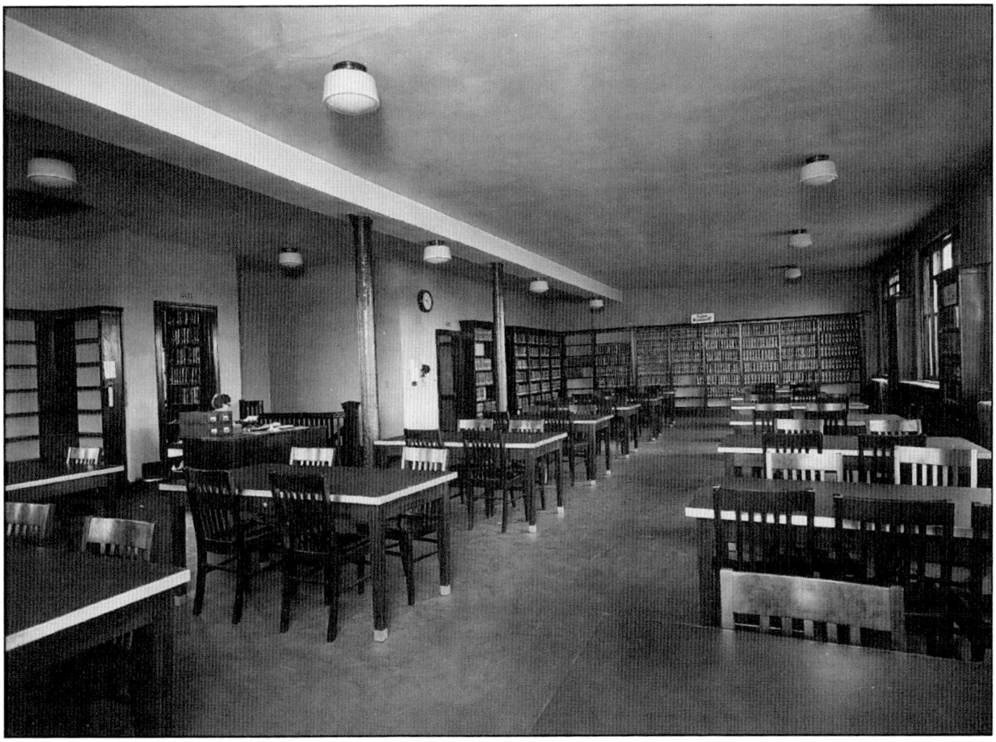

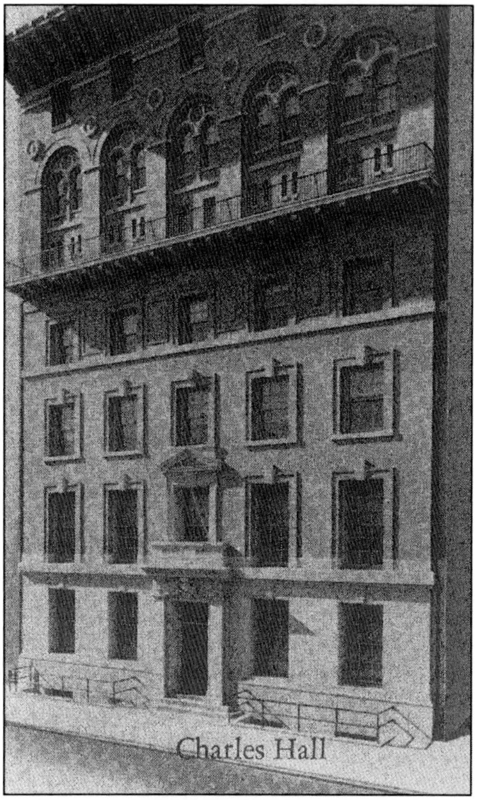

Charles Hall. The increased enrollment following World War II again made necessary an expansion of the university's physical plant. In April 1947, the university purchased the former Baltimore Athletic Club building. The building was completely renovated for the college's use. The six-story building at 1420 North Charles Street was renamed Charles Hall, at left, and provided recreational facilities, a cafeteria, several classrooms, a gymnasium, lounges, and offices. The lounge, seen in the below 1949 photograph, shows the floor where the Athletic Club's swimming pool had been. It was covered over the years and has served various functions from student lounge to office space.

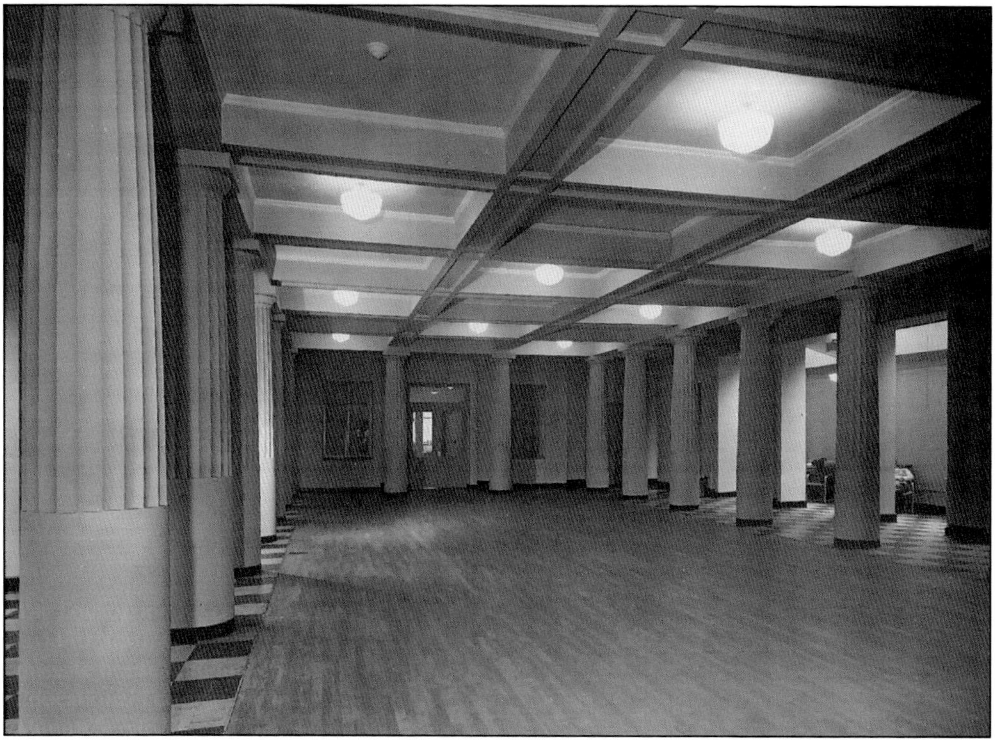

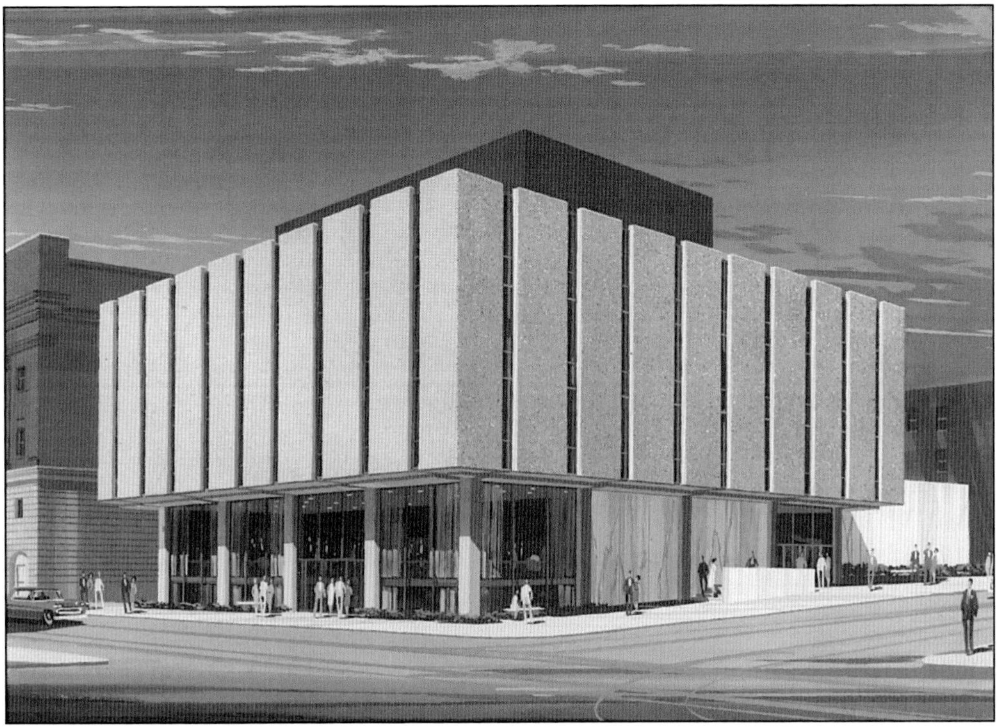

The Langsdale Library. In April 1966, the library was opened at the southwest corner of Oliver Street and Maryland Avenue. The $1.5-million building was named for longtime president of the board of trustees R. Loran Langsdale. The building is a reinforced concrete core and precast concrete panel structure. The library can accommodate 125,00 volumes and has an auditorium that seats 450 people.

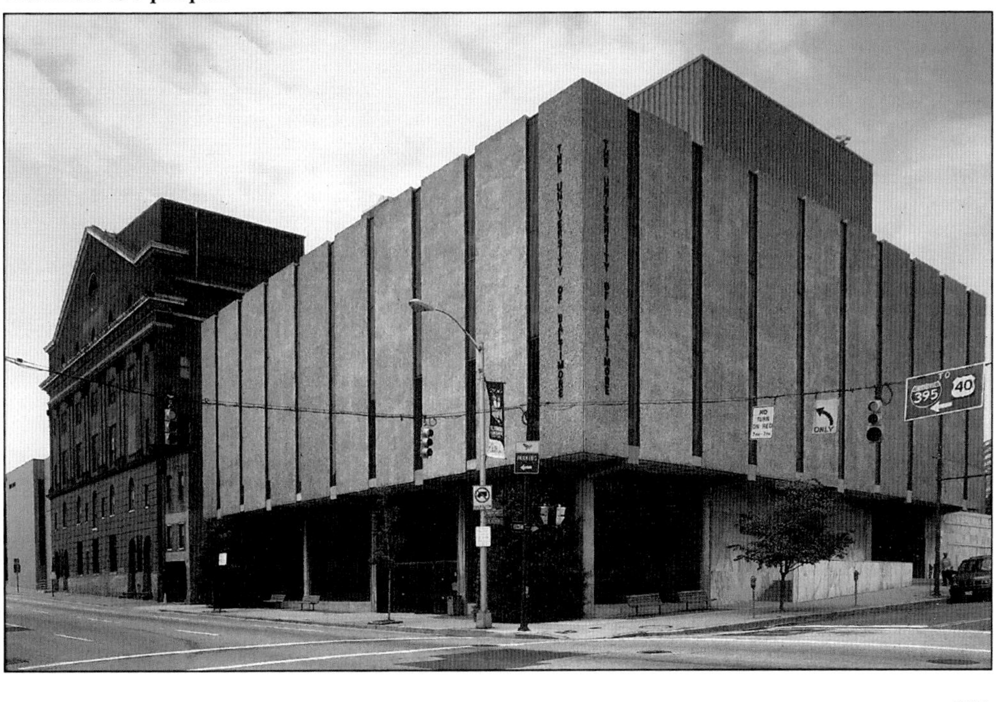

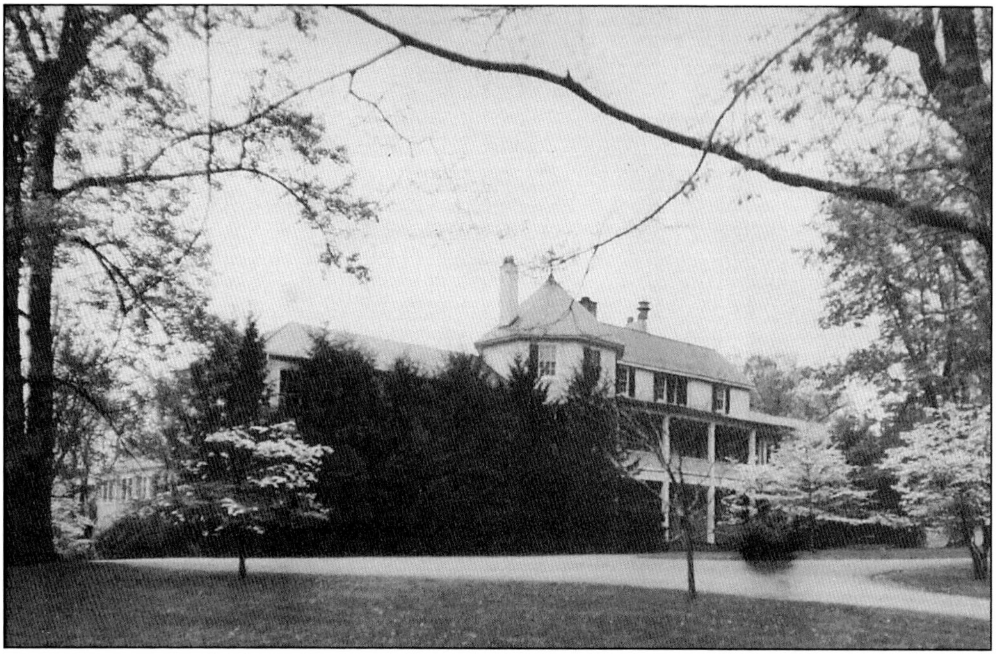

MOUNT WASHINGTON CAMPUS. The continued growth of the institution made it desirable to provide campus facilities for varsity athletics and other undergraduate activities. In the spring of 1952, the university purchased the 45-acre tract of land on Rogers Avenue, which had been formerly occupied by St. Paul's School, and thereby made provision, not only for the immediate needs of the university, but also for future ones.

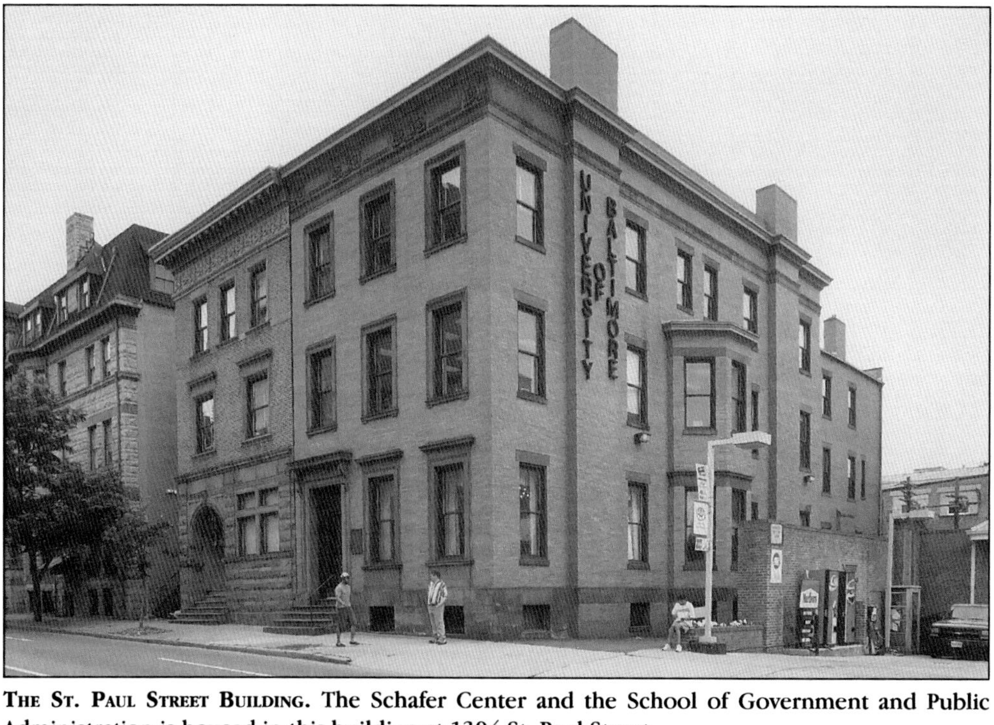

THE ST. PAUL STREET BUILDING. The Schafer Center and the School of Government and Public Administration is housed in this building at 1304 St. Paul Street.

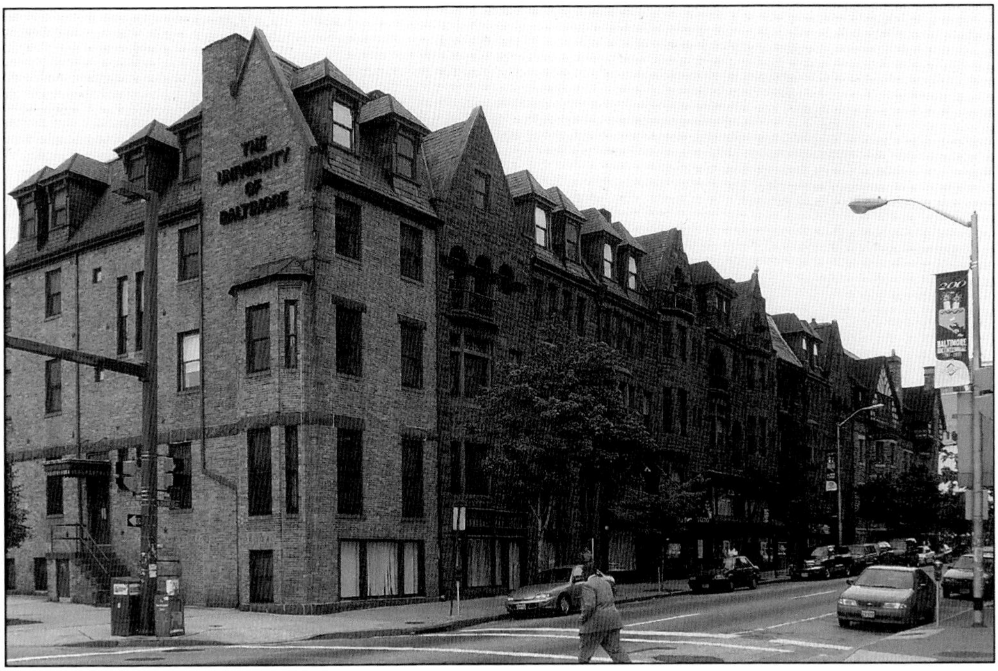

The Charles Royal Building. Located at the 1300 block of North Charles Street, at the corner of Mount Royal Avenue, the Charles Royal Building houses the Publication Design program.

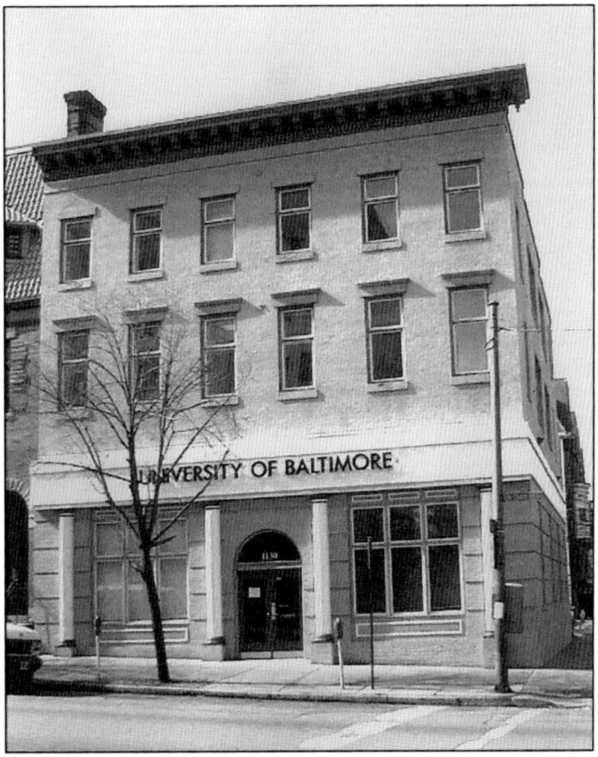

The Foundation Building. Located at 1130 North Charles Street, this site houses the university's Educational Foundation and Alumni Services.

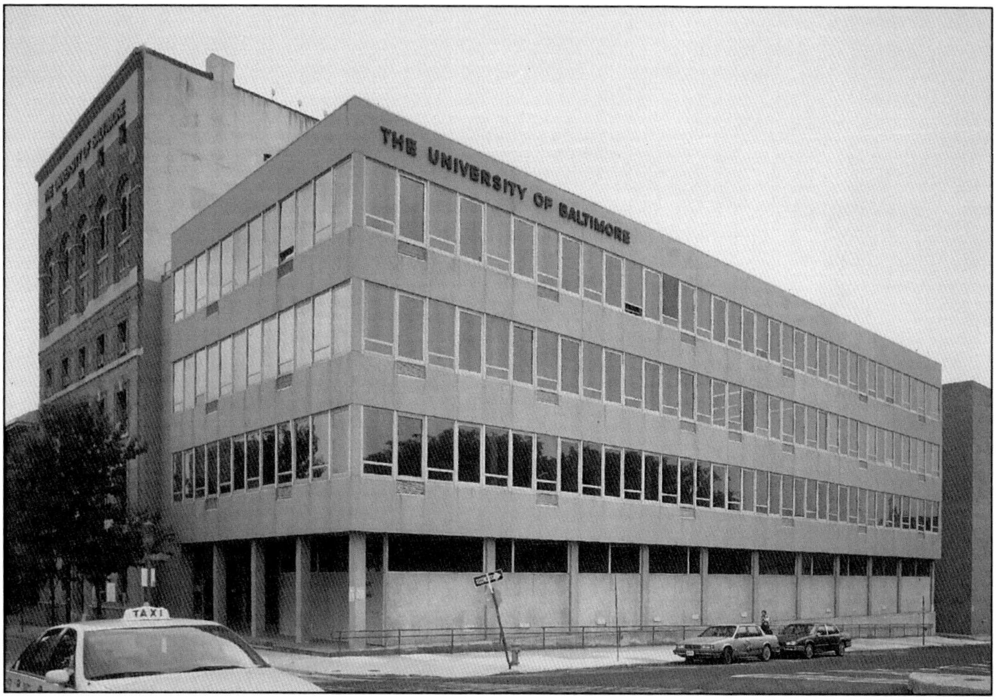

The Charles Hall Annex. In 1961, construction of the Charles Hall Annex began. The four-story building would include a lobby, a bookstore, a library, and additional classrooms. The new building is connected by corridors with the Charles Street building.

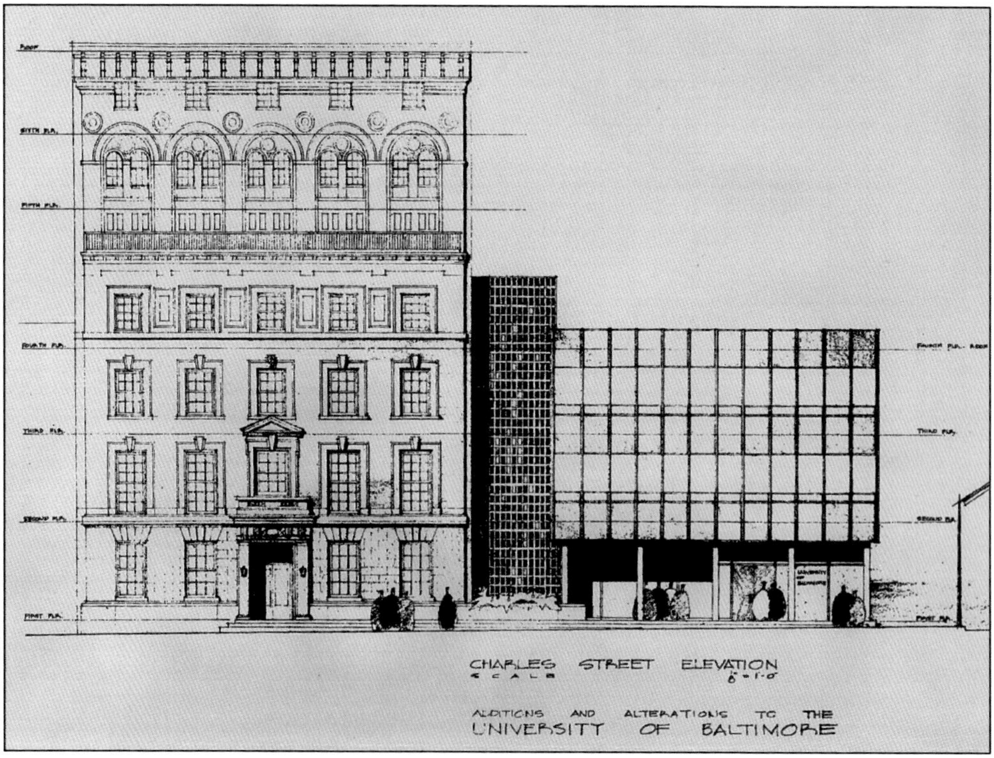

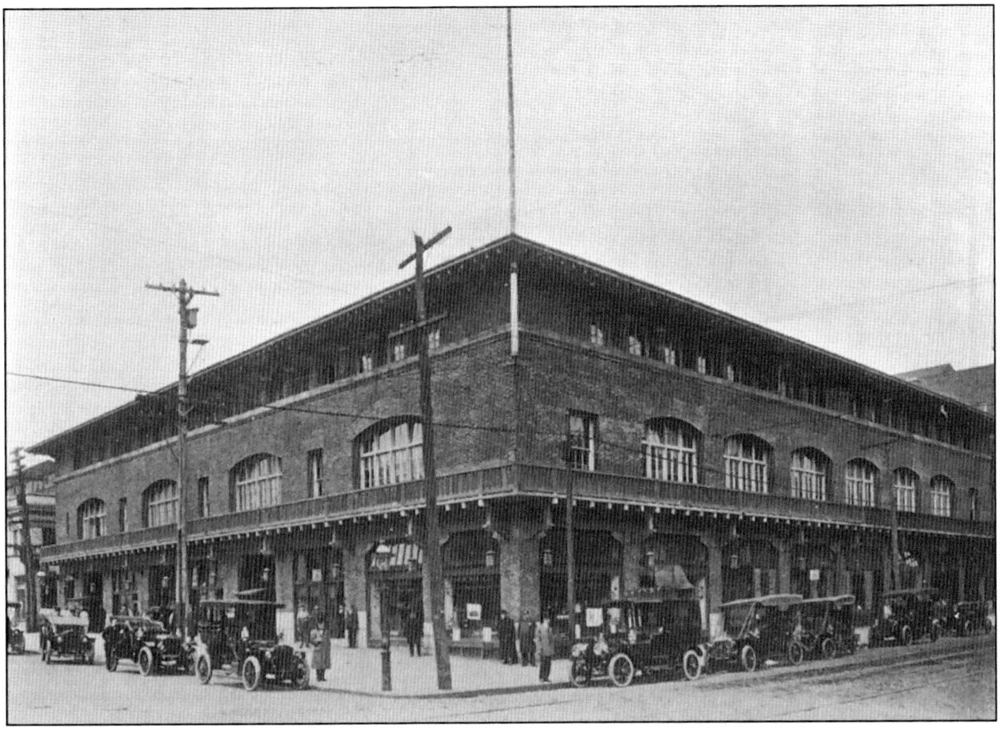

The Garage. Located on the corner of Charles Street and Mt. Royal Avenue, the garage was built in 1906 for the Baltimore Automobile Headquarters, which provided repairs day and night. It contained bowling alleys, billiard rooms, shuffle boards, a roller skating rink, and first-class dining.

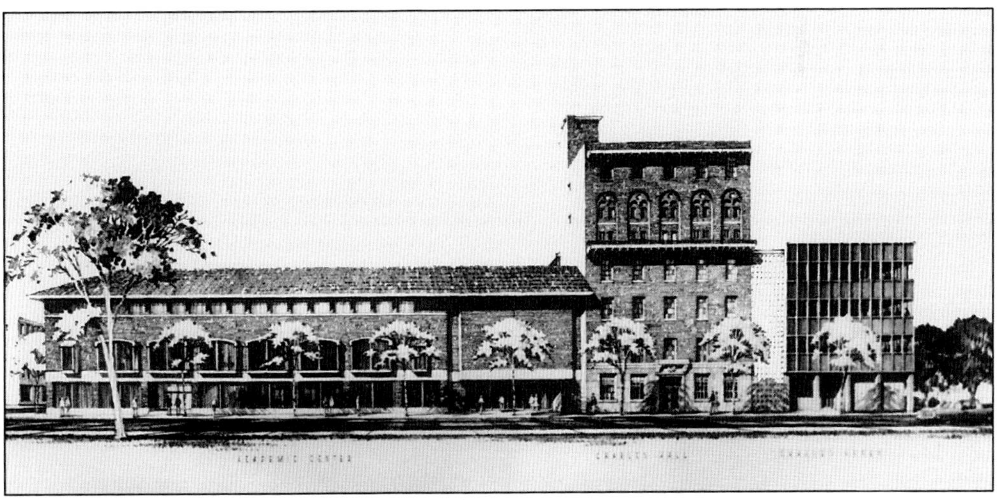

The Academic Center. In 1970, these architectural plans were drawn for the renovation of the former garage as the university's Academic Center. Construction began shortly thereafter and was completed in 1971.

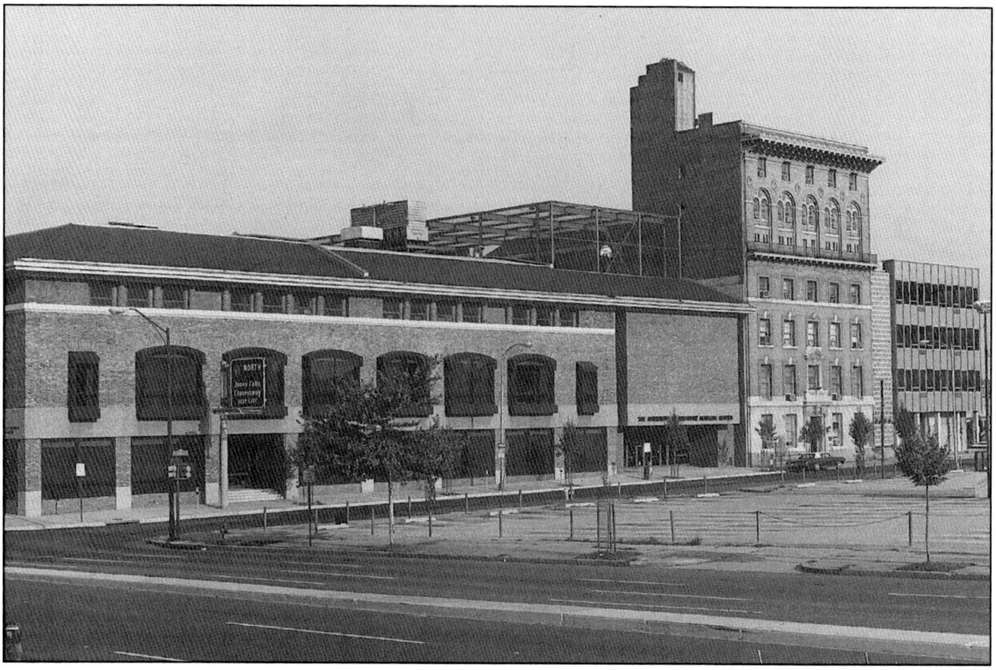

Two Views. In the photo above, the campus along the 1300 block of North Charles Street, includes, from left to right, the Academic Center, Charles Hall, and the Charles Hall Annex. In the view below, the campus is seen from Pennsylvania Station and includes, from left to right, the Thumel Business Center, the Academic Center, Charles Hall, the Charles Hall Annex, the Angelos Law Center, and Langsdale Library.

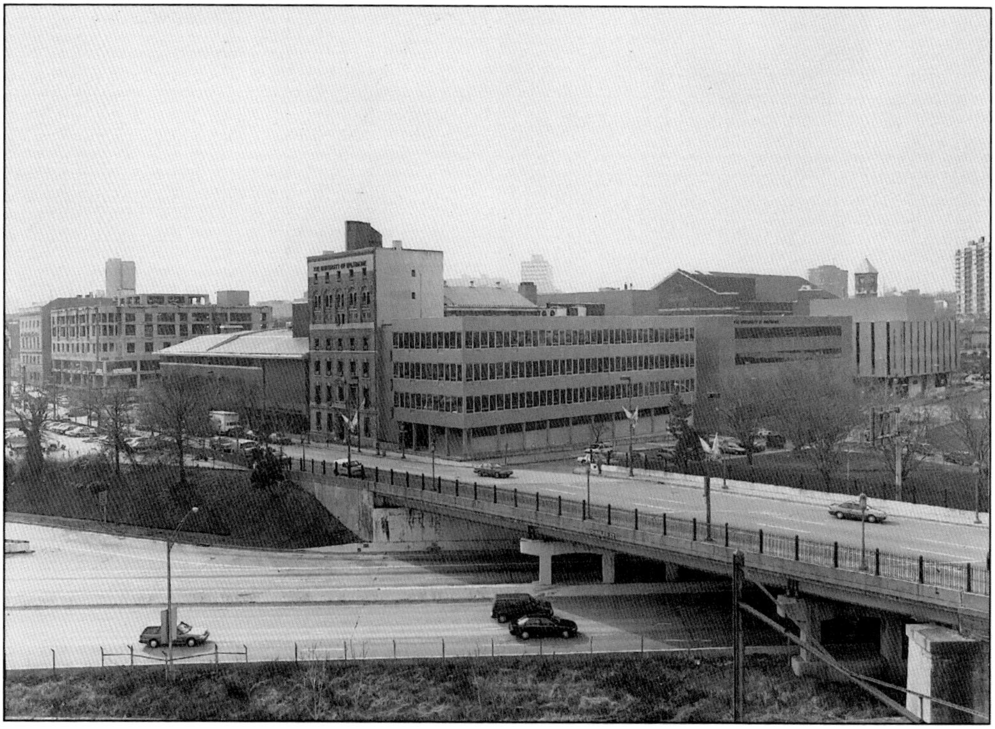

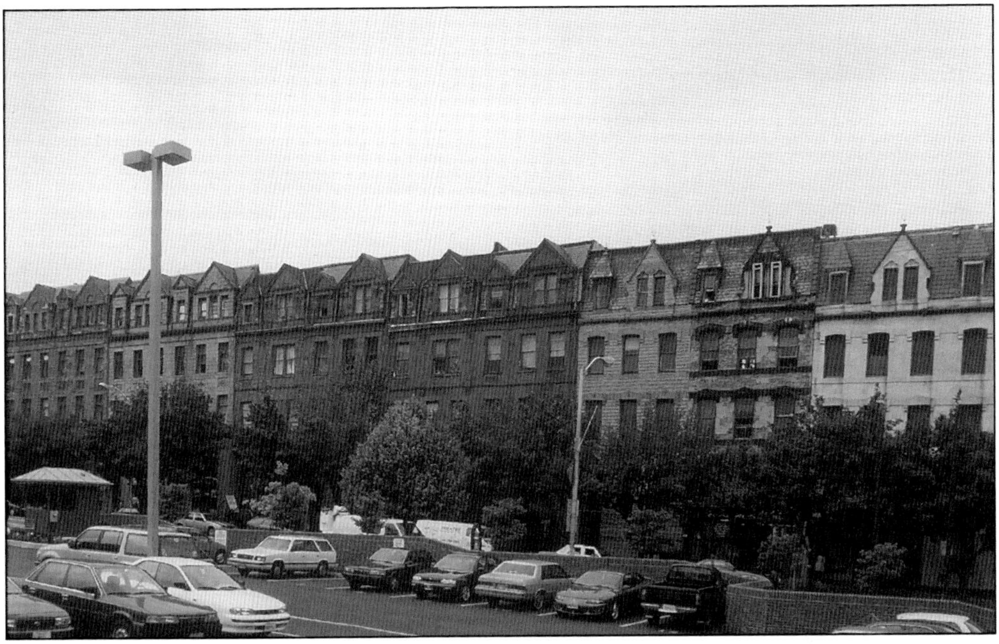

Queen Anne Belvedere Apartments. Located in the 1200 block of Charles Street, the Educational Foundation has entered into an agreement with a private developer to renovate them for market rate housing, which would make them available to UB students who want to live near campus.

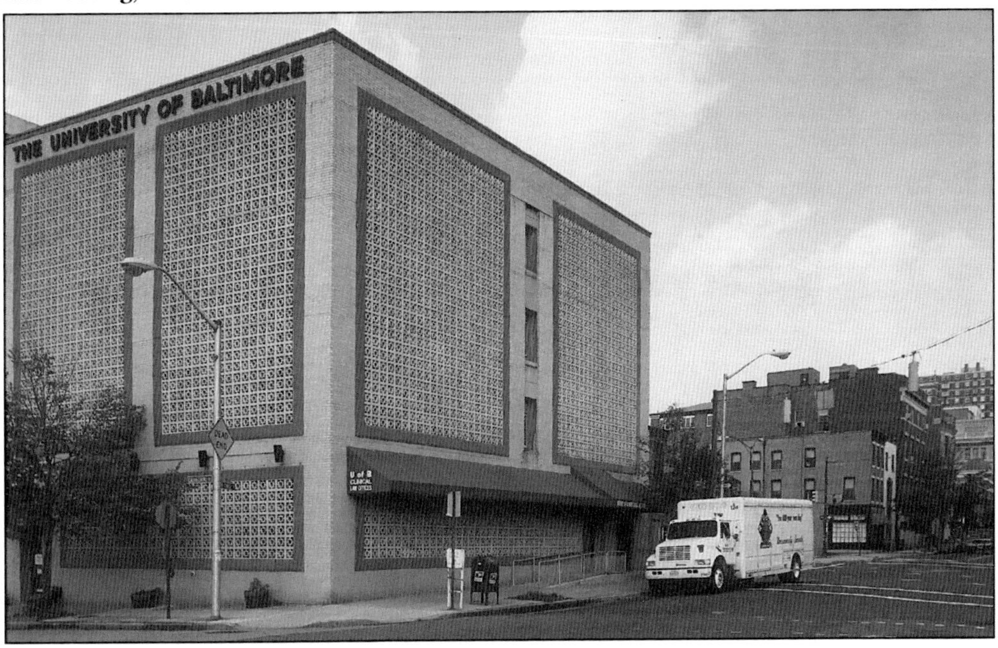

Law Clinics. The School of Law offers a wide variety of law clinics in a facility unrivaled by any others in the area to students. Seen here is the newly refurbished clinic offices at 40 West Chase Street which have state-of-the-art offices for interviewing clients, a library stocked with resource materials, and numerous work spaces and computers for students. It houses the following clinics: Appellate Practice, Civil Clinic, Community Development, Criminal Practice, Disability Law, and Family Law.

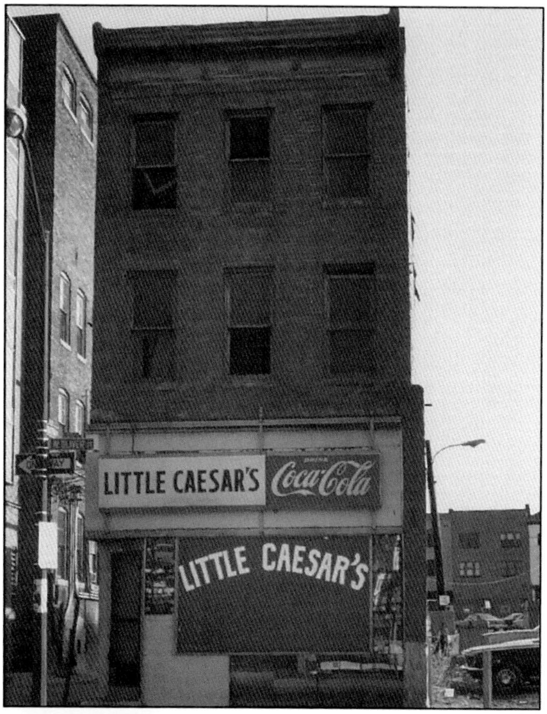

Little Caesar's. Located on the site of the future Angelos Law Center, Little Caesar's became something of a UB institution. Alumna Bonnie Hall remembers, "charging across the alley to stand in line at Caesar's. I always ordered a cheesteak sub with everything on it. This was a two-dozen napkin sub. It dripped everything. After we got our subs we'd come back to the student union in Charles Hall . . . it was always a challenge to find a table."

Pat Hayes Buick. Wrecking cranes bring down the former auto dealership in preparation for the construction of the Law Center.

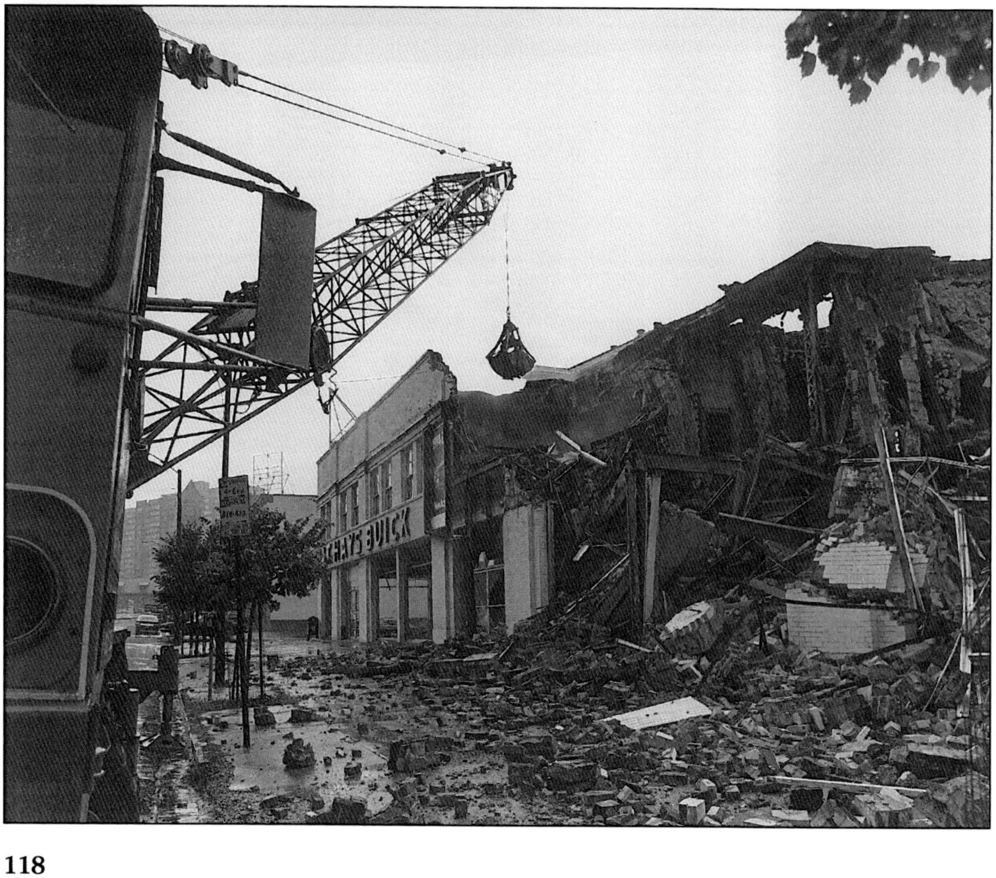

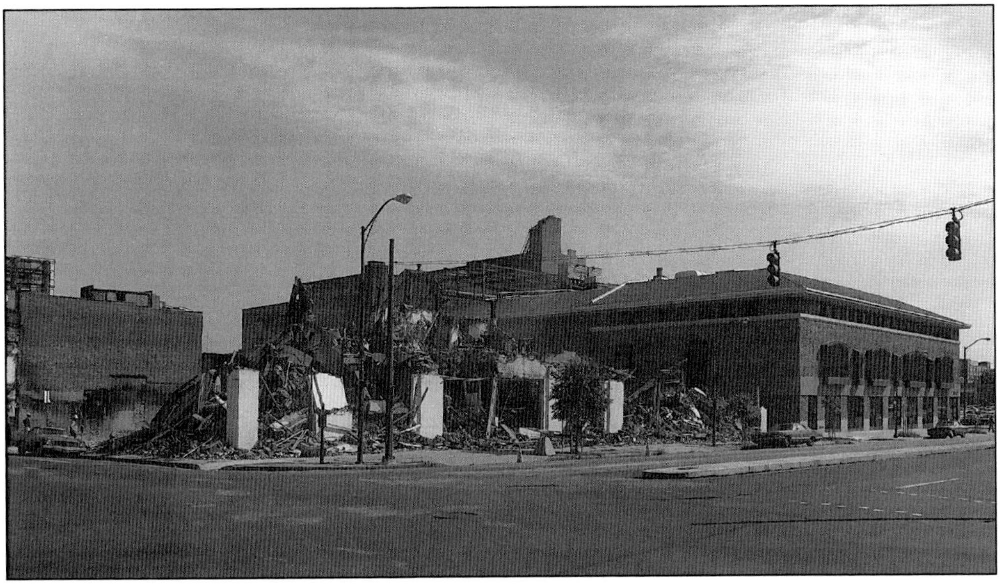

Before and After. Construction was begun on the Law Center in 1980 (above). It was officially opened on September 29, 1982. The plaza in front was dedicated two years later, in May 1984 (below).

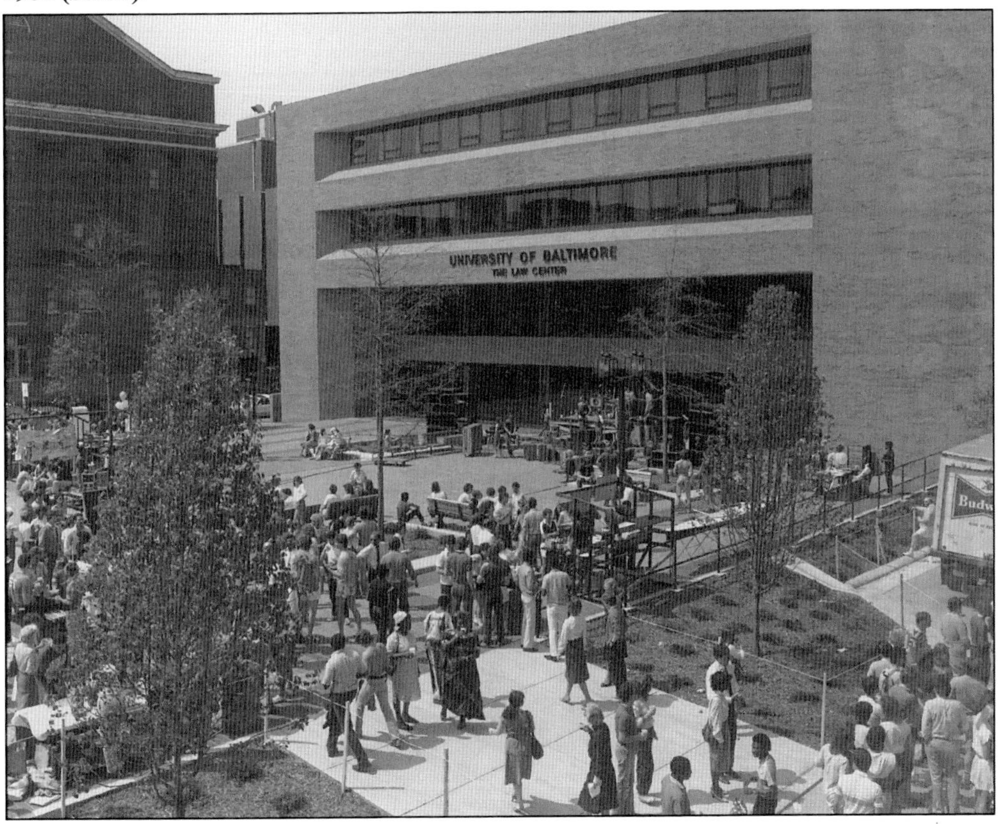

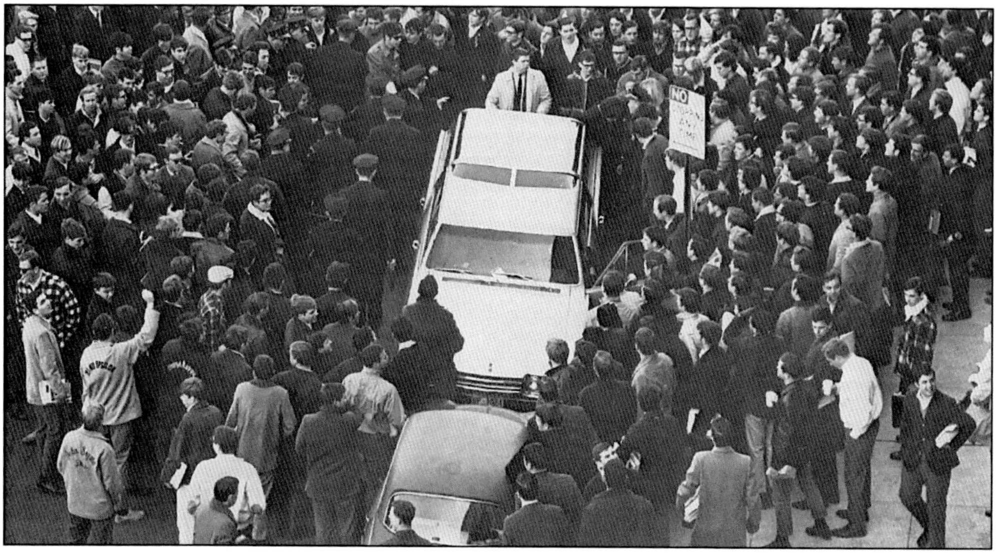

PARKING. In 1969, increases in student parking rates and the lack of parking space led students to leave their classes and block Charles Street in protest, as shown in the above photograph. Almost 20 years later, the university built the Biddle Street Parking Garage (below), seen looking southwest from the corner of Maryland Avenue and Biddle Street.

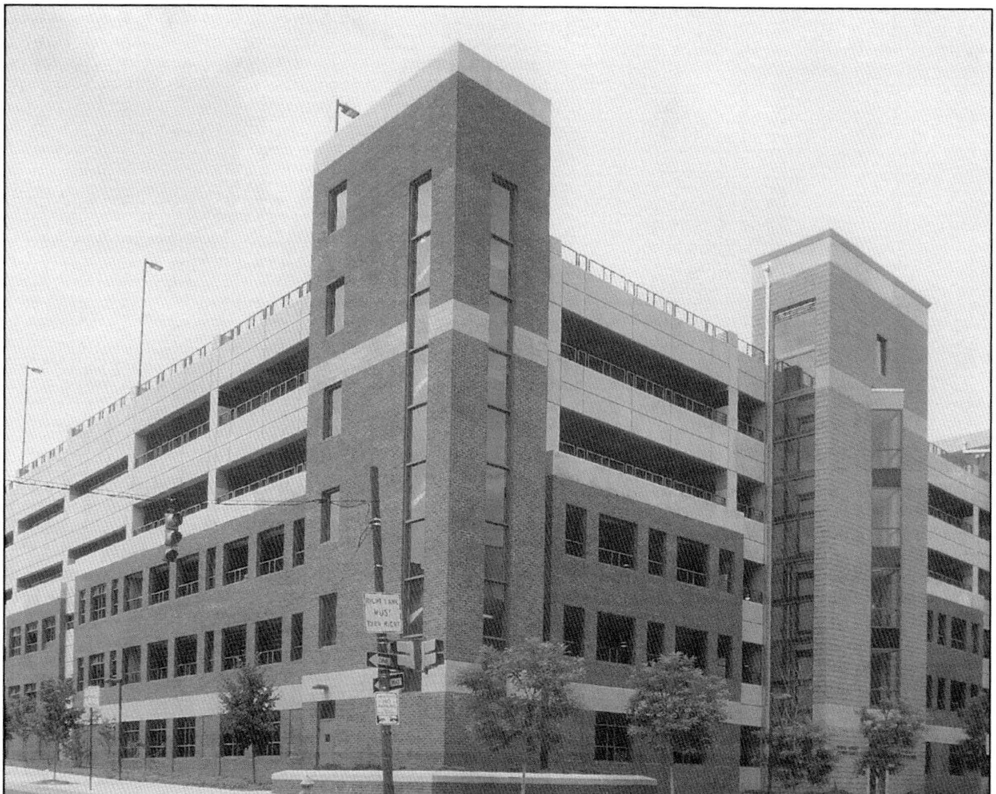

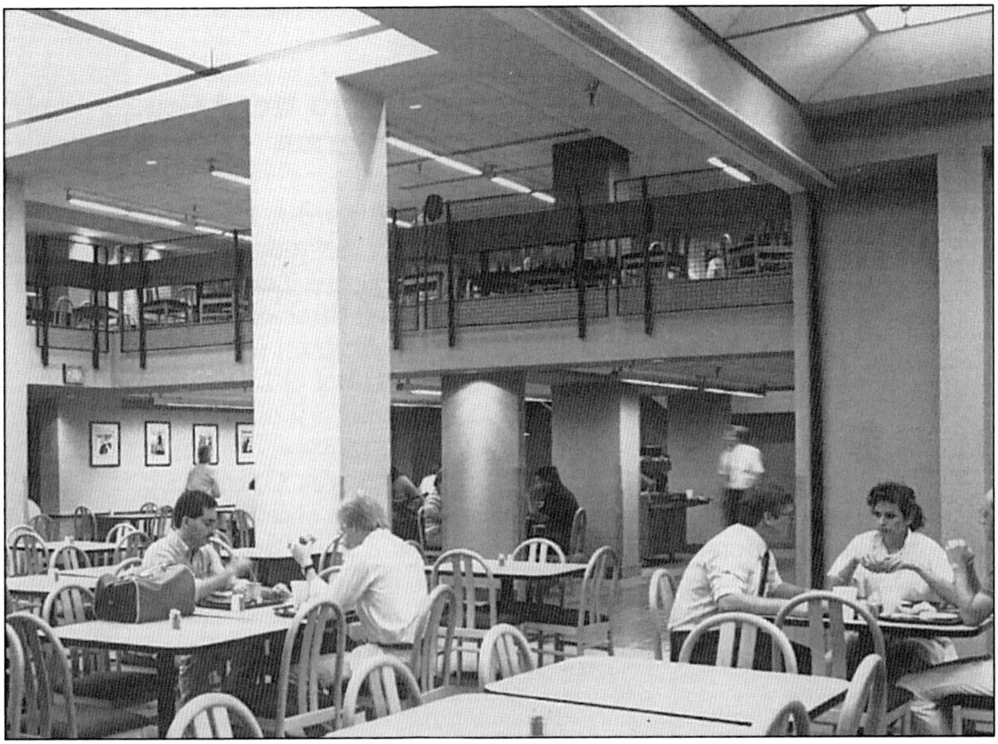

Poe's. Located in the lower level of the Law Center is Poe's Publick House. The facility includes a cafeteria, a pub, and a suite of conference rooms and features high ceilings, abundant skylights, and commissioned artwork depicting the writings and personality of the dining center's namesake, Edgar Allan Poe.

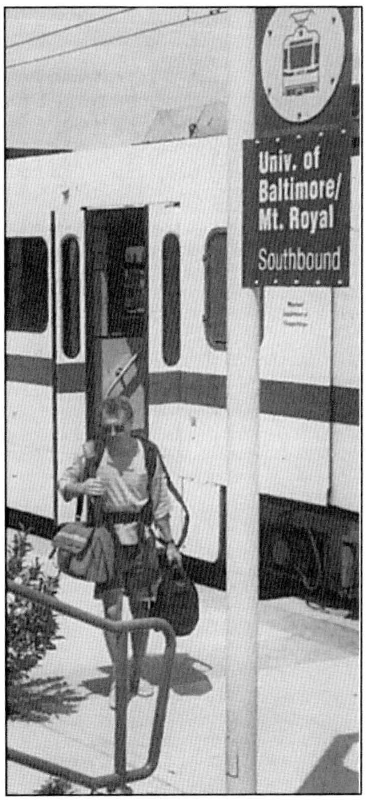

Light Rail. In the spring of 1992, the University of Baltimore Light Rail Stop was opened.

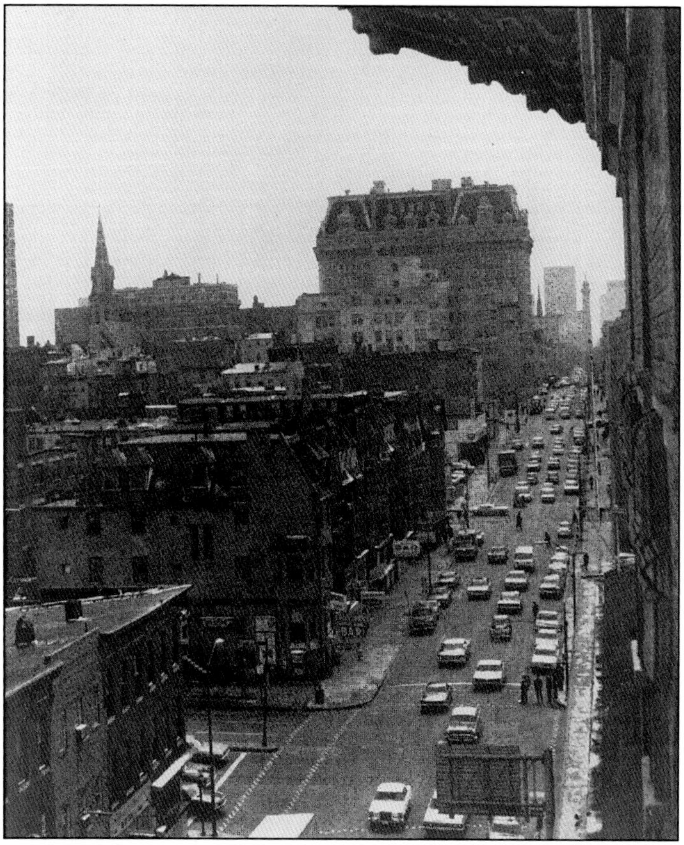

A Changing Landscape. The 1960s photograph at left, taken from an upper window of Charles Hall looking south, shows the same view as seen in the below photograph taken in the 1990s. The most apparent change is the disappearance of the numerous bars renovated as university buildings.

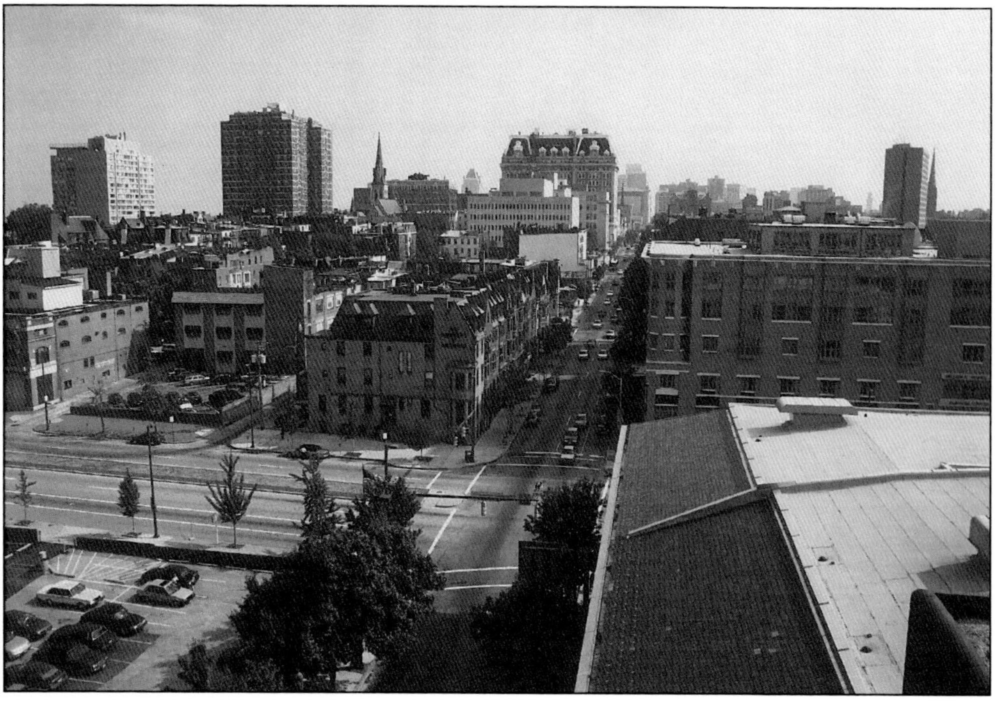

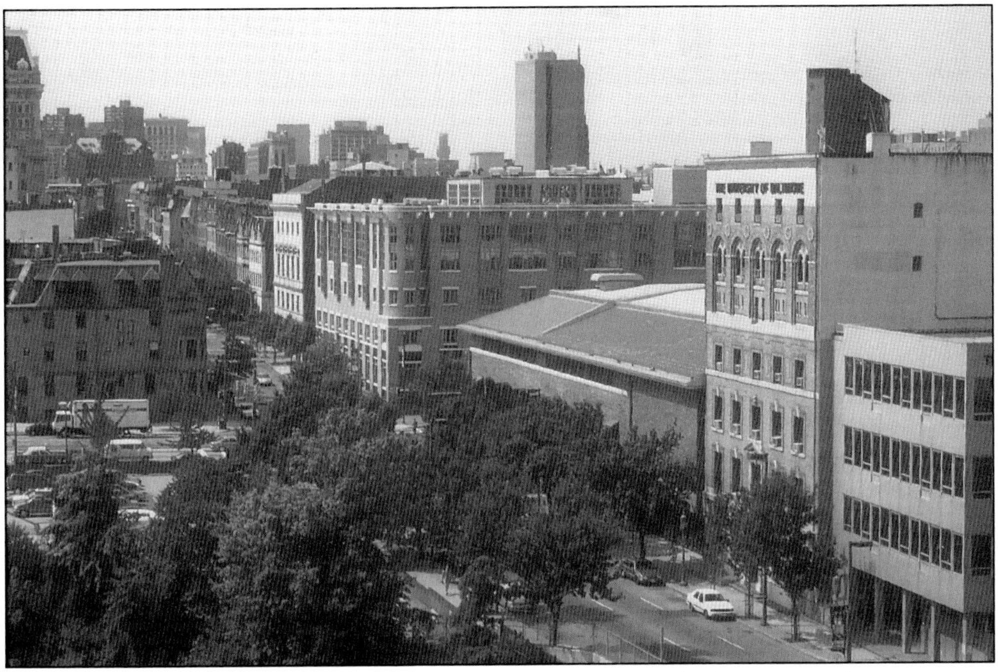

Looking South. This recent photograph, taken looking south on Charles Street at the intersection of Mt. Royal Avenue, shows, from left to right, the Charles Royal Building, the Thumel Business Center, the Academic Center, Charles Hall, and the Charles Hall Annex.

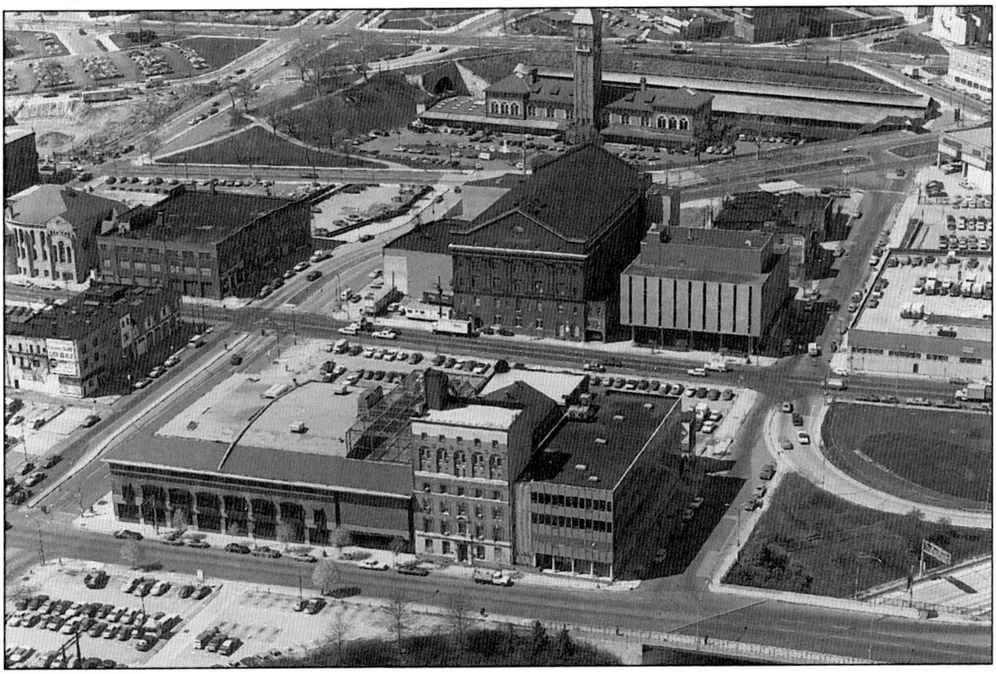

An Aerial View. Here is the campus and surrounding area as it appeared in 1980. Pictured are the following, from left to right: (forefront) parking lots, the Academic Center, Charles Hall, and the Charles Hall Annex; (background) the Lyric Opera House, Langsdale Library, and the Mt. Royal Train Station (behind the Lyric).

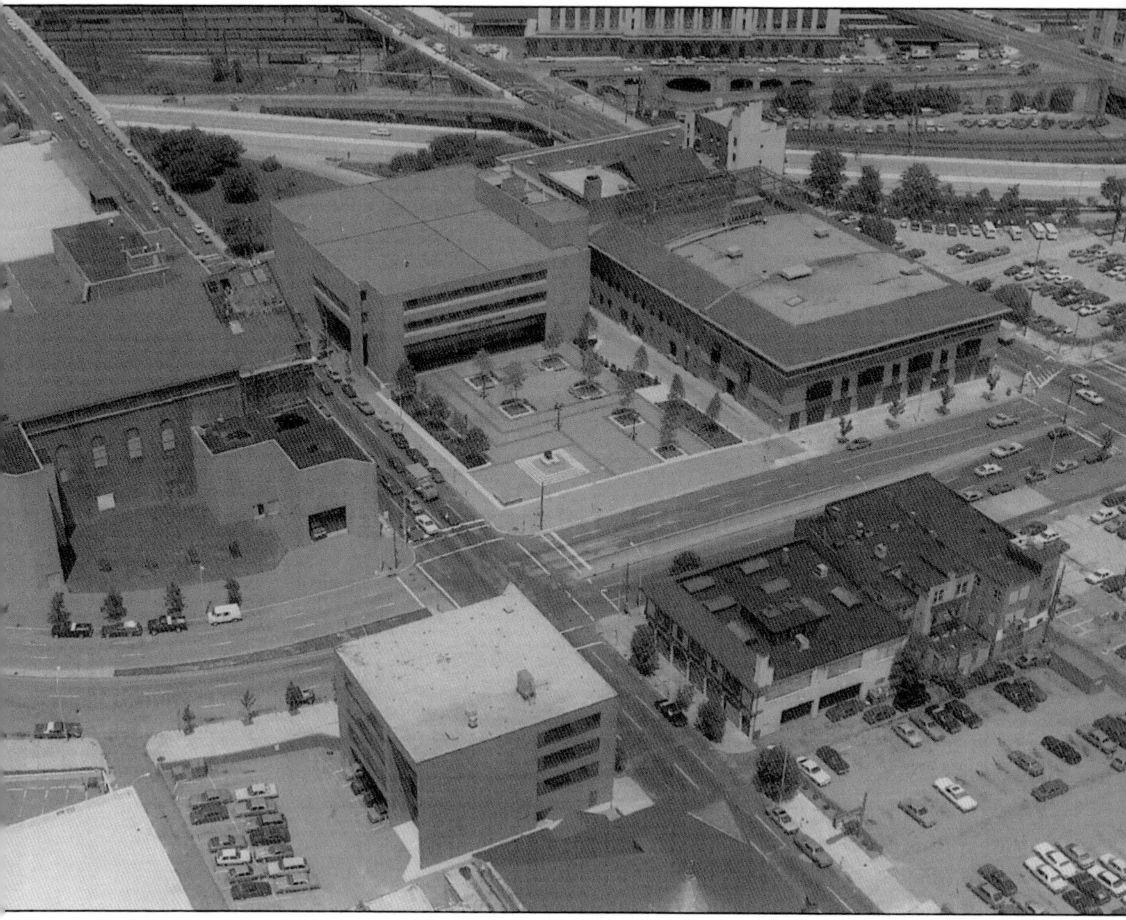

Another View. This aerial view taken in 1990 looking northeast, shows the campus. The visible buildings are the Law Center (left) and the Academic Center (right), bounded by Maryland Avenue on the west and Charles Street on the east.

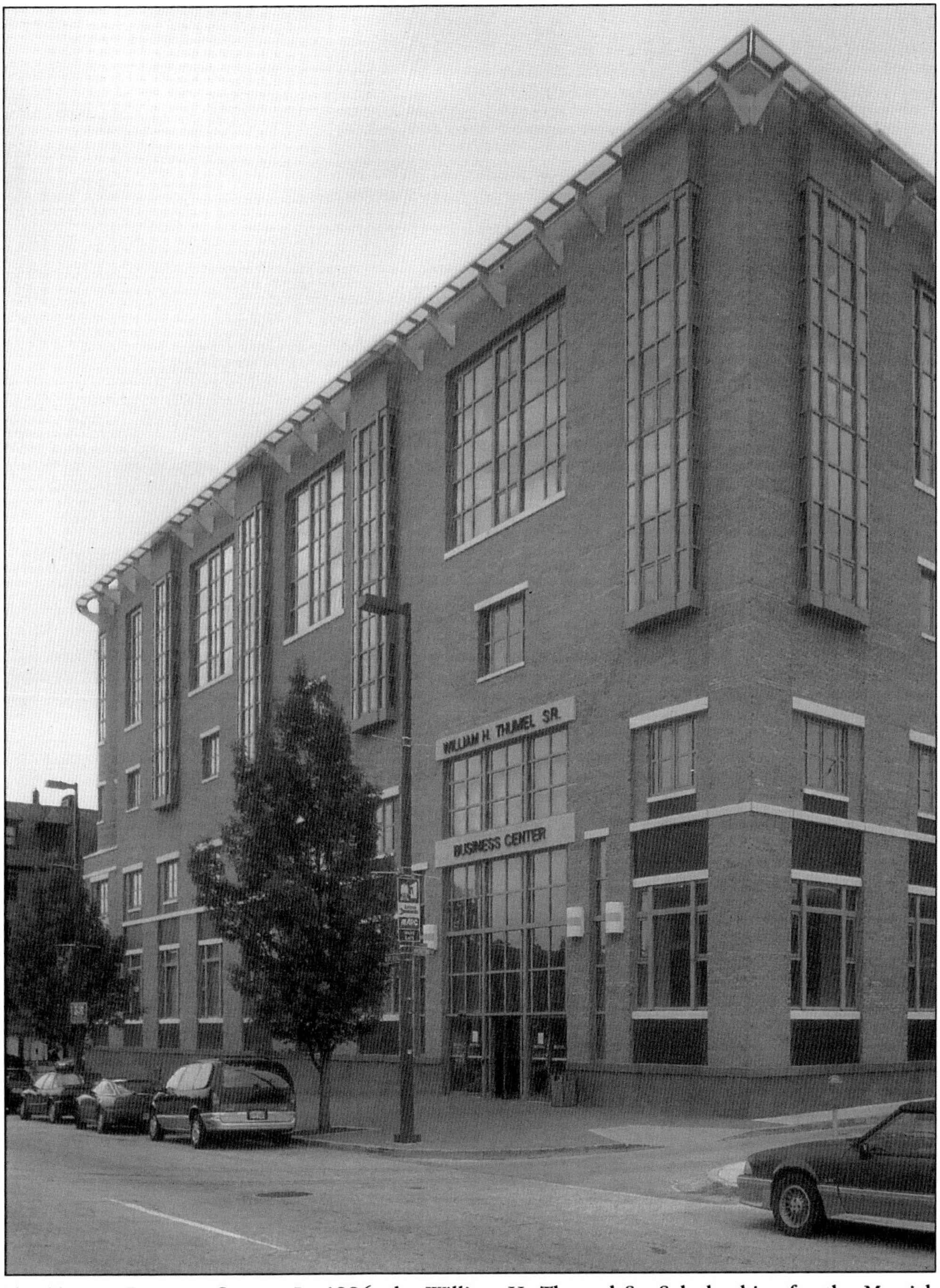

THE THUMEL BUSINESS CENTER. In 1996, the William H. Thumel Sr. Scholarships for the Merrick School of Business was established by a gift of $1.4 million from UB alumnus William Jr. to honor his father. In recognition of this generous support for higher education, the University of Maryland Board of Regents authorized the new home of the Merrick School of Business, located on the southwest corner of the Mt. Royal Avenue and North Charles Street, as the William H. Thumel Sr. Business Center.

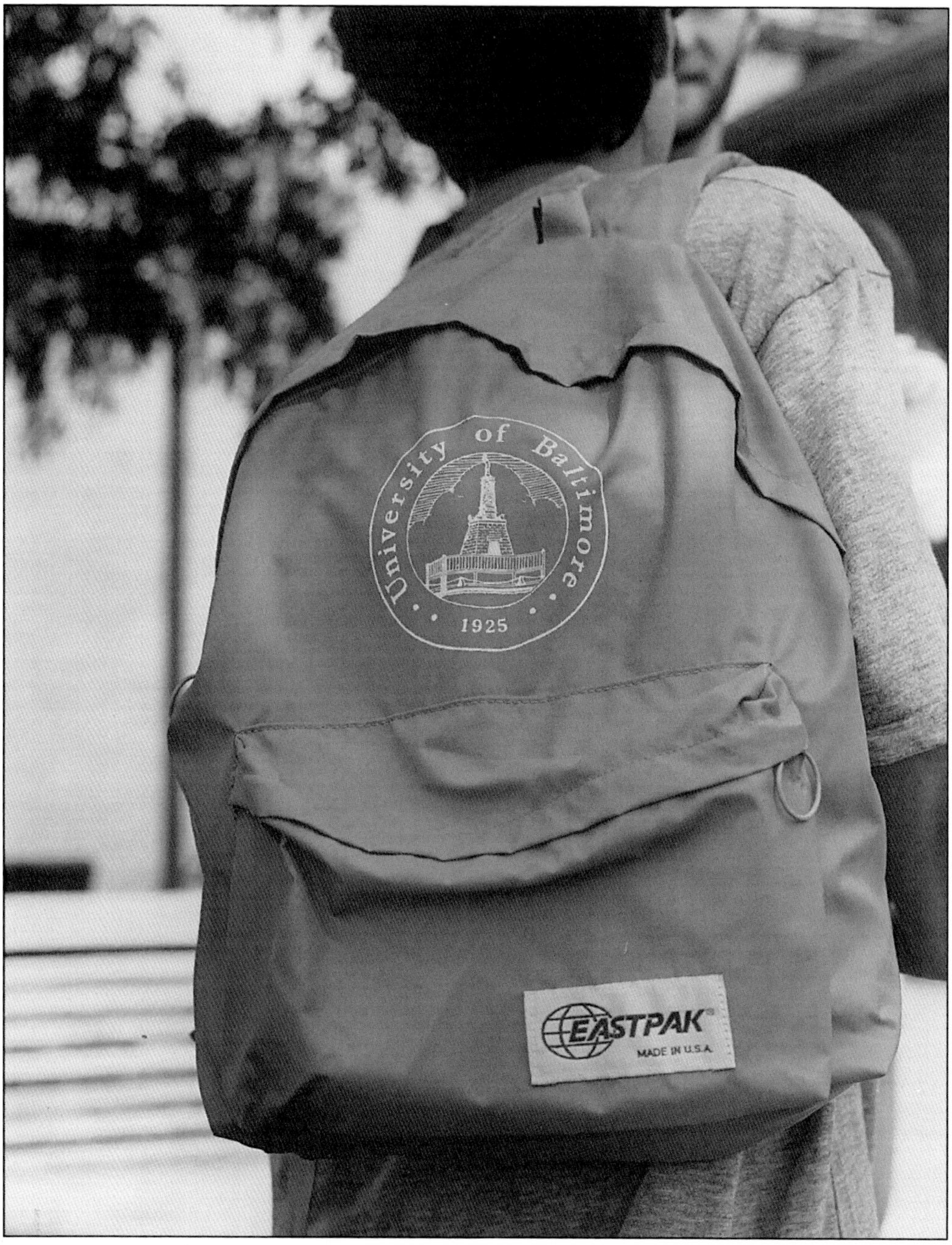

The School Seal. The university's seal incorporates the Battle Monument, which is also the official seal of the City of Baltimore. The monument commemorates the defense of Baltimore during the War of 1812.

ACKNOWLEDGMENTS

A work of this kind is a labor of love, not simply because it provides an opportunity to compile in one volume a collection of photographs from a variety of sources that include, yearbooks, brochures, and publications (to name a few), but it has allowed me to work with members of the administration, faculty, staff, students, and alumni in selecting images representative of the university's history. There a few people to whom I am especially grateful: H. Mebane Turner, Myrna McCallister, Beverly Randall, Don Paddy, Carol Garitty, Fred Hopkins, Ellen Zinner, Jessica Elfenbein, Ann Clewell, Frank Szymanski, Tami Taylor, Ron Bond, Bob Pool, and the staff of University Relations. Last, but certainly not least, are the members of my staff and students in the Archives and Special Collections Department, Langsdale Library, who have given of themselves tirelessly and with good cheer from conception to final production: Ann C. House, John Mealey, Giselle Haitsuka, and Adeyemi "Yemi" M. Oreagba. The words "thank you" can never really express my appreciation for all your efforts. To my family and friends, and most importantly, David Amos, I thank you for your patience and understanding during this undertaking.

The bulk of the photographs are housed in the Archives and Special Collections Department, Langsdale Library in the University of Baltimore Collection (Series XV). Almost all of the photographs that were taken over the past 30 years are the work of Richard Lippenholz. Richard is a 1974 graduate of the University of Baltimore with a BS degree in business. He has served on the alumni board, is a professional photographer, and has been a valuable resource in suggesting photographs for inclusion and providing background information for the captions. He is truly representative of the students the university has educated and the loyalty and dedication of its alumni.

Many of the early photographs originally appeared in the yearbooks published by the senior class, starting with the first graduating class in 1928 and, with only a couple of exceptions, published yearly until 1975. The numerous publications and brochures that have been and continue to be published have provided a valuable source for filling in the gaps after the yearbooks ceased publication. The photograph on p. 49 is the work of Doug Hansen.

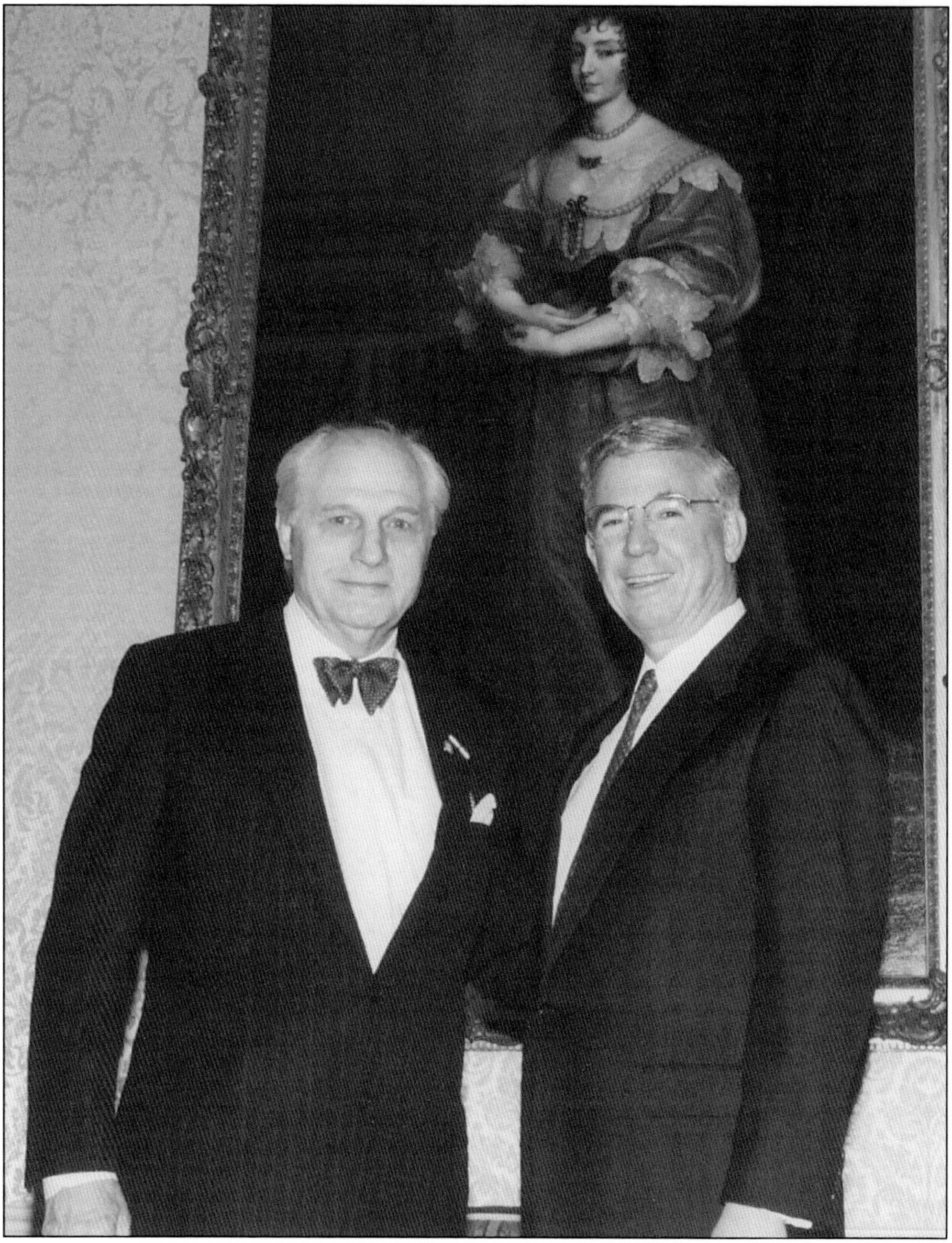

President Turner. Dr. Turner served as provost before being named president in December 1969. On April 8, 2000, the university celebrated the 30th anniversary of Dr. Turner's presidency with a "Bow Tie" Ball at the Baltimore Hyatt Regency Hotel. In recognition of his outstanding dedication and leadership, the Educational Foundation used the event to announce the creation of the H. Mebane Turner Scholarship Fund. The Turner Scholarships will be awarded on the basis of academic excellence and financial need to full-time students enrolled at the university. In this photograph, Dr. Turner (left) is congratulated by Governor Parris Glendening at Government House.